All things bright and beautiful,

All creatures, great and small,

All things wise and wonderful,

The Lord God made them all!

CECIL FRANCIS ALEXANDER

♡ *Palisades Pure Romance*

UNLIKELY
Angels

BARBARA JEAN HICKS
ANNIE JONES
DIANE NOBLE
LINDA WINDSOR

Palisades is a division of Multnomah Publishers, Inc.

This is a work of fiction. The characters, incidents, and dialogues are products of the author's imagination and are not to be construed as real. Any resemblance to actual events or persons, living or dead, is entirely coincidental.

UNLIKELY ANGELS
published by Palisades
a division of Multnomah Publishers, Inc.

"Cupid's Chase" © 1998, 1999 by Barbara Jean Hicks
"Fool Me Twice" © 1998, 1999 by Annie Jones
"Birds of a Feather" © 1998, 1999 by Diane Noble
"A Season for Love" © 1999 by Linda Windsor

International Standard Book Number: 1-57673-589-3

Design by Andrea Gjeldum
Cover art by Aleta Jenks

Scripture quotations are from:
The Holy Bible, New International Version (NIV) © 1973, 1984 by
International Bible Society, used by permission of Zondervan Publishing House

The Holy Bible, King James Version (KJV)

Holy Bible, New Living Translation (NLT) © 1996. Used by permission of Tyndale House Publishers, Inc. All rights reserved.

Palisades is a trademark of Multnomah Publishers, Inc., and is registered in the U.S. Patent and Trademark Office.

Printed in the United States of America

For information:
MULTNOMAH PUBLISHERS, INC.
P.O. BOX 1720
SISTERS, OREGON 97759

99 00 01 02 03 04 05—10 9 8 7 6 5 4 3 2 1

CUPID'S CHASE

BARBARA JEAN HICKS

One

"HEY, KINCAID!"

Reid pulled his head out from the cabinet he'd been cleaning as the kitchen doors swung inward. Franco Fortunato strolled in and leaned jauntily against the counter. Franco, to his credit, hadn't used the fact that he was the boss's son to try to get out of the closing shift tonight. Not that Lorenzo Fortunato would have let him.

"Hey yourself," Reid answered cheerfully. "Side stands all done?"

Franco snapped his damp towel in Reid's direction. "Scoured clean. Am I ready to party! What do we still have to do?"

"Not much." Reid straightened his back and stretched his shoulders. "Your choice, buddy: finish the cabinets or marry the condiments?"

Franco shuddered and raised his hands as if to protect himself. "Don't use that word around me!"

"What—marry?" Reid grinned. "Getting some pressure from the girlfriend, Franco?"

"Nah." Franco hesitated, uncertainty blurring his usual brash self-confidence. "She broke up with me last week. *After* she got her Christmas present. Women!"

"Yeah. Women. Tough luck, man."

Franco's cocky expression was already back in place. "I'll get over it. Plenty of other fish in the sea. The deejay setting up in the dining room, for instance. What a knockout!"

Ah, the resiliency of youth. Except that Reid knew

from experience a lost love wasn't as easy to get over as Franco pretended, youth or not.

"You got a date for the party tonight?"

"No." Reid didn't elaborate. He could have invited someone to the year-end party the Fortunato brothers were throwing for the restaurant staff, but seeing in the new year with a woman he knew only casually felt too much like making promises he wasn't ready to keep.

He wondered how long it would be before he got beyond casual with a woman again. He hadn't been serious about anyone since high school. Since Rae Ann. No time, for one thing—between waiting tables and directing the music program at the church, his four-year degree had already stretched out to nearly seven. But now that all he had left was student teaching…

It was something to think about. Not all women were like Rae Ann.

He took out the mustard jars and the cruets of oil and vinegar for cleaning and refilling. "Is the New Year's Eve party an annual bash, Franco?"

"Since I was a kid. Uncle Leander and my father go all out for it, too. I'm talkin' serious fun."

"Yeah?" Reid was dubious. Lorenzo he could see throwing a party in appreciation of his employees. But Leander? Leander was such a tightwad his brother probably had to sit on him to get him to put out the money. Leander still had Nonna Pippa—at seventy-five—working the hostess desk for him.

Was it Leander who got out every day to sweep the sidewalk? Was it a busboy he could have paid minimum wage for the work? No, it was his old mother bending her back over the broom. "One day, I retire," Nonna

Pippa would say, coming in off the street to sink onto a bench in the waiting area, a sheen of perspiration on her upper lip.

And while Lorenzo knew everyone who worked at Fortunato's by name, Leander rarely showed his face outside his office, tucked into a corner of the flagship restaurant near Seattle's Pioneer Square. He'd certainly never said hello to Reid.

Franco rambled on about last year's New Year's Eve party while Reid listened with half an ear. Reid had been working part-time at Fortunato's Ristorante for four months now. The Italian restaurant was a classy place, his best job since he'd started waiting tables as a college freshman to help pay his way through school. His manager worked with his class schedule, and the upscale clientele he served regularly left 20 percent tips on tabs higher than Reid's monthly food budget.

He felt lucky to have landed the job. It was rare to have a position at Fortunato's without a family connection. By now, he almost felt as if he did: Lorenzo and Leander's mother insisted Reid call her *Nonna* Pippa— Grandma Pippa—just as her eight grandchildren did. She was every bit as delightful as her name sounded rolling off his tongue.

It was Nonna Pippa who'd told him the history of Fortunato's Ristorante. The family business begun by her sons Lorenzo and Leander twenty-seven years ago had expanded to four locations in the Seattle area over a period of twenty-two years. "But this location, she is the first," Nonna Pippa told him. "Like home for this old woman."

Five years ago the Fortunato brothers had franchised

the operation, and now there were Fortunato's Ristorantes everywhere. "Even Rome," the family matriarch told him proudly. "Even Genoa!"

The twang of a steel guitar sounded from the dining room.

"All right!" Franco shoved the last rack of glasses under the counter. "Let's party!" He gestured toward the dining room. "Check out the redhead running the music, Kincaid. She looks like some fun."

Reid followed him out the door. The main dining room was enormous, wrapped in a sweeping mural of vineyard-covered hills. The tables and chairs had been pushed against the walls, leaving the hardwood floor open for dancing. Dozens of green, red, and white balloons floated against the ceiling, their long streamers of curling ribbon hanging and swaying like seaweed in coastal waters. Across from the bar, which was crowded with chilled bottles of Asti Spumante, stood a long buffet table laden with food. A makeshift stage with a half-assembled sound system stood against one wall. Franco's redhead was for the moment nowhere in sight.

A crowd of people in semiformal attire stood around the marble fountain in the foyer, talking and laughing. A pretty teenager in a short velvet dress—another of Lorenzo's seven children—was draping a glitter-emblazoned sash across the marble cupid in the center of the fountain.

The front door unexpectedly banged open, and the girl nearly lost her footing on the edge of the fountain as a blast of cold air whooshed into the room—along with something small, furry, and very wet. Two little girls, as identical as the frilly pink dresses they wore, tore after the creature, down the stairs, across the foyer, and straight for the table in the dining room.

"Tiara! Aurora!" the pretty teenager scolded as she recovered her balance. "You know that cat's not allowed in here!"

Reid doubted the twins even heard. They were by this time under the table in hot pursuit of the bedraggled little alley cat Nonna Pippa had recently adopted. Spumoni, the old woman called the scrawny calico, "because she is many flavors in one." Hard to believe the stray had been feasting on gourmet Italian dinner scraps; she was still as skinny as she'd been when she'd first appeared in the alley outside the kitchen at Fortunato's a month ago.

And nearly as skittish. Normally, she couldn't be tempted inside. Not that Leander and Lorenzo would have allowed a cat in the restaurant, of course, but Nonna Pippa would have liked to share her upstairs apartment with Spumoni.

That clearly wasn't going to happen. Spumoni was the quintessential scaredy cat. She wouldn't let anyone except Nonna Pippa hold her, though she did allow Reid to pet her now and then, and lately had even been rubbing up against his legs when she saw him. It must be wild out tonight for the poor little thing to have ventured inside at all. Reid sincerely hoped the cat would escape the twins and find a nice warm hiding place in the restaurant where she could wait out the storm in peace.

He glanced again at the stage, where Franco's redhead had reappeared and was plugging a cord into a microphone. He did a double take. It couldn't be—

She looked up. A grin broke across her features. "Reid! Where you been?" she called across the room.

Franco yelped. "You know her? Be still, my heart! Introduce me, Kincaid."

"She's a little old for you, Franco," he answered dryly.

"Not enough to—"

"She's my mother."

"Ohh-kay." Franco suddenly changed direction. "Think I'll see if Marcella needs any help over here...." He headed for the group by the fountain.

Reid hurried across to the makeshift stage. "Mom! What are you doing here?"

"Told you I had a gig for New Year's Eve, darlin'."

"I know, but—why didn't you tell me it was here?"

She grinned again, her green eyes sparkling. "Wanted to surprise you," she drawled. Even after twenty years in Seattle, her faint accent revealed her Texas roots.

"Mom, you never cease to surprise me." Reid eyed her outfit, a short black denim skirt and jacket studded with gold stars and worn with a hot pink satin shirt and matching cowboy boots. Her red hair, topped by a black, gold-banded cowboy hat, bounced around her shoulders. Her recent trip to the Caribbean had doubled the number of freckles on her nose and cheeks. Franco's mistake had been an honest one; she didn't look nearly old enough to be his mother.

Dolly Kincaid reached over and scraped at a spot of dried pasta sauce on her son's tuxedo shirt. The sleeves were still rolled up, and a black bow tie hung loose around his neck. "You're not wearin' your workin' clothes to the party, I hope."

"Something wrong with my clothes?" At her look of horror, he added, "Mom, I'm kidding! I brought a turtleneck and a blazer. I'm on my way to change. What about you? You sure you're not supposed to be at the western barbecue pit down the street?" he teased.

She placed her hands on her hips and tossed her hair. "Get with the picture, darlin'! You never heard of spaghetti westerns? Besides, I'm honorin' a special request with this outfit." She lifted one eyebrow in a saucy look he didn't know what to make of.

"Oh? Just who was it who hired you for this gig?"

"Someone who just loves my heart-wrenchin', toe-stompin', deep-thinkin' country music."

"Deep-thinkin'?" Reid rolled his eyes. "Mom, I'm afraid you've gone off the deep end! Promise you won't tell anyone you're my mother?"

"You kiddin'? Gonna make sure everybody knows, son!" She gave him an exaggerated wink, then turned her attention to the knobs and levers of her karaoke equipment. "Be ready, darlin'."

But no warning could have been enough to prepare Reid for the night that lay ahead.

Carina Fortunato turned down the wick on the kerosene lantern swinging over the dining table. The twelve-volt light she'd left burning over the sink in the tiny galley cast ghostly shadows across the cabin.

Even in the protected marina with the sails furled tight, on a night like tonight the sloop rolled like Uncle Lorenzo rolled when he walked. The north wind wailed and moaned. The halyards clanged against the mast and echoed through the cabin. Carina hadn't liked the noises when she first moved aboard, but by now they seemed comforting. The wind and the rain were out there; she was inside, warm, dry, and protected.

The *Portofino* had been Carina's home for more months than she cared to think about. Not that she hadn't enjoyed being a live-aboard, especially in August and September, when the weather in Seattle was as close to perfect as it got this side of heaven. Her father had torn himself away from work to join her for a sail at least half a dozen times. A record.

"Why did you buy the boat when you never use it?" she'd been asking him for years. But she'd been glad he had it when the contractors started to tear apart her house to replace the ancient pipes and wiring and strip the shingles from the roof. There was a reason she'd gotten the little bungalow for such a bargain; she was lucky she hadn't flooded it out or burned it down before she discovered how much work it needed.

"Two months, max," the contractors had assured her. That had been five months ago.

She pulled her warmest coat off the hook in the forward stateroom and slipped it on. Temperatures were expected to dip into the twenties tonight, which was cold for Seattle.

Not a night to be out, but everyone would be. It was New Year's Eve.

She punched in the number for the ristorante on her cellular phone. The line was busy. Maybe Babbo was trying to call, wondering where she was.

The party would be in full swing by now. Uncle Lorenzo and Babbo—her father—had closed the dining room an hour early, at nine o'clock, to clear the floor for dancing and to set up the buffet table. The yearly bash was Leander and Lorenzo Fortunato's thank-you to their hardworking staff. Lorenzo cooked and Babbo poured the vino, like in the old days.

Uncle Lorenzo was probably swinging Zia Felicia around the dance floor even now. For a man who liked his pasta as much as Uncle Lorenzo did, he could hoof it with the best of them. Felicia would be wearing sequins, her eyes would be closed, and for once the permanent crease between her brows would be so slight as to be barely noticeable.

Babbo might be dancing with the widow Giotti. Carina sincerely hoped he was. She'd hinted a month ago that he invite the widow for New Year's Eve. She was a nice woman, alone for almost two years now, someone her father had known through the church for as long as Carina could remember.

"She comes to Fortunato's for dinner twice a week," Carina had told her father. "She eats a lot. She brings her friends. You ought to thank her properly."

"She does eat a lot," was all Leander had said in response.

He hadn't dated at all since his short-lived marriage to April Dawn had ended. What a disaster that had been. It was no wonder he'd steered clear of women since.

But the widow Giotti was nothing like April Dawn. Surely her father knew that. Especially now, after spending a week with her on that cruise ship over Christmas. They had to have bumped into each other, maybe talked a little, danced a little, shared some fun. A lot of fun, Carina hoped. It would be so nice for Babbo, having a good woman in his life.

"What's this?" Babbo had frowned when Lorenzo

handed him the cruise packet at Thanksgiving.

"Your Christmas present from the family," Nonna Pippa said, beaming.

"Because you need a vacation," Zia Felicia told him.

"Because we need a vacation," Lorenzo said. When Babbo worked too hard, everybody suffered. Uncle Lorenzo wasn't afraid to call a spade a spade.

"But at Christmas?" Leander shook his head. "Christmas is to share with family."

"Family you got coming out your ears," Uncle Lorenzo said. "Every day in this business. Go have a good time without family for a change."

"But a cruise?" Leander protested. "Cruises are for doddering old—"

Carina's pleading look had stopped him. "It's a gift, Babbo. Accept it with grace."

So he had—much to the family's relief.

But three days before Christmas, an hour before the cruise ship Ysolda was scheduled to leave the dock in Miami, he'd called his daughter's office in Seattle.

"So did you know all along about the widow Giotti?" he demanded without even saying hello.

"What about the widow?"

"The cruise. The widow. The widow on the cruise."

"Well, of course! She told me about it, Babbo. That's what gave me the idea."

"Which idea?" he asked suspiciously.

"Why, the cruise!" She should have known he'd take a dim view of anything that smacked of matchmaking. And sending her father on a cruise she knew the widow was taking more than smacked.

"Oh, Babbo, what's so bad about wanting to see you

have a good time?" she asked. "Can't you just enjoy yourself?"

Was it wrong of me, God? she prayed more than once while he was away. *To arrange this thing without asking him?* She didn't like thinking she was meddlesome. And she especially didn't like thinking Babbo might have reason to be angry with her. *You know I only want him to be happy....*

The extent of her relief when he came back home refreshed and energetic told her how anxious she'd been. "I did enjoy myself, very much." He gave her a bone-crunching hug.

She hadn't gotten the details yet. He and the widow had been home only two days.

Hitting the redial button on the phone, she lifted it to her ear again and waited. Two rings, three, four.

Nonna Pippa was probably dancing with her broom.

She smiled at the picture in her mind. Her grandmother was seventy-five years old and still insisted on sweeping the sidewalk in front of Fortunato's every morning and every afternoon. Weather permitting, which in Seattle meant she did take a good number of days off.

Zia Felicia carried on about it, of course; having customers greeted by an old woman nearly as broad as Lorenzo, with a shapeless apron over her shapeless dress and her stockings slipping down around her ankles, didn't project the proper image. And she didn't like the fact that the old woman hung about the dining room during the evenings, "getting in the way of the hostesses," either. But Leander said it made her feel useful and refused to send her upstairs to her apartment all alone. Besides, since the fifth-floor apartment was only a short elevator ride from the ristorante, it would have been difficult to keep her away.

The ringing stopped. Finally!

"Fortunato's Ristorante, Signore Leander here."

She could hardly hear his voice over the noise and music in the background. "Babbo! I didn't think *you'd* answer the phone. How's the party?"

"Such a good time, cara! Where are you?"

"Just leaving the boat. My neighbor was late getting back. I knew he'd want to see his baby." Carina had been cat sitting for a week while the live-aboard across the dock had been away. A big, friendly, black-and-white tabby, Sneakers was nothing like that skinny, skittish calico Nonna Pippa insisted on feeding in the alley behind the restaurant. What good was a cat you couldn't even get close to?

"Such a good girl you are," Babbo said. "Always thinking of others. Come soon! We'll save a karaoke song for you."

"Karaoke!" But she was speaking to the dial tone. She held the phone at arm's length, her eyebrows lifted in surprise, then dropped it into her leather shoulder bag. Karaoke?

A blast of cold air greeted her when she climbed through the main hatch a moment later. She tightened her scarf around her head and snuggled deeper into her heavy camel-hair coat. Her high heels tottered precariously as she stepped off the boat and onto the pier.

At the end of the dock she turned the handle on the metal gate and swung it open, eyeing the steep angle of the ramp up to the parking lot. This was not going to be easy. High heels and low tide were about as incompatible as Leander and April Dawn.

She gripped the handrail and started up the ramp. *Please, God, let the widow Giotti be at the party.* A nice, respectable woman, the widow was. A lady.

Babbo needs a lady, God. You must see that.

Nineteen years he'd been alone after Carina's mother died, but he was too busy building the business and raising a daughter by himself to think about being lonely. Until April Dawn. She'd been hardly older than Carina, but the woman had a way about her that could make a man think he was lonely even when he wasn't.

Carina hadn't liked her from the start. But Babbo was a grown man. She hadn't voiced her misgivings.

What a mistake! April Dawn had not an ounce of conscience in her. After less than two years of free-spending, high-living, game-playing marriage, she'd left him. And taken him to the cleaners in the divorce. One thing about April Dawn—she wasn't stupid.

As for Babbo—about most things, he was practical and down to earth.

But when it came to women, he clearly needed help.

Two

LEANDER FORTUNATO WAS POURING DRINKS BEHIND THE BAR. He was a handsome man, in a craggy sort of way, Reid conceded. Tall and lean in contrast to his brother's portliness, he looked at the world through sharp, dark eyes under heavy black brows and a thatch of gray hair. A wiry mustache tickled his upper lip under a strong Roman nose. Reid wondered where he'd been to have such a tan in the middle of winter. Somewhere other than Seattle, that was certain.

"Ah, Signore Kincaid!" he said as Reid approached the bar. He held up a bottle. "Vino?"

Reid lifted his brows in surprise. Leander knew who he was after all. "No, thank you. A soda will do."

"How about a *granita? Nocciola*—hazelnut. *Mia favorita*." Before Reid could answer, he was filling a tall glass with shaved ice. He turned to reach for a bottle of syrup from the row behind the counter, selected one, and poured a generous dollop over the ice. "A splash of syrup… a little latte…fill with soda water," he said as he added each ingredient. "And here she is!" He placed a tall spoon in the glass and handed it to Reid with a flourish.

"Grazie." Reid hesitated. "I didn't realize you knew me, Signore Fortunato."

"Try it," Leander prompted, pointing to the glass, as if Reid's approval were of the utmost importance.

Reid took a spoonful of the creamy iced drink, closing his eyes as he savored the sweet, nutty concoction.

Maybe he'd misjudged Leander. He opened his eyes and nodded. "Mmm—good."

Leander clapped his hands together, beaming. "You are the one Mama calls *Zampogna.*" He stretched his arms along the bar and leaned forward.

Reid grinned. Nonna Pippa had thought his name very odd. "Like the pipe of reeds?" she'd asked, mimicking the playing of panpipes when he'd first come to work at the ristorante.

And so he'd become Zampogna, the reed pipe. He'd even brought his clarinet and saxophone to work to show Nonna Pippa how appropriate her nickname was.

"She's something else, your mama," Reid told Leander. He eyed the man over the rim of his glass as he took another spoonful. "But I worry that she works so hard."

Leander laughed heartily. "Mama will work till the day she dies—God forbid it should happen soon."

Reid's feelings of goodwill toward Leander quickly evaporated. He turned away from the bar with a sour taste in his mouth that had nothing to do with the granita.

There were Fortunatos everywhere he looked, from Franco, acting as if he hadn't a care in the world, to Nonna Pippa, who had actually abandoned her apron for the occasion. Her dress, as shapeless as the dresses she wore for everyday, glittered with rhinestones. He caught her eye and waved.

"Zampogna!" she called, gesturing.

"Go say hello to Mama," Leander urged. Reid was already on his way.

"Signora Pippa." He lifted her hand for a kiss when

he reached her side. "You look smashing. Will you honor me with a dance?"

It didn't take much to talk her into a turn around the dance floor to his mother's lively music. Nonna Pippa loved to dance.

He grinned at his mother over Nonna Pippa's head as he guided her around the floor. Dolly Kincaid was in splendid form tonight. She'd already started to warm up the crowd for karaoke with her upbeat patter and a couple of twangy country songs she'd wailed out between the dance tunes. Everybody loved her.

It was hard not to like Dolly, Reid reflected as he spun Nonna Pippa under his arm. She was great fun, vivacious and good-humored. A little quirky. Compassionate. Tenderhearted in the extreme. Reid worried about people taking advantage of her.

He'd had his share of arguments with his mother, of course—they both had strong opinions, a stubborn streak a mile wide, and the same quick temper. But since his father had deserted them eight years ago, when Reid was seventeen, to marry someone "younger and more interesting," Reid's role with Dolly had been more like father than son.

Not that she encouraged him. "Reid McAllister Kincaid," she'd told him more than once, "I know you're tryin' to help, but I really can take care of myself."

When he finished his dance with Nonna Pippa, Reid led her to the stage where Dolly was pulling CDs from her portable library.

"Nonna Pippa, I'd like you to meet my mother, Dolly Kincaid. Mom, I've told you about Signora Pippa."

Dolly reached down to take the old woman's hand

between hers. "I'm so pleased to meet you, Signora Fortunato. You must be very proud of your sons and their families."

The Fortunato family matriarch bowed her head modestly. "The pleasure belongs to me. You got a fine son, too, Signora. And can he dance!" She patted Reid on the cheek. "A good boy. I got my eye on him for Carina Sabine."

"You do?" Dolly and Reid said in unison.

It was the first Reid had heard of it. He'd never met Leander's daughter, though her office was in the same dark corner of the restaurant as her father's. As director of training for the franchise operations, she was often out of town. Apparently when she was home, she worked during the early hours of the day. In his four months working dinner shifts, he'd never run into her.

"She's older than I am, isn't she?" Reid asked.

The old woman looked surprised. "One, two years. What does it matter? You are a man. She is a woman."

Can't argue with that logic, Reid thought, grinning. At least not with Nonna Pippa. Somehow he'd gotten the idea that Carina Fortunato—Carina Sabine Fortunato—was much older than twenty-six or -seven. Maybe because she held such a responsible position in the Fortunato family business. But then, she was Leander's daughter. His only child, in contrast to Lorenzo's seven.

"You're quite enough for me, Nonna Pippa," he teased. "What would I want with your granddaughter?"

She snorted. "*Basta*—enough." But she looked pleased. "Carina will come, and you will see. Now you got to say hello to *mia famiglia.*" She took him by the arm and led him around the room to greet the rest of the clan, beginning with Lorenzo's wife, Felicia—who was as unlike her large, jovial husband as a pumpkin and a pickle—and moving on to all seven of their children, eldest to youngest in proper order.

There was Romo, attached at the hip to his new bride, and Franco, in earnest conversation with a different girl every time Reid saw him. Marcella, with her big brown eyes and flirtatious smile, had several young men following behind her like puppy dogs. Salvatore, who at fifteen had nearly the girth of his father, didn't move away from his spot next to the buffet table for more than a few minutes at a time. The ten-year-old twins, Tiara and Aurora, were holy terrors, chasing each other around the restaurant and nearly knocking Nonna Pippa off her feet. Fortunately, they seemed to have forgotten all about Spumoni.

Finally, there was six-year-old Santo in his pint-sized tuxedo, who despite the fact that he was clearly spoiled by everyone, was respectful, polite, and serious beyond his years. He, too, took Nonna Pippa for a clumsy but determined turn around the dance floor.

"Be lookin' in those notebooks for a song to sing," Dolly told the crowd breathlessly after she'd regaled them with what Reid knew was one of her favorite country songs, Pam Tillis's "Mi Vida Loca." "My Crazy Life." Dolly called it her theme song.

She'd trilled her tongue like a Spanish cowboy and tripped into a high-pitched "yi, yi, yi, yi, yi!" that had Felicia stamping her high heels like a flamenco dancer. "Brava!" Leander had cried from the bar.

Reid might be biased, but he'd never seen a karaoke hostess as good as his mother at getting people up on stage. She flattered and coaxed and cajoled with the best of them, but mostly she so clearly was having the time of her life that everybody else wanted to be in on the fun.

"Leander Fortunato," Dolly drawled into the microphone, "you come out from behind that bar sometime tonight, you hear?"

"You got a duet?" he called from across the room. "For me and you?"

"I think I can find somethin'," she answered, her tone coquettish.

Reid frowned. Was his mother flirting with Leander Fortunato? Just how had she landed this gig tonight, anyway?

Feeling a need for air, he escaped the crush of people around the dance floor and made his way to the fountain in the foyer, dropping down onto its marble edge next to Santo, who was scraping a bowl of orange *sorbetto* with his spoon.

"Pretty good?" he asked the boy.

Santo nodded but said nothing. They sat quietly, listening to the sound of water trickling from the fountain as if it were music. The winged statue of Cupid, his bow pulled back and his marble eyes vacant, seemed to be aiming his arrow directly at Reid's heart. Copper and silver coins glinted in the fountain's pool like pieces of private dreams rubbing shoulders with each other.

Fortunato's Ristorante had one of the most dramatic entryways of any building Reid had ever visited. A sweep of curved marble stairs descended from the ornately detailed bronze-and-copper doors at street level to the elegant waiting area with its marble fountain and velvet-upholstered benches on either side.

A flash of movement outside the high, street-level windows caught Reid's eye. He pointed. "Look, Santo."

To the right of the doors, a Pembroke Welsh corgi and a pair of jeans-clad legs with white athletic shoes attached were splashing through the puddles on the sidewalk. The corgi's short legs took a dozen steps for every one of his person's. It was a wild night for walking the dog.

The legs slowed, and the corgi strained at its leash as a miniature poodle and a pair of stretch pants tucked into stylish boots approached from the opposite direction. Another pair of die-hard Seattleites, undeterred by the wind and rain.

The jeans stopped. The stretch pants stopped. The poodle wagged its tail, and the tailless corgi wagged its entire hind end. They barked joyfully, touched noses, and then, as both pairs of legs moved on, reluctantly left each other behind, peering over their shoulders. "Love at first bark," Reid observed.

Santo looked at him solemnly.

A pair of nicely turned ankles in high heels appeared through the window in the wake of the late-night dog walkers, the length of their owner's stride indicating a pair of extra long legs beneath the coat that swished around them. Legs with a purpose, Reid thought as they disappeared at the end of the last window.

The front door opened, and the legs reappeared suddenly with an entire woman attached. A very lovely woman. Reid sat up straighter.

"*Who* is *that?*" he breathed.

"My cousin, Carina," Santo said.

Reid stood up automatically, spine straight and shoulders back, clasping his hands behind him. Carina Fortunato commanded attention.

Unbuttoning her coat, she stood at the top of the stairs and surveyed the scene as if she owned the place. Which in a manner of speaking, she did. Or would one day.

She descended the stairs. Beneath her camel-hair coat she wore a brown suit with a fitted jacket and a short straight skirt. A gold heart hung on a rope chain around her neck. She moved like Spumoni, sinuous and surefooted.

There was a catlike quality to her face as well. Prominent cheekbones and a square jaw narrowed to a small but resolute chin. Her short, dark brown hair was brushed behind one ear and left to swoop over the opposite cheek from a deep side part. Gold earrings gleamed against her olive skin. Her nose was long and straight, her lips full. Very Italian, he thought. Sophia Loren Italian.

His eyes met hers for a brief moment as she reached the bottom of the stairs and began to slip out of her coat. Her eyes were toffee colored and somnolent.

Suddenly she stopped, her head snapping away from him and her coat dropping unnoticed to the floor. "Babbo!"

He automatically stooped to retrieve the coat, turning his head at the same time to follow her stunned gaze. Dolly had somehow cajoled Leander up on stage. Each of them held a microphone. The introduction to Natalie and Nat King Cole's "Unforgettable" boomed through the speakers.

Dolly was really playing this one up, Reid thought, rolling his eyes at his mother's theatrics. She'd removed her cowboy hat and pushed her red hair off her face. The hat she held across her heart. She looked about twenty years old—no, younger. She looked like a love-struck teenager, gazing up at Leander as if she adored him, stars in her eyes and all.

He frowned as Leander started to sing, gazing down at Reid's mother with a look of adoration mirroring her own. Whoever would have thought Leander had such talent—not just the singing but the acting, too?

"Babbo!" Carina cried again. "What is he *doing up there*?"

Three

REID'S HAZEL EYES AND BLOND GOOD LOOKS WERE LOST ON Carina after a brief initial impression. The sight of her father on stage with microphone in hand wiped out everything else. And then when he started to sing...

Babbo didn't sing. At least, she'd never *heard* Babbo sing. Not along with the radio in the car. Not in church, where he held the hymnal as far away as he could and frowned at it. Growing up, she'd never even heard him sing in the shower. Where had he acquired such a voice?

And where had he gotten the daring to get up on a stage? Babbo never got up in front of people. "Terminal stage fright," he called it. Even conducting business, Leander wrote the presentations, but Lorenzo delivered them. Life had always been that way. Her father admired Carina profusely for the work she did as a trainer for the franchise stores. "All those eyes on you!" he'd say. "Everybody listening!"

"I just pretend they're in their underwear, Babbo," she'd tease him, just to see his horrified expression.

She glanced at the urban cowgirl sharing the stage with her father. Definitely not the widow Giotti. The deejay, then. The karaoke hostess.

Whose idea had karaoke been? Lorenzo, maybe— Lorenzo tended toward the flamboyant.

Even "flamboyant" seemed a mild term for her father's singing partner. Carina took in the glittering gold stars on the woman's skirt and the eye-popping pink of her shirt and boots. Her hair was the color of ripe persimmons, no exaggeration. Big, poufy, country-western hair.

She was not the kind of woman Carina was used to seeing in the elegant, upscale atmosphere of Fortunato's Ristorante. How on earth had she gotten Babbo on that stage? He was singing his heart out like a regular Pavarotti.

The duet sounded halfway decent—no, she conceded, it was actually good. She shook her head, still not quite believing it was her father up there singing. And apparently enjoying himself.

The voices stopped. The music stopped. Babbo and the redhead were still gazing into each other's eyes. No one was clapping. Carina looked around and realized everyone else was as stunned as she was.

Her father lifted the microphone once more, his eyes searching the room and stopping when they spotted her. "Ah, cara! We've been waiting for you before we make the announcement!" Leander pulled the redhead close and nestled her under his arm, where she seemed to fit perfectly.

Announcement! What was going on?

"Reid, darlin'?" the redhead called out, lifting a hand to shade her eyes as she searched the room. A diamond so gargantuan it could only be a fake winked on one finger.

Carina felt a movement at her side and glanced over to see that the blond man who'd been standing with Santo at the fountain was now at her elbow, raising his arm to acknowledge the woman on stage.

Reid, darlin'?

"Tonight you must all meet Dolly Kincaid," Leander said. *"Mia fiammetta."* His face was flushed, and he was wearing a silly grin. For that matter, so was the woman.

"Mia fia-*what?*" the man next to Carina muttered fiercely.

"Fiammetta. His 'fluttering flame.'" Carina wondered if she sounded as shell-shocked as she felt. "Who on earth is she?"

"What in the world is she doing with *him?*"

Leander answered both their questions as if he'd heard. "On Christmas Eve, aboard the cruise ship *Ysolda* in the Caribbean, it was my great good fortune to meet this *bella donna*—this beautiful lady," he said. "A gift from God. She has taught me to sing again, my Dolly."

His eyes again found Carina. "God and *mia famiglia* I have to thank for this: Mama, Lorenzo, Felicia, Carina." He blew kisses around the room.

"And now—" He paused dramatically. "And now Dolly Kincaid and I would like to invite you to our wedding!"

A moment of stunned silence, then a "Bravo!" from Lorenzo, and the room erupted.

Leander grabbed Dolly and swept her into a back-bending kiss. When they came up for air, flushed and breathless, Dolly Kincaid threw her cowboy hat in the air. "Yi, yi, yi, yi, yi!" she cried and caught the hat on its way down.

Without further ado, Carina fainted.

Frankly, Reid was glad for the distraction. He felt Carina sag against him and grabbed her just in time to keep her from crumpling to the floor.

"Valentine's Day," Leander was saying. "Everyone's invited!"

Valentine's Day! Reid pulled Carina back from the edge of the crowd and laid her on one of the benches in the foyer. Getting married in six weeks after meeting Leander eight days ago? Had his mother gone crazy?

Santo was the only other person in the crowd who'd seen Carina faint. Reid sent him for a glass of water and began to slap Carina's face gently, one cheek and then the other. Her eyes opened just as Santo returned and threw the water into her face.

She sat up abruptly, blinking and sputtering. It was all Reid could do to keep from sputtering himself, as Santo looked on with an owlish expression. Perhaps he should have explained he'd wanted the water for her to *drink*.

"What are you doing?" she gasped.

"Good, your color's coming back." Reid fished for a handkerchief in his pocket and thrust it at her. "Sorry about the drenching," he added. "Your cousin got a little carried away. Are you all right?"

She closed her eyes, shook the water from her hair, and dabbed at her face with the handkerchief. "No, I'm not all right! I'm wet. What are you doing?" she asked again.

"Reviving you," he answered patiently. "You fainted."

She looked up at him as if she had no idea who he was or what he was talking about. "What do you mean, fainted?"

He ignored her for a moment. "Santo, find Nonna Pippa for me."

The boy nodded solemnly and disappeared into the crowd. Reid sat down next to Carina. "Keeled over. Passed out. Swooned."

"I know what *faint* means," she said irritably, sitting up. "Why would I have fainted?"

He raised his eyebrows. "I must say it seemed like an overreaction. But I got the impression you were about as thrilled with the engagement announcement as I was."

Carina stopped mopping her brow and buried her face in the handkerchief instead, groaning and mumbling unintelligibly.

"What?"

She dropped the hankie into her lap. Her hair was mussed and her mascara smudged beneath one eye. Somehow it made her more approachable. "I just can't believe he'd spring an *engagement* on me!"

"I know what you mean," Reid muttered.

"What could this woman want but Babbo's money? This—this karaoke hostess?" She grimaced, as if the words pained her. "Why does he *do* this to himself? What's so hard about choosing a *lady*?"

"Dolly Kincaid happens to *be* a lady," Reid said, his voice frigid. "She also happens to be my mother."

"Your mother!" She looked at him, aghast. "Who *are* you?"

"My name is Reid Kincaid. I've worked here since September." *Little you or Leander would know—or care.*

"And you're the one who introduced my father to that—to your mother?"

He narrowed his eyes and set his mouth in a grim line. "If he were the last man on earth, I wouldn't wish your workaholic skinflint of a father on my mother."

"I beg your pardon?"

"You heard me. My mother deserves to be happy. Leander Fortunato doesn't have a clue how to treat a woman like her."

"A woman like her," Carina repeated. "A woman like her! *Look* at her, man! She's nothing but a—a dance hall girl! How do you think she got her hooks into my father? And *why,* do you think? I will not let another gold digger ruin his life!"

"Gold digger? Excuse me if I find your judgments ironic, considering your father is a hardheaded, cold-hearted penny-pincher who doesn't deserve a woman with one-tenth the warmth and love my mother has to offer."

"Now, wait a minute!"

"Look, he's so cheap he makes his own mother do the grunt work around here so he doesn't have to hire someone. Seventy-five years old and sweeping the side-walks. His own mother!"

Carina opened her mouth, but nothing came out for a moment. "You haven't the faintest idea what you're talking about," she finally sputtered. "Nonna Pippa would wither away and die without her work to do."

Reid wouldn't listen. "And you have no idea what *you're* talking about. My mother doesn't care about money! My father gave her a generous settlement—which she'll lose by marrying your father, by the way—and she's perfectly capable of making her own living, anyway."

"Oh, she's *divorced.*" Carina's voice dripped with derision. "I'll just bet she got a generous settlement."

They glared at each other.

"Carina Sabine?"

They both looked up at the sound of Nonna Pippa's anxious voice.

"Santo says you had a fainting spell."

"She's fine." Reid couldn't contain his fury. He stood. "If you'll excuse me, *I'm* the one not feeling so good."

Nonna Pippa hovered over Carina anxiously, cradling the scruffy little alley cat that had somehow managed to worm its way into the old woman's affections.

Carina sat up, shaking her head in an effort to clear it. "I'm all right, Nonna."

Her grandmother looked at her with her bright black eyes. "You are swooning for Signore Kincaid, si?"

"I would as much swoon for Signore Kincaid as for the man in the moon," Carina answered darkly.

Nonna Pippa's eyes widened. "A fine boy, Signore Kincaid." She stroked her calico cat, who purred like an ancient lawnmower just about ready to give up the ghost.

"You wouldn't think so if you'd heard what he said about Babbo. *Babbo!*" she wailed, suddenly remembering. "Nonna, how could he? This cowgirl with her impossible orange hair and her yi-yi-yi. Dolly! April Dawn! How *could* he?"

"She is no April Dawn," Nonna Pippa said firmly. "A good woman, this Signora Kincaid."

Carina drew her brows together in a scowl.

Nonna Pippa held up a warning finger. "Only a good mother could have a son so fine."

"What are you talking about, Nonna? Who is this boy who makes you forget about watching out for your own son?"

"I see that my son is happy. As for Zampogna Kincaid—he is my friend. Even my Spumoni likes him!"

Carina snorted. "You let that skinny upstart of a *cat* choose your friends? And what do you mean, 'Zampogna?'"

"This cat you poke fun with," Nonna Pippa said, setting her chin, "knows good from bad like me and you know night from day. As for Zampogna—his name in English is Reid, si? A funny name, like the reed pipe. So I call him Zampogna, the Reed."

This was serious, Carina thought with alarm. Nonna Pippa had a nickname for Reid Kincaid. Somehow he'd wormed his way into her affections. Were they in on this together, then? The son and his mother, to con the entire family? Were Kincaid's harsh words about Babbo only meant to throw her off?

"Zampogna is good for this old woman," Nonna Pippa said stubbornly. "Use the brains God is giving you, child! A man who knows how to be treating the old ladies knows how to be treating the young ladies, too."

Carina's jaw dropped, but only for a moment. She snapped it shut, narrowed her eyes, and raised her chin to the same angle as her grandmother's. "I cannot believe what you're suggesting!"

Nonna Pippa glanced again across the room and shook her head in disgust. "You two are the pair tonight, anyway, with your sour faces. On the eve of the new year! I go to dance now," she called over her shoulder as she stalked away. "I think so should you!"

Carina's eyes flew past her grandmother straight to Reid Kincaid, who was standing alone across the room with his arms crossed, glowering. They *were* a pair, she admitted to herself as she realized that she, too, was standing with her arms crossed, wearing an identical frown.

She dropped her arms and tried to smooth her expression, but Dolly and Babbo suddenly moved across her line of vision, her father doing fancy footwork she hadn't even known he knew how to do. Her scowl returned. She realized that she was rapidly twisting the ring on her pinkie finger. Her father had given her the ring on her sixteenth birthday—a small gold ring with a cupid's arrow piercing its ruby heart.

If she hadn't been so happy with the gift, she might have seen it even then as a warning sign of Babbo's fatal weakness for romance. To marry a woman like April Dawn! To believe now he was in love with Dolly Kincaid—after knowing her a week!

Uncle Lorenzo was doing deejay duty on the stage. How much were they paying this woman, Carina wondered peevishly, for Uncle Lorenzo to play her music for her while she danced?

Her eyes found Reid again, flickered away, then returned to spend a moment taking inventory. What was it about him that had taken in Nonna Pippa so completely?

His reddish blond hair was straight, thick, and well cut, short on the sides and longer on the top, falling over his forehead in a boyish way though he couldn't have been much younger than she was. Tall and broad-shouldered, he was quite good-looking, or would have been if his expression hadn't been so forbidding. Was that it, then—his good looks? Nonna Pippa wasn't ordinarily taken in by a pretty face.

"My Spumoni knows good from bad like me and you know night from day."

Good from bad? Ha! Kincaid had called her father a workaholic skinflint! If Nonna Pippa had heard him say *that,* she'd have changed her tune. Spumoni or not!

So Babbo did work hard. It wasn't a secret. But since when was working hard a thing to be ashamed of? Furthermore, Fortunato's Ristorante wasn't work to Babbo, it was family. It was home—just as it was for Carina.

She twisted her ring in furious agitation. To hear her father called a hardheaded, coldhearted penny-pincher! Just because a man was careful with his money—that made the man a skinflint? No, it did not.

Besides, look at how generous he'd been when he was married to April Dawn. The one time he *hadn't* been careful with his money, and look where it had gotten him.

Oh, Babbo! What are you doing with this—this karaoke queen, this Dolly?

She raised a hand to push the hair away from her face and realized she was still clutching Reid Kincaid's hankie, now damp and smudged with makeup. Who carried handkerchiefs these days, anyway? She traced a finger over the initials embroidered in one corner. He must have known she'd ruin it, but he hadn't hesitated.

Reid turned his head, his eyes meeting hers across the room in a direct gaze. For a moment they seemed to spark fire, glinting golden in the soft light of the chandelier. Carina wondered irrelevantly if they crinkled at the corners when he smiled.

If he smiled.

He looked away again, his grim expression unchanged. Had he been smiling when he stood at the fountain watching her come in? Carina wondered. She couldn't remember.

So what if he was or he wasn't, she thought, irritated that she would even wonder. What did it matter to her? The only thing that mattered was Babbo. She would have a big job talking sense into her father, but she had to do it. She couldn't bear to see him with a broken heart. Carina didn't like this Reid Kincaid, who insulted Babbo with his unfounded and unflattering opinions, but she could see that, under the circumstances, he might become an ally. He didn't want this wedding between her father and his mother any more than she did.

She made a beeline toward Reid as the song ended and tapped him on the arm just as Dolly and Leander stopped breathless and beaming in front of them.

The moment was pure chaos. "Cara!" Her father grabbed her by the shoulders and kissed her on both cheeks.

"Reid!" Dolly cried at the same time, putting her arm through her son's and leaning into his shoulder.

"My two favorite women—"

"The man of my dreams—"

"—must get to know her—"

"—you'll love him like I do—"

"—so glad you two are getting to know each other!"

Carina wanted to shout, "We are not getting to

know each other!" She realized, however, that Babbo wouldn't even have heard. He and Dolly were in a world of their own.

She managed to murmur a greeting, but offering congratulations was outside her ability to act. Dolly didn't appear to notice her coolness any more than her father had.

"A dance with your old Babbo?" Leander asked her at the same time Reid Kincaid pulled his mother onto the dance floor.

How could she say no?

"Babbo—" she said as he grabbed her hand. "Babbo, we need to talk."

"So talk!"

"You must know what I'm going to say. Babbo, you've known this woman a week. How can you marry her? Have you forgotten April Dawn?"

"Dolly is no April Dawn," Leander said, parroting Nonna Pippa's sentiments. "Wait till you get to know her. You'll see."

"I don't have to know her. She's after your money!" She felt Leander stiffen.

"Nonsense. I will not allow you to talk this way. If you knew Dolly like I know Dolly, it would not enter your head to think such a thing."

"Knew her like—Babbo, you've known her a week!"

"Maybe so—" He held up his hand when she started to interrupt. "Okay, so I met her a week ago, no 'maybe' about it. But—I cannot explain it, cara—I also feel I have known her all my life. She is part of me." His voice was tender in a way it rarely was these days. He gazed soulfully across the room.

She knew without looking that his eyes were following Dolly and Reid Kincaid around the dance floor.

She shook her head, refusing to accept his decision. "What was so wrong with the widow Giotti?" she asked. "A perfectly respectable woman."

Leander sighed. "Respectable isn't enough, cara. You should know. Haskell T. Robbins III is respectable enough."

Haskell was the attorney she'd said good-bye to six months ago after a year of dating off and on. "Respectable" was a good description of Haskell, all right. He was solid. A man with prospects. But when she'd found herself happier during their "off" times than their "on," she'd known it was time to let go. Although with Haskell, there had been other issues. Between him and the widow Giotti there was no comparison.

"I just thought you'd meet a woman of means on a cruise, Babbo—"

"I know exactly what you thought," Leander said, his voice flinty. Carina knew that tone of voice. Her father was digging in. Carina used that tone, too. Stubborn as all get-out, both of them.

She ignored his interruption. "A woman of substance. Not some karaoke singer working on the boat!"

Leander frowned. "Now you got something against working women?" His voice was harder than Carina had heard it since she was sixteen and he'd told her she absolutely could not go out with Emilio Pazzo, a boy who wore black leather, had a pierced ear, and played drums in a rock band.

Ironic, isn't it? a little voice whispered inside her head.

"But a woman who makes her living this way!" she said, ignoring the voice.

"Helping people to have a good time—a wonderful calling, si? Cara, you don't know how I've needed to have a good time. I did not know it myself. Did not know how I had buried my heart when your mama died, God rest her soul. Did not see how working, working, working, never taking time to sing, to dance, to play made me less than I am meant to be. Look at my Dolly, would you!"

He turned so Carina could see her across the room, dancing with Reid. She looked young enough to be his sister instead of his mother, alight with life and laughter. As they watched, her smile faded, and she shook her head at something Reid was saying. Light rippled along the length of her persimmon-colored hair like a river of fire.

"Ah, that hair," Leander sighed. His voice had lost its hard edge and held something akin to awe.

Carina shook her head again. Hopeless. Positively hopeless. What was she going to do?

Four

"Mom, I just don't get it. What's gotten into you?"

"I love him. He loves me," Dolly said simply, as if that explained everything. She twirled under Reid's arm.

He pulled her back toward him. "Leander Fortunato doesn't know the first thing about love."

"And you're the expert on love, now, are you?" she asked, her green eyes flashing. "You seein' someone I don't know about?"

"I'm not seeing anyone," he said irritably. At least she hadn't brought up Rae Ann.

"Ahh." How could she put such a world of meaning into one simple syllable?

"He can't possibly make you happy."

"He does."

Reid rolled his eyes. He was getting nowhere. "You could have warned me, at least. Do you think it was fair, not telling me before you announced it to the world?"

"You'd have done just what you're doin' now," she said stubbornly. "And I don't mind tellin' you it's none of your business."

"Mom, be practical—"

"You're far too practical for your own good, darlin'."

He pretended she hadn't interrupted. "You met him a week ago."

"Best week of my life," she said, her green eyes starry. "So far. Have a feelin' it's only the beginnin'."

"I've worked for Leander Fortunato for four months, Mom. I—"

"Don't know the first thing about him." Dolly held up her hand. "Reid, that's enough. I'm a grown woman. I know what I'm doin'."

"He's no different than Dad."

The sudden hurt in her eyes made him immediately sorry. He knew she was remembering how his father had told her he was filing for divorce.

"You're not interesting to me anymore," he'd said, not bothering to wait until Reid had left the room. "You haven't been for years—with your prattle about babies and the PTA and volunteering at the church."

"I stayed home because you wanted me to!" she'd protested.

His look of disdain could have frozen water in a glass. "Whatever."

Interesting, Reid thought, was the fact that the young lab technician Dr. Kincaid had moved in with was now at home, pregnant with their second child, and living Dolly's old life. *Interesting* was the way Dolly had reinvented herself in the last eight years. Reid had thought about pointing out the irony of the situation to his father but doubted it would serve any useful purpose.

"I'm sorry, Mom. I just meant—well, Leander's obviously married to his work the same way Dad is. From everything I've seen, he's self-absorbed and cheap on top of it. You deserve more than that."

Dolly shook her head. "You don't know him, Reid."

He bit his lip, knowing it wouldn't do any good to say she didn't know him either.

"I want you to be happy for me."

"And I want *you* to be happy, Mom. I just wish—"

He stopped at the warning look in her eyes. *I wish you'd think about it.*

"I'd better get back to work." She let her arm slide off his shoulder as the music ended. "Lorenzo's eyes are looking glazed."

Carina tapped Reid's arm a few minutes later as he stared bleakly at the stage where his mother was helping Salvatore through an old Beatles tune, joining in when he faltered, fading out as he gained confidence.

"Care to dance?"

He agreed only because he thought she might want to apologize for the things she'd said about his mother. It crossed his mind that he owed her as much for what he'd said about Leander, but he couldn't bring himself to say he was sorry. Where was the line between truth and courtesy?

"Look," she told him as they swung around the dance floor, "I've been watching you, and you're no happier about this match—this mismatch—than I am. Maybe we can help each other out."

"What did you have in mind?"

"It's crowded here. And public. Will you meet me in my office? Five minutes." It felt more like a command than a request, but he didn't argue as she spun around and strode away, her dark hair bouncing with the energy of her retreat.

Pretty or not, Reid liked Carina Fortunato about as much as he liked strep throat. She was arrogant, high-handed, and cold. But her concern about his mother and Leander's impending marriage was as real as his own, however different their reasons might be. Maybe they could call a truce long enough to figure something out, come up with a plan.

Anything to keep his mother from making this horrible mistake. Could any two people possibly be more mismatched than Dolly and Leander?

He could see the yellow light spilling through the half-open door to Carina's office when he walked down the dim hallway behind the kitchen a few minutes later, balancing a cup of cappuccino in each hand. A peace offering of sorts. Something to smooth the way. Clearing his throat to let her know he was there, he entered without knocking.

He glanced around the small office in surprise. He didn't know what he'd expected, but certainly not teddy bears. They were everywhere: peeking between the notebooks on the shelves, around the corners of the computer on the desk, even through the leaves of the silk ficus in the corner.

Jumbo, giant, large, small, mini. White, black, cinnamon, beige, brown. Bears in dresses, bears in pants, bears in glasses, bears in hats. Beautiful and plain. Elegant and ordinary. Curly, plush, plaid, flowered, and everything in between.

His mother, too, collected teddy bears. He never would have guessed Carina Fortunato and Dolly Kincaid would have had a single thing in common, and already he was wrong.

Carina didn't explain the stuffed animals, and he didn't ask. On a personal level, they had nothing to say to each other. This meeting in her office, while the party in the dining room raced toward midnight, was strictly business.

"Thought you might want something to drink." He set the cups on her desk.

"Leaded or unleaded?"

"Decaf. I can live without a caffeine rush at this point."

She nodded as she picked up one of the cups. "Thanks. I have a feeling I'm not going to get much sleep tonight as it is."

She lifted the cup to her lips and took a sip, then set it back in its saucer and met his gaze. "All right. Let's get down to business. We agree we've got to break up this ridiculous match between your mother and my father, right?"

He bristled despite himself. "Ridiculous because you think my mother's a gold digger?"

"Look, Kincaid, it's nothing personal, okay? I'm sorry if I offended you. I'm just trying to watch out for my father, all right? He met your mother a week ago. A week ago! He's not so smart sometimes about love. Who else has he got but me to watch out for him?"

"Who else has he got? Who else has *he* got?" Reid, still standing, crossed his arms over his chest. "And who do you think my mother has but me? You don't have to tell me they've known each other only a week. My mother is the *only* reason I'm here talking to you instead of having a good time at the party." He drew a steadying breath. How did she so easily get under his skin?

"So we do agree."

"We agree they have no business getting married. That's what we agree on. Period."

Carina's brown eyes flashed. "Period. What else could we possibly agree on?"

Really—she was so irritating! "What I'd like to know," he said stiffly, ignoring her question, "is how your father just happened to end up on the same cruise my mother was working. Doesn't it seem a bit more than coincidental?"

She crossed her arms and narrowed her eyes. "Frankly, yes. Very convenient—the karaoke hostess meeting the wealthy businessman from her hometown in the romantic Caribbean. Finding out her son works for him."

Reid bristled again. "You make it sound like I had something to do with your father taking that cruise!"

"You're telling me you didn't set this whole thing up, you and your mother?"

He snorted. "I thought I'd made my feelings abundantly clear about this—this mismatch, as you call it. As I recall, it was your family Leander thanked for sending him on the cruise—and I believe he named you specifically."

"I didn't think he'd fall in love with the—" She stopped at Reid's glare. "Okay. I heard the widow Giotti was signed up for the cruise," she said. "A good match for my father, the widow Giotti, but he refuses to take the initiative. I thought the change of scenery, the moonlight in the tropics…maybe he'd see her in a different light. I thought they might bump into each other on board, spend a little time together. Have a little romance."

Reid groaned. "The widow Giotti! I wait on her two, three times a week. I heard her talking to friends one night a few months ago. She wanted to take a cruise for Christmas, get away from the cold and the rain and the kids. Of course I told her about Mom and the *Ysolda*. I was making conversation!"

Carina looked aghast. "It's all my fault," she said. "Now I *know* I've got to do something. I can't let her—" She looked up at Reid and stopped, as if thinking better of whatever it was she'd intended to say.

At least she was making an effort to be civil, he thought.

"I did this; I can undo it," she said, her chin firm and her mouth set.

Reid pulled up a chair and sat down across from her. "Listen, I made some…" He searched for the right words. "Some strong statements about your father. Can we just agree that Dolly and Leander aren't right for each other and leave it at that? Without either of us bad-mouthing anyone?"

"Yes!" She sounded relieved. "We were both a bit—"

"Defensive?" Reid supplied.

"I was going to say childish."

Reid lifted a hand to the back of his neck and massaged the muscles before responding. "Yeah. You're probably right."

Their eyes met and held for a moment before Carina looked away. "You're Dolly's only son?" She picked up her coffee cup once again.

"Yes." Her only child, he might have added. Her protector. "It hasn't been easy for Mom these last few years."

"Nor for Babbo—Daddy." She sighed. "He tells me I'm too much the mother and not enough the daughter with him, but he doesn't see how much he needs me."

Reid looked at her thoughtfully as she sipped her

cappuccino. Maybe she wasn't so hard and brittle as he'd thought. Maybe she loved her father as much as he loved his mother, was driven by the same kind of protective urge. Maybe they could help each other after all.

"We don't have much time," he said, keeping his eyes on Carina as he set his empty cup and saucer on the floor next to his chair. "The wedding's supposed to be in six weeks. You have a plan?"

Carina grimaced. "I've tried to reason with Babbo, but he won't be reasoned with. I figure we'll have to go underground."

Reid nodded. "Mom wouldn't listen to reason, either. What do you think?" He shifted uncomfortably. "Sow the seeds of doubt?"

Carina looked every bit as uncomfortable as he felt, Reid thought as he watched her twist the ring on her finger. "What's left?" she said. "We can't lie, though. That would be wrong."

"Isn't it just as wrong to mislead them?"

"Wouldn't it be wrong to let them fall into a disastrous marriage? Here's the way I see it: Our parents think they're in love. Which is to say, they're not in a rational state of mind. In a word—" She paused as if for dramatic effect. "They're handicapped."

"Yes!" Reid agreed. "Incapacitated, even."

"Exactly. They can't be held responsible for their actions or decisions."

"So we've got to make their decisions for them."

"Exactly." Carina slapped her hand on her desk.

The sound made Reid's nerves jump. Or was it the voice of his conscience jangling so harshly?

"Our motives are pure," she argued, as if she could

hear his doubts. "We love our parents. We want the best for them."

Reid nodded, trying to push his uncertainty into a dark corner of his mind. "If we don't watch out for them, who's going to?"

"Miaow!"

He jumped. So Spumoni had found her way to the back of the house. And apparently discovered Reid's coffee cup on the floor.

Frankly, he was glad for the distraction.

The cat looked up at him, her eyes half-closed in contentment as she licked cappuccino froth from her little kitty lips. Then she rubbed against his leg, rumbling loudly, like an engine badly in need of a tune-up.

"What's that cat doing in here?!" Carina leapt up from her chair.

One thing about Spumoni, Reid couldn't help but thinking as the little calico bolted for the door—she wasn't stupid.

He, on the other hand—

He looked at Carina standing over her desk, her expression fierce and her dark eyes flashing.

What in the world was he getting himself into now?

Five

She couldn't believe it. Spumoni acting as if Reid Kincaid were her best friend, for crying out loud, when the scrawny little thing wouldn't let Carina within a dozen feet! And it wasn't because Kincaid was any more approachable than she was, either. In fact, the man had a fuse about as short as her own.

On the other hand...

He hadn't been so hard to deal with once they'd laid down some ground rules. Once they started to focus on their common goal.

And once she decided to make it a point not to insult his mother.

Still, that her grandmother's cat would prefer Kincaid to Carina!

"You go on ahead," she said shortly.

He nodded and left without another word.

It was just a precaution, she told herself a few minutes later as she made her way through the kitchen and back to the party. No sense in raising anyone's interest, disappearing and reappearing together. People saw things, people got ideas, people talked.

She could almost forgive Reid's insults to Babbo; clearly he was in a protective mode where his mother was concerned. Much the way she was with her father. He was only trying to save Dolly from making the same mistake she wanted to keep Babbo from making. From the sound of it, he loved Dolly as fiercely as she loved Babbo.

Of course his love would make him nearsighted about Dolly's faults, if not completely blind to them. Not such a bad thing in a son. She'd just have to keep her own eyes open, that was all.

Maybe Nonna Pippa was right about "Zampogna." Maybe he was a "fine boy." He probably would know how to treat a young lady, as her grandmother had suggested. Perhaps under different circumstances…

She glanced around the dining room as she pushed through the kitchen doors. While she and Reid had been cloistered in her office, someone had handed out party hats and whistles. "Ten, nine, eight, seven…"

The countdown to the New Year! Dolly and Babbo were both on stage with microphones in hand. "Six, five, four, three…"

She spotted Reid with Nonna Pippa near the buffet table.

"Two, one. Happy New Year!"

The noise in the dining room nearly drowned out the popping of fireworks outside as the entire city welcomed in the new year. Nonna Pippa reached up to kiss Reid on the cheek. He gave her a hug, grinning widely, then caught sight of Carina, watching him from across the room. His smile faded, but he raised his hand in a smart salute. *We'll get through this,* his eyes seemed to say.

She nodded and looked away. Dolly and Babbo were entangled in another back-bending kiss on stage. When they straightened, Dolly hit a button on the CD player and lifted the microphone. She began to sing "Auld Lang Syne."

Leander joined in, linking his arm through Dolly's and beckoning Santo and the twins up on stage to join them. By the end of the verse, everyone in the room stood in a circle with arms linked, swaying back and forth and singing lustily, or at least stumbling through the words they knew. Carina stood between her cousin Marcella and Zia Felicia, who was flushed and smiling. For the first time this evening, she felt hope that everything would work out as it was meant to.

Babbo would come to his senses once he got back to work. The widow Giotti would seem more sensible and sane to him than this flamboyant cowgirl who had turned his head for the moment with her exuberance and her persimmon-colored hair.

She'd thought it best not to discuss with Reid the details of her plans to sabotage their parents' romance since she'd decided to prove to Babbo that Dolly was interested only in his money. Reid couldn't be objective; he'd be insulted at the idea. Why push his buttons?

He hadn't shared the specifics of his plans, either, and she hadn't asked. They'd simply agreed to keep an eye on their respective parents, to help each other sow the seeds of doubt, and to keep each other posted on their progress. Carina even gave him the number for her cell phone, a closely guarded secret, so he could reach her on the boat.

The party began to break up not long after midnight. Dolly went to work tearing down her audio equipment, and Carina offered to help.

Dolly had caught her long hair in a band at the top of her head to keep it out of her way while she worked. Even after several hours on stage, she looked fresh and energetic, her lightly freckled skin flushed like a girl's, and her sea green eyes clear and bright. Still, if she was

Reid's mother, she couldn't be all that young. Certainly not as young as April Dawn.

She banished the thought as soon as it appeared. If she kept comparing Dolly and that woman, she wouldn't be able to keep a civil tongue.

"How long have you had your business?" she asked as she helped Dolly lift a large speaker from its stand. It seemed as good a question as any to start a conversation.

"Four years now," Dolly answered. "Part-time, of course. I've never been able to make a livin' at it."

Carina was startled to hear her admit she didn't make enough money to support herself. If she were after Babbo's fortune, she wasn't bothering to be subtle about it.

"Thanks, Carina. It helps to have another pair of hands," she said as they set a second speaker on its side. Her expression was sunny. "Especially hands as capable as I hear yours are. I'm lookin' forward to gettin' to know you. Your father's told me a lot, of course."

"Has he?" Carina tried to keep her tone neutral. "I wish I could say the same. Your engagement is rather a surprise."

Dolly wasn't fooled. "You're hurt." She sighed. "My son is, too. I hope you'll both forgive us." She tossed a cord into a large plastic tub and began to coil another. "We wanted to tell you privately, but things have been so hectic since we got home. And we couldn't pass up the opportunity to announce it at the party."

Of course not. Going public as soon as possible made it harder for a man to change his mind. After the engagement was official, pride entered into the picture. She'd have to stay on her toes to keep up with this one.

"What do you think of the restaurant?"

"Oh, it's lovely. I could get used to this elegance easy!"

Carina quickly bent over a storage box, where she was packing songbooks, to hide her furious expression. *I'll just bet you could,* she wanted to say.

Biting her tongue, she said instead, "It is nice, isn't it? I hope we can afford to renew the lease when it expires next month." She sighed heavily. "It takes so much money to run a restaurant."

"Is Leander having money problems?"

Carina tried to interpret Dolly's tone. Curious? Cautious? Alarmed? "Oh, Dolly, I shouldn't have said anything. My father will be furious with me! You won't tell him, will you?"

Dolly was silent for a moment. "No, of course not. But I wish he'd told me...."

Good, Carina thought. She had Dolly worried. Now all she had to do was let nature take its course. Dolly could use whatever excuse she wanted to break the engagement with Babbo, but Carina would know the truth. And tell him.

You'd hurt Babbo that way? Better now than after they're married. Still, heaviness weighed on her heart just thinking about it.

He was clearly smitten with Dolly Kincaid. This wasn't going to be easy.

"Well, where did you come from, you sweet little thing?" Dolly cooed unexpectedly.

Carina looked up, startled.

Spumoni was wrapping herself around the red-head's pink-booted ankles.

———⊗⊗⊗———

Reid tried to think of a way to approach Leander indirectly and finally decided he didn't have it in him. He was going to have to face him man to man.

Taking a calming breath and letting it out slowly, he walked across the room to the buffet table where his boss—the boss who'd never even spoken to him before tonight—was cleaning up.

"Need some help?"

Leander looked up, his expression surprised and pleased. "Zampogna!" He studied Reid for a moment. "You wish to work, or is it the excuse to talk?"

Reid was glad he'd decided not to resort to subterfuge. Leander was too astute. "Both."

"All this to the kitchen," Leander said with a sweep of his arm. He began to gather up spatulas and serving spoons from empty dishes. "What is it you wish to say?"

Reid followed him around the table, stacking bowls and platters. "I wonder, Signore Fortunato—"

"Please—call me Leander. I do not expect you to think of me as your father, but I would like to think we might be friends."

Reid shifted uncomfortably. "Speaking of my father—I wonder how much my mother's told you about him."

Leander picked up an empty serving tray and placed it on a stack at the end of the table. "Why?"

"Because he hurt her. And I worry that you're like him."

Leander whipped his head around and stared at Reid, his dark eyes spitting fire. "What are you saying? I would never do to Dolly what your father did—abandon her for another woman! You think so, you don't know the least little bit about Leander Fortunato!"

Reid felt his jaw clench involuntarily. "My father is a doctor," he said. "Years before he left my mother for another woman, he left her for his work. His work is his life, Signore. The way Fortunato's Ristorante is yours." He met Leander's fierce gaze directly. "My mother deserves more."

The older man's mouth had hardened into a ferocious frown beneath his bristly mustache. Reid stood his ground, his chin set, daring the other man to look away.

For a full minute they stared at each other in silence, neither flinching. "I will think about what you say," Leander finally said. Then his face broke into a sudden grin. "You are a good son for Dolly Kincaid," he added approvingly. "She has told me, and now I see." He lifted the stack of trays and nodded toward the tables and chairs pushed against the restaurant walls. "If you wish to help, put together the dining room while I finish cleaning. You have had your say. I will think about it."

It was noon before Carina dragged herself out of bed on New Year's Day. It had been nearly two by the time she made it back home, still brooding about the night's events. Then she'd lain awake forever as the boat rocked and rolled in the storm. Even with her head under a pillow, she couldn't shut out the sounds of rain beating against the deck and the wind howling through the harbor, snapping the halyards against the masts in an eerie echo. When she finally did drift off, her sleep was fitful, interrupted again and again by dreams that left her heart thumping like a jungle drum.

Sunlight was pouring in through the hatch over the stateroom as she pulled on a pair of sweats, a heavy wool sweater, and a pair of rubber thongs. Sometime during the night the storm had passed. Yawning, she picked up the nylon duffel bag she referred to as her "portable beauty shop," draped a towel over her shoulders, and climbed out of the cabin. One big breath of the rain-washed air immediately made her feel more alive.

Her neighbor's black-and-white cat was sitting on the dock washing himself. She bent to scratch between his ears and felt a sudden unexpected twinge of loneliness as he dropped on his back, his green eyes squinting, and waved a front leg at her.

"At least *you* like me, Sneakers." She bent down to rub his fat tummy. "What's wrong with that Spumoni, anyway? I'm as nice as the next person."

She'd liked having the cat on the boat the two weeks Lou had been gone. During the day the big tom curled up in his second-favorite spot, the stainless steel sink in the forward head; after dinner he curled up in his favorite spot, Carina's lap, purring raggedly, like a lawn-mower in tall grass. At night he insisted she let him out. She didn't even want to know what he did in the hours before dawn, when he came around scratching at the hatch.

"You'll have to come over to visit sometime when Lou doesn't require your company," she told the cat. "I miss you already."

She gave his tummy one last scratch and headed for the women's restroom at the top of the pier. The boat had a shower, but the coin-operated shower in the marina facility was roomier and didn't drain her water tanks. The light was better for applying makeup, too. Her father hadn't outfitted the boat with a woman's beauty routine in mind.

Did Dolly sail? Did her father even know?

The thought of her father with Dolly Kincaid hurried her steps. Today was Babbo's last day of vacation. She had to keep them away from each other.

It's too late, she told herself in a panic as she scrambled for change in her bag. Babbo and Dolly would certainly have made plans to spend the day together. Why hadn't she thought last night about a plan for today? Time—she needed time. Babbo needed time. Time to get perspective, time to rethink this mad rush into marriage.

She dropped a quarter into the pay phone outside the restrooms, punched his number, and waited anxiously. They were probably somewhere together even now, confusing the issue with kisses.

When her father picked up the phone on the second ring, her words tumbled over each other in a rush of relief.

"Hey, Babbo, hope you don't have plans for tonight. I thought I'd fix dinner on the boat, that Mediterranean black-beans-and-rice casserole you like, and I've got a new video, the latest Whitbread—I thought we could watch it together, what do you think?"

"I think you gotta slow down before you lift off into orbit! And a happy New Year to you, cara."

"You too, Babbo. Well?"

"You talking your special recipe black beans and rice? With the raisins and the sweet red pepper? You make it hard for me. But it's back to work for Dolly and me tomorrow, so we got plans tonight to be together."

Carina's heart sank. Of course they had plans to be together. "Back to work for both of you?" Then hopefully, "Dolly goes on another cruise tomorrow, maybe?"

"Oh no! The karaoke work is Dolly's second job, Carina. Dolly is a teacher," he said proudly. "She gives music lessons to the little ones. Every day she goes from this school to that school to another."

"Really!" Carina didn't know what else to say at the unexpected information.

"You know," her father said, "I'm thinking this morning about how you say the widow Giotti is a respectable woman, as if Dolly is not. But what could be more respectable than a school teacher, si?"

Carina couldn't argue with that.

"And the funniest thing I gotta tell you. I'm talking to Dolly this morning on the telephone. She says she was hearing I have problems with the restaurant and did I need some help. 'I got a little saved up,' she says to me. 'You take it if it means saving the restaurant from going under.' 'Going under!' I tell her. 'If going anywhere, Fortunato's Ristorante is going *over*—in a big way! We got no need for your savings. But thank you very much. I love you for the offer.' What a woman, my Dolly!"

Carina was stunned. Offered her savings! "Why, Babbo…" She paused, then hurried on, "Why did she think you were in trouble?"

"She thought she heard, is all. I don't know who would say such a crazy thing, when the franchises are selling like hotcakes. But never mind that. Don't you see? She wanted to give me her savings, cara! So, what do you think now of your worries about she's after my money?" He sounded nothing short of triumphant.

Carina's brain felt scrambled. Offered him *money!* This wasn't looking good at all.

"Babbo," she said slowly, "why don't you bring Dolly here for dinner tonight? To the boat?" If she couldn't prevent their being together, at least she could keep an eye on them.

"My Dolly you want along, too? Cara, you make your old babbo happy. You and Dolly are gonna be friends, I know you will."

She was definitely going to need moral support. "Maybe I'll call Reid and see if he wants to come," she said. "If he's not working."

"Good!" Babbo sounded almost too eager.

Reid was scheduled to work but called back after their initial conversation to tell her he'd found someone to cover his shift. "I think we should both be there," he said. "More distraction."

"Kincaid?"

"Yeah?"

"Did you ever think you'd be chaperoning your mother's dates?"

He laughed, his first laugh since Carina had met him. A nice laugh, deep and rumbling. Something inside her resonated to the sound, and she found herself smiling.

"KINCAID!"

Reid looked across the double row of permit-only parking spots at Shilshole Marina and lifted an arm in greeting. Carina Fortunato leaned against the railing at the top of the Pier K ramp, one hand shading her eyes from the late afternoon sun.

She was full of surprises, Reid thought as he zigzagged through the parked cars toward her. He'd never have figured her for a live-aboard. Last night she'd seemed so at home in the elegant atmosphere of Fortunato's Ristorante that he'd pictured her living that way, in a villa overlooking the sound, if not somewhere on a cliff above the Mediterranean. Last night in her velvet-trimmed suit and gold jewelry, at least until he'd seen her with her makeup smudged and her hair mussed, she'd looked sleek and expensive and completely unapproachable.

This afternoon Carina looked more like the proverbial girl-next-door. She'd pulled a bright orange windbreaker over a yellow-striped knit shirt. Her baggy jeans were rolled up at the ankles, and her deck shoes, worn without socks, had seen their share of salt spray. As Reid stepped over the curb, a puff of air blew her dark hair away from her face. Her skin glowed golden in the lowering sun. He felt warm just looking at her.

She touched his sleeve. "Thanks for coming, Kincaid."

"Yeah. I figure we're in this together." He followed her down the ramp, standing aside as she unlocked the metal gate to the pier and pushed it open.

The *Portofino* was docked a hundred feet farther on. Reid let out a low whistle as they approached. "Wow! She's a beauty! I'd guess a Liberty?"

Carina nodded, looking pleased. "Liberty 458. You know sailboats."

"My old roommate's family had a little Coronado 15," he said. "Fun, but nothing like this. So she's a forty-six footer!"

"She was the only boat Babbo could find that had enough clearance in the cabin for all six-feet-five inches of him." Carina climbed the stairs and jumped across to the deck with catlike grace.

"What's it like, living aboard?"

Carina slid back the hatch and opened the doors to the cabin. "Sometimes it's cozy, and sometimes it feels like I'm trapped in a sardine can. To tell the truth, I'll be happy when the remodeling's done on my house and I can move back home."

"You have a house?" he asked, surprised. It wasn't unheard of, he supposed, for a working woman of twenty-seven, but after seven years of struggling to pay for school on his own, he could barely imagine what it would be like to own a house.

Carina looked up as she descended the stairs. "Right now, 'fixer-upper' is more accurate. When I bought her, I was naive enough to think all she needed was a little elbow grease and paint. Big mistake!" Sighing, she added, "I knew she'd have to be reroofed at some point, but I didn't know how soon. Or that all the wiring and plumbing would have to be updated. But hey, at least she's mine."

He followed her down the stairs into the cabin. "You seem awfully sure she's a girl."

"Of course! Houses and boats are always girls." She took his jacket and hung it next to the stairs.

"Once upon a time, hurricanes were always female, too," he said with a grin.

The *Portofino* was beautiful inside. The louvered cabinets, built-in drawers, and closets were all polished teak, and the sole—the cabin floor—was inlaid with strips of lighter-colored holly. The two forward state-rooms seemed dark and cramped, but the captain's state-room in the stern, with an overhead hatch and row of rectangular portholes along the back of the bunk, was light and airy, cozy without feeling crowded.

Reid liked the efficiency of the main cabin as well as its aesthetics. Supplies were tucked into every available nook and cranny, including beneath and behind the cushions on the benches and underneath the stairs. The galley was barely big enough to turn around in but housed an under-the-counter refrigerator and freezer, a gas oven and stovetop, a microwave, and a double sink, as well as cabinets for food and dishes.

"She's a beautiful boat, Carina." Reid slid behind the dining table. He watched as she lifted the glass from the lantern hanging over the dining table and lit the kerosene-soaked wick with a match. A warm glow filled the cabin.

"She is, isn't she?" Carina set a platter of cheese and crackers and a bowl of salmon dip on the table. "I wish Babbo would take more time—" She stopped.

Afraid of confirming his claim that Leander was a workaholic? Reid wondered. So Signore Fortunato didn't spend much time on his boat. How much time would he spend on Dolly Kincaid?

"Help yourself," Carina said, withdrawing to the galley to busy herself with dinner.

They kept their conversation neutral, Carina apparently as reluctant to bring up their parents' impending marriage as he was. What more could be said? They both knew what had to be done.

Reid told Carina about his classes in music education at the university and his hopes to someday head a high school choral program. He'd been directing the choir and the congregational singing at his small church since he'd been a senior in high school, and he'd never wanted to do anything else.

Carina confessed her love for art and literature in college and the struggle she'd gone through before deciding to take the franchise training job with Fortunato's. "I spent my senior year of college studying art history in Florence. I loved it, but I missed Babbo and the restaurant like crazy. It's home to me. It always has been."

She was smart and intense and interesting. She was beautiful.

Reid couldn't keep his eyes off her. He tried. He told himself he was being foolish. She was attractive, yes, but not more so than a lot of other women he'd known. He hadn't had a serious relationship with anyone since Rae Ann, but he'd dated several women, some of them very pretty.

But he'd never found any of them, not even Rae Ann, as compelling as he found Carina. Besides, when

Rae Ann left him, she'd been just a girl. Carina was a woman. Smart, successful, confident. There was no comparison.

She looked up and caught him staring. Her toffee-colored eyes were startled. A faint flush appeared along her cheeks as their eyes remained locked for an intensely intimate moment. When she finally broke the gaze, Reid realized he'd been holding his breath.

Neither of them spoke for a moment. Then, as if the moment of connection hadn't happened, she asked him, her voice trembling only slightly, "Want to help with dinner?"

I can do this. I can pretend as well as she can that that look meant nothing. Besides, he wasn't willing to contemplate what it *might* have meant.

Struggling to change mental gears, he eyed the narrow aisle where she stood and asked, "You think we'll both fit in the galley?"

She laughed, a low, musical sound that made him want to reach across the space between them and take her hand. *Get a grip, man!* He crossed his arms over his chest. *You are here for one reason, and one reason only.*

"You could toss this Caesar salad right there where you sit." She held up a plastic bag and a large stainless steel bowl. "I want it done before Babbo gets here. He'd be appalled to know I make my salads from a kit."

"From a kit? *I'm* appalled," he teased. "Apparently you didn't inherit your Uncle Lorenzo's cooking skills."

"Who had to? I grew up in the restaurant. The food was always there. Babbo's impressed I can make this one meal we're having tonight. I've never told him it comes out of a box."

"Speaking of Leander…" Reid frowned and looked at his watch. "What time are he and Mom coming?"

Carina glanced at the chronometer on the wall across the room. "They should be here in ten minutes." She leaned over the sink and set the bowl and the bag of salad greens on the table. "So get crackin', Kincaid!"

Reid was sprinkling the Parmesan cheese over the dressed romaine when he heard footsteps overhead. He could feel the sudden tension in the atmosphere and his own stress level rising as the main hatch opened. He looked across the sink at Carina. She was twisting her ring and biting her lower lip.

Oh, well, it was fun while it lasted.

Carina tried not to show her surprise as Dolly Kincaid made her way down the steps into the cabin. She looked like a different person from the flashy urban cowgirl of last night's party, though she still exuded the same kind of energy. Her hello was as breathless and eager as an excited puppy barking joyfully at its first cat, not yet knowing what a cat could do.

"Thanks for your invitation to supper, Carina," she said. "I do so want to get to know you."

It was all Carina could do to keep from rolling her eyes. The woman may have lost her cowgirl outfit, but she still had her affected Texas drawl.

Dolly's eyes darted around the boat as Leander helped her out of her navy pea jacket. *Assessing its value?* Carina wondered, her jaw tightening. No way was Dolly getting her hands on the *Portofino*.

"Oh, my—this is lovely!" Dolly turned in a full circle

as she took in everything. Dressed in jeans and a bulky, apple green sweater, her red hair pulled back in a loose chignon at the nape of her neck and her makeup subtly applied, Dolly didn't look anything like the scheming gold digger from the night before. In fact, she looked like a very nice woman.

All the more dangerous. Carina would have to keep her wits about her; Dolly was clever.

"Sit down," Carina said, her tone more abrupt than she'd intended. No one seemed to notice. Except for Reid, perhaps; he met her eyes briefly before deliberately turning his attention to her father.

She found his eyes intriguing; last night in his off-white turtleneck and neutral houndstooth blazer she'd thought them hazel, that color used to describe any pair of eyes not blue or brown or green. She'd changed her mind. Already tonight she'd seen them thistle gray and olive green, and once, in that moment when she'd looked up to find him watching her, a brown so deep they seemed almost bottomless. Chameleon eyes.

Stop it! Concentrate on Dolly and Babbo.

"You're quiet tonight, cara," her father said as she finished serving the plates and sat down to dinner with her guests. "What are you thinking?"

She looked at her father, then at Dolly, and then at Reid. *I'm thinking how confusing life gets sometimes. I'm thinking how little control we have over our own hearts, let alone anyone else's.* "I'm thinking maybe you would like to ask the blessing on our meal, Babbo." She reached one hand out to him and the other to Dolly and closed her eyes.

"Thank you, God, for the love Carina shows by

sharing this meal she made with her own hands."
Leander squeezed her fingers. "Let this love she shows
be returned a hundredfold. Amen."

"Amen," Dolly repeated softly and squeezed her
hand on the other side.

Carina quickly retrieved both her hands and made
a show of unfolding her napkin and placing it on her
lap. The blessing made her squirm inside. God knew her
motives had nothing to do with love.

They do! she argued with herself. *Whatever I'm doing,
it's for love of Babbo.* But her heart felt heavy.

The casserole and salad and crusty Italian bread got
rave reviews around the table, but Carina hardly tasted
the food. She tried to join in the conversation here and
there—pleasant, polite, getting-to-know-you talk, nothing too serious, nothing that might cause conflict.

"Seconds, Babbo?" she asked as Leander cleaned his
plate of rice and beans. At his nod, she got up and lifted
the lid of the pan on the stove.

He cleared his throat. "So you kids gonna congratu-
late us on our engagement, or what?"

She stopped with the serving spoon in midair and
looked at Reid. He choked and coughed, his face going
red, and reached for his glass of ice water. For a long
moment no one said anything.

Dolly finally broke the silence with a nervous laugh.
"Well! Talk about your awkward moment."

Carina placed the spoon back in the pan, and Reid
set down his glass. Then they both spoke at once.

"Leander's right—"

"I'm sorry, Dolly—"

"—haven't said—"

"—so rude of me—"

"Congratulations," they finished in unison. But even with their voices joined together, it sounded weak.

Leander, scowling fiercely, opened his mouth as if to speak, but Dolly held up her hand. "No, Leander, we need to talk about it. They have a right to their reactions."

"And so do we!"

Dolly took Leander's hand across the table, gripping his fingers hard enough to make her knuckles turn white. "Reid. Carina." She looked from one to the other. "We know how sudden this seems to you. Our engagement. It is sudden. For us, too."

Her thumb began to make small circles on Leander's hand. To calm him or to calm herself? Carina wondered.

Dolly looked at her son. "Haven't you ever had the sense that when somethin' happened in your life, whatever it might've been—well, that it was meant to be?" She shifted her gaze to Carina. "The feelin' that this somethin' had been in the works for eons, but the universe was waitin' for just the right time to let you in on it?"

Reid and Carina exchanged glances. "I'm not sure what you mean," Carina said carefully.

Dolly looked at Leander and smiled. The lines between his brows and on either side of his mouth eased.

She turned again to Reid. "Darlin', after your father left, I really didn't think I'd ever fall in love again. It wasn't just the hurt of his betrayin' me. After I'd worked the hurt through, I realized I'd lost myself lovin' your father. A good part of myself, anyway. Tryin' to figure out what it was he wanted, tryin' to please him.

"After he left, I started figurin' out what it was that *I* wanted. What pleased *me*? I thought about how much I loved music and how much I loved kids." Her eyes returned to Carina. "The divorce was a hard thing, the hardest thing in my life, but it did somethin' good for me. I didn't see it right away, but now when I look back—well, it was almost like comin' out of retirement. I started the karaoke business, and I made up my mind to finish the teachin' degree I'd started way back before Reid was born."

She smiled again at Leander. "I told God that if he wanted me to have another partner, he'd have to bring him to me because I sure as anything wasn't goin' to go lookin'."

Leander squeezed her hand. "And I was finally saying to God a similar thing."

"I was clear about what I wanted," Dolly added. "'He'd have to be strong enough for a strong woman,' I told God, 'because now that I know who I am, I can't ever go back to bein' less.'"

"For me, it was a longer journey," Leander said. "There was for years a ristorante to keep me busy, and then another and another and another. I did not miss a woman in my life." He looked at Carina. "Except for your mama, God rest her soul. Your mama I missed like a part of my soul was gone. She spoiled me a good long time for any other woman."

He looked a little sad for a moment, Carina thought. Was it because his memories of her mother were strong, or because they had faded after so many years?

Still, his voice was cheerful as he went on. "And,

too, I had from you and your nonna enough female influence to make me happy and keep my thinking straight." His eyes twinkled. "Carina to surprise and delight me, her nonna to nag me," he explained to Reid. "And Lorenzo and Felicia to keep having children for me to be uncle and godfather to. A good life I was having."

He sighed dramatically. "Then Carina was off to Florence. A year she was away! Such a year it was for her, and so proud her babbo was! But lonely, too. I saw that she would be having her own life once she came home—and so she should. I saw that I should be having my own life, too." The sadness had crept back into his voice.

Carina wanted to say something, tell him she'd never meant for him to feel abandoned, that she could never have stayed away from Fortunato's for too long. But she couldn't speak around the lump in her throat. Her father was right. He had known when it was time to let go.

At least for her sake.

For his own, she thought, it should have been sooner. Maybe then a woman like April Dawn wouldn't have gotten her hooks into him.

"In business," Leander said to Reid, "a better partner than my brother Lorenzo I could never find. In business, I am a smart man." He tapped his head with two fingers. "In love…" He sighed heavily and held a hand over his heart. "In love I think I am not so smart. With April Dawn I learned—"

"Who?" Reid interrupted.

"My former wife. In name alone," he added hastily. "She did not want to be the wife I wanted. But with her

I learned a lesson: when I am lonely, my heart does a lousy job to find a partner right for me. So I tell God, 'God, next time around I let you choose.'"

He stopped.

Carina felt light-headed. "You're saying God brought you together."

Leander nodded. "For me to meet my Dolly on this cruise I did not even want to take—it was like a miracle."

"And I felt from our first meetin' that Leander was a gift to me from God," Dolly said.

"But how did you *know*? How *do* you know?"

They looked at each other, smiling, and said in unison, "We just do!"

"God spoke the word in both our hearts," Dolly added.

"Now," Leander said, "I have a word of my own, but for Zampogna's ears only." He wiped his mouth with his napkin and folded it neatly. "You will walk with me down the dock?"

"Please do, darlin'," Dolly urged. "I'll help Carina clean up here. When you get back—well, I've been lookin' forward to that Whitbread video."

Carina, who was feeling a bit as if the tide had rushed in and swept the sand from beneath her feet, jumped on the topic as if it were a life raft. "You know about the Whitbread?" Among serious sailors, the grueling 'round-the-world race was a common reference point; if Dolly knew about it, she'd had at least some exposure to sailing.

"Reid and I took sailin' lessons from an Aussie who crewed in the '92 race. He had tales to curl your hair."

"I thought his stories would scare Mom off of sailing." Reid laughed. "Did I have her pegged wrong! All those years, I had no idea how much she loved adventure."

"The real me was under wraps," Dolly said. "No more."

Leander shook his head. "No more." Admiration shone from his eyes. "What a woman, my Dolly!"

Seven

REID AND LEANDER'S STROLL ALONG THE PIER WAS QUIET. Leander made a comment here and there on a boat or two that caught his eye. Reid responded to his observations but didn't initiate conversation. He was too busy wondering what it was Signore Fortunato wanted to say to him away from the two women.

He found out, finally, when Leander stopped at the end of the pier and looked out over the dark sound, his hands hooked behind him.

"I have been thinking about your concern," he said. "That I am the same as your father. Leaving the wife behind for the work."

Reid remained silent.

"You are right when you say Fortunato's Ristorante is my life," Leander continued. "But also you are wrong. Mia famiglia is my life. The ristorante is not the building, not the accounting books, not even the fine food my brother makes. The ristorante is my brother himself. Lorenzo. And his wife, and their sons and daughters— my nephews and nieces—and Mama and Carina. They are why Fortunato's Ristorante is my life."

Reid tugged at his earlobe. He hadn't thought of that. "But it's still work, Signore Fortunato," he argued. "Long hours of work away from Mom."

"And Dolly will be long hours away from me in the schools," Leander said. "But now that I see how well things run at Fortunato's without me, I will take the holidays she takes. Sometimes I will go with her on the cruises, and sometimes she will take off the time from singing to sail with me on the *Portofino*."

"You've decided this since last night?"

"We talked this morning about it, your mother and I. This is the key, Zampogna, when you find a woman to love: to talk about what you are thinking, to listen well, and to make the compromise. All the time, to keep doing it." He turned his eyes to Reid. "I want to tell you I have made the pledge to your mother, that she will always come first for me. And now I make it to you." He held up one hand. "So help me God."

Reid was silent for a moment. "You'll need *some-body's* help if you hurt her," he said fiercely.

Leander's smile showed white in the dark. "You protect your mama like I protect mine," he said approvingly. "Mamas need their sons, but sometimes you gotta let them do what they decide." He laughed. "Like my mama working in the ristorante. 'I let you know when I want to retire,' she tells me when Felicia talks about it not looking good, an old woman working the way she does."

"Nonna Pippa *wants* to work?" Carina had implied as much before, but Reid hadn't wanted to believe it.

"Fortunato's is *her* life, too, Zampogna. What would she do with her days if not for the work?"

What would she do with her days without the work? Reid had never thought to ask.

By the end of the meal, Carina knew for certain the misgivings and twinges of conscience she'd been feeling over her behavior—and pushing to the back of her mind—were more than social programming. As surely as God had made it clear to Dolly and Leander that he'd brought them together, he was making it clear to Carina that she made him very sad.

In fact, she was quite sure that God had been trying to get through to her ever since she'd decided to do him the favor of taking charge of Babbo's life. As if she knew best. As if God couldn't work his will without her interference.

"Judge not, that you be not judged," he'd been whispering. And something about considering the plank in her own eye before she worried about the speck in someone else's. Something about love, too: *"Love worketh no ill to his neighbor,"* he'd been reminding her.

No ill to her father. No ill to a friend, as Dolly was surely going to be.

Forgive me my presumption, God. Forgive me my unfounded criticism and my lack of love. And thank you for a chance at happiness for Babbo....

"Penny for your thoughts," Dolly said gently, her eyes searching Carina's face.

"I'm very glad you came for dinner, Dolly Kincaid." She took a deep breath. "And I'm very glad you and my father have found each other."

With her son and fiancé gone, Dolly might easily have called Carina on the carpet for misleading her about Leander's finances. She'd have had every right to question Carina about her motives. But all she said was, "Thank you. I'm very glad you're willin' to share him with me." Generous, gracious, a lady through and through. It was easy to see why Babbo had fallen in love.

As they cleaned up together, Dolly regaled Carina with colorful tales about teaching, growing up in Texas, and what a good son Reid was when he wasn't trying to control her life.

"I know he doesn't mean to drive me crazy," she confided. "It's just that the divorce brought out all his protective instincts. Maybe he'll lighten up now that I've met your father."

Carina had to duck her head to hide her expression. If Dolly only knew.

When Reid and Leander returned to the boat, they were talking amiably—if not enthusiastic, at least respectful of each other. She wished now she hadn't asked Babbo and Dolly to stay for the sailing video; she and Reid needed to talk. "Things aren't the way we thought," she'd tell him. "I think we need to back off. I think we need to let them make their own decisions."

What if he wouldn't back down? What if he'd already said something to Babbo on their walk to give him second thoughts about the engagement? What if he hadn't bought the story that their parents' relationship was from God?

Have you?

I have, she answered back. The couple's candor had disarmed her. God himself had disarmed her.

Watching the sailboat race on video, Dolly and Leander happily sandwiched between their children behind the table, actually turned out to be fun.

"Whew! Sailing the Inside Passage this summer will seem like nothing after that," Leander said when the video was over.

Carina looked at her father curiously. "You've got sailing plans?" The Inside Passage, known for its breathtaking beauty, was the narrow waterway between the coast of

British Columbia and the long string of islands that stretched from Vancouver Island all the way to Alaska.

"Our honeymoon has to wait till I'm out of school," Dolly explained. "Leander's promised to take me all the way up to Desolation Sound on the *Portofino* come July."

"Babbo!" Carina was surprised and pleased. "You've talked about making that trip since you bought the boat! I'm glad to hear you're finally going to do something about it."

"Dolly makes me remember how important it is to play." Leander pulled her toward him. They gave each other foolish, adoring smiles. Carina looked at Reid, who was sitting back with his arms crossed, watching his mother and her father with a thoughtful expression.

"Your house better be done by then, cara. If not, we gotta boot you off the boat."

"If my house isn't done by then, I'm moving back in with you."

Her father pretended dismay. "I gotta talk to that contractor tomorrow morning, first thing," he declared. "And speaking of tomorrow morning, we gotta be getting home soon."

Carina found herself reluctant to see the evening end. Filled with laughter and lively conversation, the sloop felt more like home than it had since she'd moved on board. Forget a cat when she moved back to the house—she needed a roommate. She glanced at Reid, who was slipping into his brown suede jacket. Or…

Carina Sabine! What are you thinking?

The four of them walked together from the boat to the parking lot. Reid lingered behind as Dolly and Leander drove off, waving.

"Your mother is a nice woman."

"Your father—he surprises me."

Carina scuffed the asphalt with the toe of her shoe. "I know we made a bargain, Reid Kincaid. But sometimes when the circumstances change—"

"Or your understanding of the circumstances."

"Or your understanding of the circumstances," she agreed. She looked up, startled. Their eyes met in a look as intense and intimate as the one they'd shared earlier in the evening.

"Are you thinking what I'm thinking?" she finally asked.

"I'm thinking your father is good for my mother."

"And vice versa."

"I'm thinking we were wrong to try to break them up."

She breathed a sigh of relief. "I wasn't feeling so good about it," she said. "That still, small voice kept nagging."

"I know what you mean."

Her breath caught in her throat. "You do?"

"I heard it, too. And tried to ignore it. Mom and Leander took care of that."

She nodded.

"Carina." His eyes under the streetlight were a dark, fathomless brown. She imagined she could see into his soul. Her heartbeat quickened at what she thought she saw there.

Reid reached across the space between them and stroked her cheek, gently, as if her skin were something delicate and fragile, as if she herself were precious beyond measure. "I'm thinking something else," he said quietly.

Her breath caught. His gentle caress had set her limbs to trembling. "I'm thinking the same."

Funny the little details she remembered about that moment later on. The warmth of his hand. The fringed shadow of his eyelashes across his cheek. A ship's foghorn sounding through the night in the distance—a sound of longing. The smell of clean skin as he leaned forward and kissed her lightly on the lips, a kiss of wonder and promise.

There was a spring to her step as she strode back down the ramp and let herself in the gate. They had a date, lunch on Saturday. Two nights, a day, and a morning to get through first. No matter; anticipation would keep her company.

Reid glanced at his watch, frowning, and once again searched the faces of the weekend crowd streaming through the main courtyard of Grand Central on the Park, the renovated century-old building at the heart of Pioneer Square. He didn't take it as a good sign that Carina was late for their first official date. He himself had been ten minutes early.

"Reid!"

There she was, pushing through the crowd toward his table. He waved and stood to pull out her chair, his frown of irritation changing to one of concern. Something was wrong; he could see it on her face.

"Carina?"

She dropped her leather handbag on the table and sank into the chair. "Have you talked to your mother?" Her voice was strained.

Reid's heart jumped. "No, not since dinner the other

night. Carina, what's happened?"

"The engagement is off—Babbo just told me."

"What?"

"Reid, we can't let them break up. They were meant for each other!" She looked as if she might burst into tears at any moment. "It's my fault. I planted the seeds of doubt in Babbo's mind, and now he says I was right— Dolly only wanted his money, and he'd been a fool again like he was with April Dawn."

"Where on earth did he…how…like April Dawn!" Reid was dumbfounded.

Carina had told him the whole story of Babbo and April Dawn in a long phone conversation after his dinner shift last night. He empathized wholeheartedly with Leander. April Dawn had married him for his money; Rae Ann had left Reid for his lack of it. The dynamic was the same. Their version of "love" had been nothing more than self-interest.

"Babbo wanted her to sign a prenuptial agreement." Carina looked as if she might cry.

Reid looked at her blankly.

"To protect himself," she continued. "In the event of divorce."

"Well, that sounds reasonable. Especially after his experience with April Dawn."

"Reasonable! How can you say that?" Carina's expression was horrified. "To bring up the topic of divorce six weeks before the wedding? No wonder Dolly threw the ring in his face and stormed out!"

"She did *what*? You mean my mother broke off the engagement just because he asked her to sign a prenuptial agreement? What's wrong with her? She knows what happened with his last wife. She should know it's only a precaution. Just a piece of paper."

"If they have to take precautions, why are they getting married?" Carina sounded less distressed and more indignant now. "Of course you'd take his side. You men all stick together."

"Now wait a minute—"

"How can there be love when there isn't trust?" she interrupted. "It isn't Dolly's fault they've broken up. Babbo's wrong. It's ridiculous, this prenuptial thing!"

"But—" Reid stopped. They weren't going to get anywhere arguing. "It doesn't matter whose fault it is," he said soothingly. "What's important is that they work this out. Compromise. Your father knows that that's the key to making love work. He told me."

"I already tried that tack. He set his chin the way he does and said, 'On some things there can be no compromise.' Stubborn old coot."

"I'll talk to Mom, but I think you'd better lay off Leander."

"Oh, you do, do you?"

Reid cringed at her sarcasm.

"You barely know him, yet you think you know better than I do how to deal with my father?"

"On this issue…I just think I understand is all."

She didn't answer, but her silence was thick with anger.

He sighed. "Carina, let's not fight. I'll talk to Mom tomorrow. She has to know how much Leander loves her."

"How could she know?"

"They both just need some time to cool off. You'll

see. The whole thing will blow over in a day or two."

Carina stood and grabbed her bag from the table. "I don't believe it *should* blow over," she said, her expression stormy. "I'm not in the mood for lunch. I'll see you later."

He watched in dismay as she marched off and disappeared into the crowd. If first dates were any indication of a couple's future, he and Carina were already doomed.

And he'd been so sure...

In a foul mood, he returned to his Wallingford apartment, changed into sweats, and drove to Discovery Park where he went for a long run through the woods. The steady rhythm of his feet pounding against the path restored his sense of calm, enough that he made it through his dinner shift later that evening without snapping anyone's head off.

His mother was missing from church the next morning, which was unusual. He found her afterward holed up at home, still in her pajamas and robe and looking miserable.

"I'm not feelin' well," she told him through a crack in the door.

"Mom, I know about your disagreement with Leander. Let me in."

"Disagreement? Don't know where you got your information, son, but disagreement's too mild a term. Leander and I have parted ways." But she let him in, reluctantly, and left him with the Sunday paper while she dressed.

He had no more luck reasoning with her than Carina had had with her father. She wasn't angry, only very sad. "If Leander doesn't trust me enough to know I would never, ever do what that woman April Dawn did to him, then he doesn't know me at all," she said. "He doesn't love me the way I thought he did."

"Maybe he thinks if you won't do what he needs you to do to set his mind at rest, you don't love *him* enough." Reid tugged at his earlobe.

His mother seemed not to have heard him. "You were right about Leander from the start, darlin'," she said ruefully. "He thinks more about his money than he does about me. At least I found out before I married him."

Reid's heart sank. "I didn't know Leander then, Mom. I was wrong about him. He could make you happy."

She shook her head and got up from the sofa, but not before he saw her eyes swimming in unshed tears. "Please, darlin'." Her voice choked. "I can't talk about this anymore."

He watched her walk across the room and into the kitchen, her shoulders slumped. What had he and Carina done?

More to the point—how were they going to fix it?

Eight

WHEN CARINA WAS FEELING STRESSED, SHE CLEANED. BY EARLY evening on Saturday the *Portofino* was spotless. She'd even washed down all the interior woodwork with Murphy's Oil soap, a job she'd been putting off for weeks.

After a quick dinner of soup and a sandwich, she spent the evening doing laundry in the marina facility near Pier K. She tried to lose herself in a good mystery while she waited through the cycles, but images of Dolly and Babbo kept appearing on the pages: singing together on New Year's Eve, holding hands at dinner, snuggling while they watched the Whitbread video. Talking about their plans. Telling their children with such joy and sincerity how they knew their meeting was a miracle, a gift from God.

She slipped into the pew next to Leander at church the following morning but heard little of the sermon—though probably as much as Babbo did. Afterward, when she invited him to lunch, he said he had things to do at the office and couldn't take the time. She knew it was just an excuse.

Reid was either out or not answering his phone; she tried to ring him several times throughout the afternoon and finally decided to intercept him at Fortunato's before his dinner shift. Between lunch and dinner, Babbo and Uncle Lorenzo provided a limited menu for the staff at reduced prices, and Reid had said he often took advantage of the perk.

She owed him an apology. And she wanted to explain. If she could make Reid understand, then maybe there was hope for Babbo.

Reid walked in the door with only two minutes to spare before his shift began. He met her eyes directly. "I don't want to fight, Carina."

"I know. It was wrong to walk out on you the way I did. I'm sorry."

"Are you?"

She brushed an imaginary piece of lint off his sleeve. "I wasn't mad at you. I was mad at me," she said. "I feel as if it's all my fault, the trouble between Babbo and your mother. I don't know if he'd have even thought of drawing up a prenuptial agreement if I hadn't questioned Dolly's character."

"It's no more your fault than mine," Reid said. "I don't know if Mom would be having such a fit about signing the stupid prenup if I hadn't told her I thought Leander was a cheapskate." He clocked in on the computer in the serving aisle just as Franco breezed through the swinging doors from the dining room.

The other waiter raised one eyebrow and lifted a corner of his mouth in a cocky grin at the sight of Carina straightening Reid's bow tie. "Marcella's seating your section," he said. "You've got a four-top."

"Thanks, Franco." Reid pulled a tray off the overhead shelf and placed four water glasses on its skid-proof surface. "I've been at Mom's all afternoon, or I'd have been here sooner," he told Carina. "No luck changing her mind."

"Babbo hardly talked to me in church this morning."

"Mom didn't even go." He dug the plastic scoop into

the ice bin and filled the glasses with ice cubes, then topped them off with water. "We need to talk, Carina."

"I know." She hesitated. "Want to come over to the boat after work?" At Reid's look, she quickly added, "Just to talk."

"Just to talk? Alone on the boat with you at night, as bad as we're both feeling?" He shook his head, his expression filled with both longing and regret. "I don't think that would be a good idea."

She saw her cousin out of the corner of one eye, obviously eavesdropping, and turned her back on him. "Then how about breakfast tomorrow morning?"

Reid nodded. "I have my student-teaching orientation tomorrow, but not until ten. Meet you at Charlie's at eight?" he asked, naming the coffee shop in the Port building at the marina.

"All right."

He was out the door, the tray of glasses balanced in one hand.

Carina was already seated at a window booth, sipping coffee and staring out over the marina when Reid arrived at Charlie's a few minutes after eight on Monday morning.

She smiled at him as he slid in across from her, a smile that warmed him from the inside out. He couldn't believe how elated he'd been last night when she apologized. When she let him know she wanted to work things out.

"Good morning. I'm glad you're here."

"Morning. You look great, Carina." He reached across the table to touch the sleeve of her ivory angora sweater, unable to resist its soft nap. The way she leaned into his hand slightly made him want to pull her into his arms.

We're here to talk, Kincaid, he reminded himself.

"I need to know why you were so angry Saturday," he said. "About me defending your father."

She avoided his eyes. "Could we order first?"

"Because if I'm not allowed to have my opinion without you getting angry," he continued as if she hadn't said anything, "this isn't going to work."

Carina's eyes met his again, studied his face a moment. "You're allowed," she finally said. "But I can't guarantee I won't get angry."

"What *can* you guarantee?"

"That when I'm wrong, I'll say I'm sorry. That I'll talk to you about it." Once more she smiled, a secret Mona Lisa kind of smile. "That being hot-blooded has an upside as well as a down."

"Coffee?"

Saved by the waitress, Reid thought, his face warm.

With their breakfast orders taken and the menus removed from the table, Carina launched into her tale.

"It's about Haskell T. Robbins III," she said. "A good man with many fine qualities. We dated for a year, off and on. Six months ago I broke up with him."

"And now you're sorry." Reid was suddenly deflated. "That's why you think Mom and Leander are making a mistake." This wasn't what he'd wanted to hear.

"You're jumping to conclusions, Reid. It's true that Haskell was a good match in some ways, but in one way he was not. A very important way: he didn't trust me." She sent him a significant look. "Every time I had a business lunch with a man, every time he thought I laughed too hard at another man's joke, every time I smiled at another man, he accused me of flirting and sulked for a week."

"*Were* you flirting?"

"Reid! No, I was being friendly." She threw her hands up in the air. "I'm Italian. We're friendly people."

He grinned. "Just teasing. You've got a lot of your Nonna Pippa in you when it comes to sociability, you know?"

"You think so?"

"Absolutely." *When it comes to stubbornness, too.* She and her father both. Could this be a good thing, the Fortunato stubbornness married to the Kincaid stubbornness? He hoped so. Because even if Leander and his mother never resolved their differences and tied the knot…

"Western omelet and sausage and eggs. Anything else I can get for you?"

He looked up at the waitress gratefully. Saved again! What in the world had he been thinking?

"We're fine," he said.

Carina smiled and nodded at the waitress, then turned her attention back to Reid. "So anyway—where was I?"

"Haskell T. Robbins III," he said. "Sulked for a week. Shall we pray?" Without waiting for an answer he bowed his head and offered a short blessing.

"Haskell," he prompted as he cut into his omelet.

Carina absently sliced her sausage into bite-sized pieces. "He was worst when I went out of town for franchise training, which was often," she said. "He called me three or four times a day, left messages at the hotel desks. The last straw was a San Francisco trip last June—he flew down to check up on me.

"We had it out right there. 'How can you say you love me when you can't trust me?' I asked him. 'I've tried to ease your fears every way I know how. What's the use? How can there be love when there isn't trust? I'm sorry,' I told him, 'but this is no good for me anymore.'"

"After the poor man flew all the way to San Francisco to see you?"

She made a face. "You're teasing again, right?"

"I'm teasing. So what did he say?"

"You can't guess? He asked me if I'd met another man." Carina shook her head. "In my book, trust is foundational for love. How much does Babbo trust your mother—how much does he *love* her—if he won't marry her without a prenuptial agreement?" She shook her head again. "She doesn't deserve the way he's treating her."

Reid was silent for a moment. "I see your point," he finally said. "You're right. Mom needs to know Leander trusts her. But he's been burned before, Carina. I know what it's like to believe someone loves you and then find out they were only interested in your money. Mom knows that's not true for her. Why can't she show him that?"

"Someone was interested in you for your money?" Carina asked instead of answering his question. "I didn't know you *had* money."

"I don't. Probably won't ever have a lot. But Rae Ann thought I would someday." He spread strawberry jam on a triangle of toast.

"Rae Ann?"

"My high school girlfriend." He sighed. "My dad's a doctor, you see. A plastic surgeon. A good one, very successful. Dad and I both assumed I'd follow in his footsteps—Dad because he's always gotten whatever he wanted, and me because I wanted to please him. Rae Ann liked the idea that I was going to be a doctor."

He bit into his toast and chewed slowly, aware that Carina was waiting impatiently for him to continue. "And?" she urged as he wiped his mouth with a napkin.

"Something happened when my dad left and my mom started figuring out she'd been living her life for him instead of for herself. Remember how she talked about that the other night? Well, I realized I was in the same boat she'd been in—wanting more than anything to make him proud of me. So I started thinking about what I wanted to do. What I was good at. What gifts God had given me that I could give back to him. That's when I started leading the singing at church and then directing the choir.

"My dad had always told me he'd pay my tuition and expenses for the first four years of college, but when I told him I wanted to be a music teacher, he changed his mind. 'You go into teaching, you're on your own,' he told me."

"Oh, Reid!" Carina looked pained.

"Yeah. But it was okay because I knew I'd made the right choice for myself. I applied for scholarships, and I got my first job waiting tables and started to save money. And I had Rae Ann—I was crazy about her. Or at least about who I *thought* she was. I had our whole life planned, our whole future. We didn't talk about it much—I just assumed.

"Then on the night of high school graduation she told me she'd been counting on being a doctor's wife. 'Teachers don't make any money,' she said. That was that."

"Oh, Reid!" Carina said again.

"I understand what's going on in your father's head, Carina. Look at what April Dawn did to him. If his thinking seems irrational to you—well, it is irrational. Way down at the bottom of his heart, he's afraid. If Mom would just understand that's what it's about!"

Carina sighed. "If only they were as sensible as their children."

He grunted. "Yeah, right. Like we haven't made a mess of everything."

Carina pushed her plate away. "We made a mess, all right. So how do we *un*make it?"

"Maybe we should just sit back and hope for the best."

She shook her head. "Unacceptable. We have a responsibility to them, Reid. I know we can come up with something."

"No more half deceptions," he warned.

"No deceptions. This time it's the truth, the whole truth, and nothing but the truth. This time, whatever we do, we bring God in on it."

Reid knocked at the door to Leander's office later that afternoon, his sharp rap against the wood sounding more confident than he felt.

"Who is it?" Leander called from inside, his voice grim.

"Reid Kincaid, Signore Fortunato. May I come in?"

He held his breath as he counted off the moments of silence from inside the room. Not more than ten seconds, but it felt like a lifetime.

"Enter," Leander finally growled.

His expression was forbidding beneath his thick gray hair and black brows. "Well? What is it?"

"I want to make a confession."

Leander's glare was suspicious. "What do you think, I'm a priest?"

"No. A man who has been wronged."

Reid spilled out his story, how he'd judged Leander without really knowing him, how he'd belittled him to Dolly, how he'd tried to talk her out of their engagement. How he and Carina had taken it into their hands to do whatever they could to break up the relationship.

"My Carina was part of this?"

"I'm afraid so. She thought she was doing what was best for you the same way I thought I was doing what was best for Mom."

"Why do you tell me this?"

"Because when you and Mom told us at dinner that night on the boat about the way you'd prayed and how you met, we changed our minds. We saw how judgmental and presumptuous we'd been. We saw that God had brought you together there on board the *Ysolda*. We saw that you were meant to be together." He took a deep breath. "We still believe that, Signore Fortunato. God has not changed his mind. Only you have. You and Mom."

"And you do not now think you are being judgmental and presumptuous?"

"I hope not. My mother loves you. She wouldn't be so hurt and miserable if she didn't. I understand, more than you can know, why you have to believe she isn't marrying you for your money. But Carina has helped me understand that my mother has to believe you trust her before she marries you." He stood. "I hope you can find the compromise, Signore. It would be very sad for you to lose each other now."

Leander stood as well. "Please," he said, his scowl easing. "Call me Leander." He thrust out his hand.

Carina was getting the tour of Dolly Kincaid's West Seattle home, which was decorated in rustic country style and held almost as many teddy bears as Carina had in her own collection, artfully displayed on window sills, tabletops, and bookshelves throughout the house.

"I have my entire collection crammed into my office at work while my house is being remodeled," Carina said. "It will be so nice to get them home again. Mid-February, my contractor tells me now."

"Mid-February," Dolly repeated sadly.

Valentine's Day was in mid-February. Dolly and Babbo's wedding day. If it were still going to happen.

She nervously twisted her ring. "I have to tell you how upset I am with Babbo."

"Did he send you?" Dolly asked, hope brightening her features.

"No, he didn't. He would be very unhappy knowing that I'm here. His little *impicciona,* he sometimes calls me. 'Busybody.'" Carina hugged herself and rubbed her hands up and down her arms. When had it turned so cold? "Maybe it isn't Babbo I'm upset with so much as I'm upset with me."

Dolly raised her eyebrows.

"May we sit?" Carina asked.

"Of course. Forgive me."

Carina shook her head. "I should ask for *your* forgiveness."

Drawing her brows together in a puzzled frown, Dolly waited.

"It's my fault, the trouble between you and Babbo," Carina said. "Mine and Reid's."

"Oh no, it has nothing to do with you and Reid, Carina! Your father and I are both happy to see you spending time together. It's how we got to know each other, talking about you—"

"I don't mean that." Carina took a deep breath. "I mean that Reid and I set about to break you up from the beginning. If we hadn't, maybe this trouble would never have happened between you."

Dolly sat back in her chair and crossed her arms. "Oh?"

Carina, looking at her lap more often than at Dolly, told her story. "I was wrong to mislead you about my father's finances," she finished. "I was sure you'd find a way to—unengage yourself, so to speak."

She looked up to find Dolly's eyes riveted on her. "You quickly proved me wrong," she added sheepishly. "Babbo told me the next morning you'd offered to loan him money. I didn't know what to think."

"You were only trying to protect him."

Carina nodded. "Like Reid was trying to protect you. Only neither of us think you need protection from each other anymore." She took a deep breath. "We think you need protection from yourselves."

Dolly frowned. "Go on."

"Reid says you're as stubborn as my father. And if one of you doesn't do something soon—" She stopped. "I don't want him to lose you, Dolly. He has his faults, but he would be very good to you. He loves you. I hope you'll give him a chance."

With a toss of her head, Dolly turned away and stared out the window. "So my son thinks I'm stubborn, does he?"

Carina's heart sank. That was all she had to say?

Hope stirred again when Dolly turned her face back toward Carina. "He's right," she sighed. "Stubborn and proud. Still, after all these years. Thank you for coming, Carina. As for your father..."

She sighed again. "All I can promise is that I will seek God's heart."

Nine

"THAT WAS SO ROMANTIC." CARINA SIGHED AS REID HANDED her into the car on the afternoon of Valentine's Day. "Babbo and Dolly singing to each other at their wedding! If I hadn't heard them New Year's Eve, I never would have believed it."

"I'm still not sure I do," Reid said. "Who would have thought? Eight weeks ago they'd never even met."

"Six weeks ago we were frantically trying to break them up," Carina added.

"Five weeks ago we were frantically trying to get them back together."

Carina laughed. "It's fitting their disagreement had such an O. Henry ending, don't you think?"

Reid nodded. He wished he could have been a fly on the wall the afternoon his mother swept through the restaurant and into Leander's office, brandishing a long plumed pen and closing the door firmly behind her.

Ten minutes later she and Leander had emerged arm in arm, flushed and triumphant, Leander tossing the torn pieces of the signed prenuptial agreement into the air like so much confetti. "The wedding is on!" he'd cried. Dolly's smile could have lit the far corners of the kitchen, especially when the entire staff broke into applause.

Taking one hand off the wheel, Reid found Carina's hand and squeezed it. "'The Gift of the Magi' all over again," he agreed. He glanced at her and almost missed the red light at the intersection. She was positively glowing. Was it only the afternoon sun filtering through the windows? The reflection of her apricot-toned dress? Or was it happiness, radiating from the inside out?

"Have I told you how beautiful you look today?"

"Only twice."

The light turned green. He proceeded through the intersection. "I'm slipping," he said.

She raised her eyebrows. "You also just missed the turn." The wedding ceremony had taken place in the West Seattle church where Reid and his mother were members, but no other place than Fortunato's Ristorante would do for the reception. Lorenzo had been preparing the wedding feast for days.

"A short detour," Reid said. "No one will notice if we're a little late."

"Reid! It's our parents' wedding reception."

"Humor me." He lifted her hand to his lips. "I guarantee you won't be sorry."

"Mmm…" she murmured, rubbing her knuckles along his cheek. The touch and the sound of her voice resonated through his body.

The last six weeks had been a wild ride. Inside the dizzying whirlwind of Dolly and Leander's romance, he and Carina had created a tornado all their own.

After their breakfast at Charlie's, they'd seen each other nearly every day. They worked together, worshiped together, played together. And talked together, endlessly. Reid couldn't imagine they'd ever run out of conversation, though Carina had told him just last night that in the beginning she'd wondered, briefly, if they'd have anything to talk about once they stopped meddling in their parents' lives.

"Still worried?" he'd asked her.

"Not an ounce."

They argued, but cheerfully, and only about nonessentials. About the essentials they agreed: commitment to family, to calling, to learning from their mistakes. And especially, after the mess they'd made interfering in their parents' lives, to seeking God's heart in everything.

They'd chased each other down the ski slopes at Snoqualmie and through the woods at Discovery Park. They'd taken the *Portofino* for a turn around Elliot Bay. They'd kidnapped Nonna Pippa for a ferry ride through the islands. They'd baby-sat Santo, Tiara, and Aurora, and afterward made a solemn vow never to have twins.

They'd wandered through the craft booths at Pike's Place Market holding hands, snuggled atop the Space Needle, and kissed in the elevator going down. The elevator attendant's bored expression hadn't even flickered, as if he were used to such foolishness.

Reid knew now exactly how his mother had felt when she'd met Leander—as if the link between them had been there before they'd ever met, and all they needed to do to fall in love was to recognize it. Accept it. And hold on tight.

With Carina, he had never felt so exhilarated, so alive, so in love.

Or, suddenly, so nervous.

He let go of her hand to pull into a parking space at Alki Beach. The winter sun, sinking toward the white-capped Olympic Mountains across Puget Sound, had the sky to itself. Not a cloud in sight—a rare Seattle day. A perfect day for a wedding.

Or a proposal.

He reached into the inside pocket of his blazer, his heart beating wildly. "Happy Valentine's Day, Carina."

"Happy Val—"

The sight of the black velvet box in Reid's hand stopped her in midsentence. "Reid Kincaid! Is that what I think it is?"

He opened the box and held his breath. The choice, on his budget, had been either a large zircon or a modest diamond; he'd opted for the diamond. It winked in the late afternoon sun.

"I know it's small," he said anxiously, tugging at his earlobe. "Someday I'll—"

"It's perfect, Reid. I love it."

He pulled it from the box and slipped it on her finger. She was right; it was perfect for her hand.

When he looked up, she was smiling at him, her head tilted to one side. "Well?" she prompted. "Isn't there something you wanted to ask?"

He grinned, his nervousness falling away. Leave it to Carina to get right to the point.

"Carina Sabine, will you marry me?"

"Absolutely! What took you so long?"

Dolly and Leander Fortunato stared at their children in open-mouthed astonishment.

"You're *what?*" Dolly cried.

"No!" Leander stormed. "I will not allow it!"

"You're so young!" protested Dolly.

"You only have known each other for six weeks!"

"Have you thought about it?"

"On our wedding day. That they would tell us this

thing on our wedding day!" Leander fumed as if Reid and Carina weren't standing right there.

"It's all our fault," Dolly moaned. "We've been so caught up in weddin' plans, we didn't see what was happenin' before our very eyes."

Leander glowered. "We've got to talk some sense into them."

"Babbo," Carina protested. "Can't you be happy for us?"

"*You* knew in a week," Reid pointed out.

"Miaow!"

Four startled pairs of eyes shifted downward. The sleek, plump, calico cat at their feet rubbed hard against Carina's ankles, looking up at her with adoring eyes.

"Even Spumoni thinks it's a good idea," Reid said— only because Carina was too shocked to say anything.

Silence. The newlyweds looked at each other. Dolly started to laugh. "Who can argue with a cat?" she asked Leander.

He threw his hands in the air. "Who can fight *amore?*" His dark eyes glittered with good humor, as if his blustering had been only a joke. He took his bride's hand. "*Mia fiammetta,* will you dance with me?"

The statue of Cupid hovering over the fountain in the foyer was as blind as ever, Reid noticed when he and Carina whirled by a few minutes later.

But had he always worn that smile?

Barbara Jean Hicks is a freelance writer in Portland, Oregon. She was a finalist for the 1999 Reviewers' Choice and 1998 Readers' Choice Awards and is a past winner of the RWA Golden Medallion Award. No pets are allowed in the 1930s apartment Barbara rents, but when the landlord's not around, she leaves her door open for the neighborhood cat. She also regularly borrows friends' dogs for walks, tail wags, and lap-sitting. Someday she hopes to have one of each, all her very own!

OTHER TITLES BY BARBARA JEAN HICKS:
All That Glitters
An Unlikely Prince
China Doll
Coming Home
Snow Swan

NOVELLAS:
"Tea for Two" in *Mistletoe*
"Twice in a Blue Moon"
in *Porch Swings and Picket Fences*

FOOL ME TWICE

ANNIE JONES

For Molly Fox, who spreads joy and laughter

For Wondergirl Jones, and all the good people who work to rescue greyhounds like her

For the staff and students of Phillips University, which recently closed its doors after ninety years of service in Christian education

and

For Rhonda Hromas and her mom, Cheryl—you got cut out of the family dedication by accident, but not out of my heart

One

"LET'S FACE IT—MANY WOMEN DREAMED AS LITTLE GIRLS THAT they would one day find and marry their prince. Many men expected that when the time came, they'd marry a girl just like the girl who married dear old Dad, their perfect fit, their very own Cinderella—except she'd look like Cindy Crawford, of course."

Ginny Sanborn looked up to acknowledge her classroom full of restless college students. "Then reality came crashing in on that youthful fantasy world, and a lot of women found themselves settling for the distant relative of their Prince Charming: The Duke of Doesn't-Scratch-Himself-in-Public."

Snickering, pens scratching over thick pads of note-book paper, and whispered responses answered Ginny's half-jest.

"And a lot of men chose not to 'settle' at all, avoiding commitment in fear that if they chose one girl, the very next day they'd meet their ideal woman, their Cindy-rella-mom."

It was Friday before spring break. Ginny's Sociology of Interpersonal Relationships class was only two-thirds full. She felt that those who had made the effort to show up today when the temptation to skip out early was so great deserved to hear something interesting and applicable to their lives. So today she decided to speak on one of her most passionate subjects—the myth of romantic love.

Ginny tugged at the hem of her fitted blazer, then

smoothed her hand up her sleek French twist. She knew not a single strand of golden hair was out of place, but she wondered if her blue suit might show a telltale sign of the hug her rescued racing greyhound, Ralphie, had given her earlier in the day. Useful or not, the gesture gave her audience a chance to soak in her statement.

She glanced out the window at the Oklahoma wind-whipped landscape and the familiar setting of the college campus. She was well into her fourth year teaching here, and Phillips University felt as much like an extension of herself as her wire-rimmed glasses did.

There had been a time when she had thought of leaving the comfort of her home and the closeness of small town and university life. She fingered the pink slip of paper with the phone message from the man who had expected her to change her entire life for him but had refused to change even his mule-headed mind for her.

Adam Buckman. Her heart skipped at the thought of the rugged cowboy whom she had dated for three years without the natural progression expected in most relationships, despite his alleged feelings for her. He'd bought himself quite a bit of time with his "I love yous," but in the end they had not been enough. Ginny had needed a more permanent demonstration. She'd needed a commitment.

Adam simply refused to give that to her. A flash of pain slashed through her at that knowledge, even six months after their breakup. If Adam could have lived his love instead of just talking about it, she would not be giving this lecture today.

She glanced down at her note cards but saw only the phone message as she said, "Not all prospects for romantic relationships are this grim, of course." She skimmed one fingertip over her secretary's scrawled note, practically stroking Adam's concise request. *"Please call."*

Sure, she thought, her throat constricting as she forced down a surge of unresolved emotion. She'd call, all right. When it snowed here in Enid, Oklahoma, in August.

"There are many references in the Bible to love, and we've already talked about the different kinds of love noted." Even though Phillips was a Christian university, she did not always put biblical references into her lectures. This time it was warranted. "But have you ever noted that when we find specifics about men and women loving one another, there are two different sets of instructions—one for wives and another for...husbands?"

She almost choked on the word. *Husband.* The one thing she would never have. The one thing Adam would never be.

No. She adjusted her glasses. She'd made the right choice in deciding not to return Adam's call. She bowed her head, scanning her notes to quell the riot of feelings these pointless thoughts had stirred in her. She mustn't let her lecture suffer by allowing herself to dwell on an impossible relationship.

"Could that be because God knows what we often don't want to acknowledge in modern society?" She gripped the edges of her podium. "That men and women are, in the way they approach this most basic bond, not just from two different worlds but from worlds that seem at opposite ends of the universe?"

Her hand moved to the pink slip of paper, and in one quick movement, she crumpled it inside her fist.

Fool me once, shame on you, but fool me twice, shame on me. That's how the old saying went. She lowered her head for just a moment to refocus her energy and rally her inner strength. Adam Buckman had made a fool of her once by leading her on as he did. She would not give him the chance to do it again.

Wham!

Ginny jumped at the slam of the heavy classroom door a few feet away. At first she refused to dignify the rudeness of the latecomer by acknowledging him or her, and she kept her gaze lowered. Then she gritted her teeth and spoke in her most authoritarian tone, "If you can't be on time for my lecture, at least have the courtesy to be quiet when you do get here."

Was her mind still in the past, or was that the sound of cowboy boots she heard striding toward the platform?

A sense of foreboding sank like a chunk of ice into the pit of her stomach. The scent of leather and bracing aftershave tweaked her nose. The sound of the footsteps halted.

Ginny jerked her head up to catch mischief flickering at her from a pair of all-too-familiar brown eyes.

"Adam," she whispered.

A shudder rippled from high in her chest straight down to her knees. Her pumps skiffed over the linoleum floor as she shuffled backward.

A hush rolled across the classroom.

Adam Buckman touched two fingers to the brim of his black hat and dipped his head. "Howdy, Gin."

"Wh-what are you doing here?"

"I've come for you, darlin'," he said in that low voice that sounded soothing yet aggressive at the same time.

She tried to swallow. Or blink. Or even breathe. But those most basic actions eluded her.

Somewhere beyond him, her students became a murmuring blur.

He stepped forward.

The sight of Adam engulfed her. His broad shoulders all but blotted out the classroom behind him. The shocked reaction of her classroom faded from her sight with each inch that Adam closed between them.

Like a pivotal scene in a bad movie, the whole event took on a surreal quality, as if it were happening in slow motion. He moved near enough for the sharp, citric smell of his aftershave to sting her nostrils.

She ran her tongue over her parted lips and retreated another step. The heel of her shoe snagged on a nick in the floor. She had to pinch the earpiece of her glasses to hold them in place.

He flashed a grin, his teeth fiercely white in contrast to the dark stubble on his cheeks.

Her heart stopped. It had to have stopped; otherwise she would have been able to do something, to say something. Instead, she just stared at the waves of deep brown hair creating a thick fringe over his collar.

A shadowy, day-old beard defined the lines of his strong jaw. His chest rose and fell in a heavy, hypnotic rhythm. She shut her eyes for an instant but could still see his image glimmering behind her closed lids. Adam Buckman was here, so close she could smell him, touch him, kiss him senseless.

Senseless. Now there was an appropriate word for

•the moment. She moved from behind the safety of the podium, ready to confront her own traitorous feelings and the man who caused them. She drew in a deep breath.

The sound of boots shifting on the cold floor answered her. Ginny glanced at his face, and from the shade of his low-fitting hat, he winked at her.

Her breath rushed from her lungs in a great whoosh. Still, she got a coherent sentence out for both Adam and her students to hear. "You're disrupting my class, Mr. Buckman."

"That's *Dr.* Buckman, ma'am." He raised his eyebrows at her.

"Dr. Buckman." Some people might think he, a veterinarian, deserved the title more than she. "You're disrupting my class, and I'm going to have to ask you to leave. I simply do not have time to talk to you right now."

"Good." The tilt of his lips was echoed by the laughter in his eyes. "Because I didn't come here to talk."

One large hand snatched her by the wrist.

Her stomach lurched. Confusion clashed with excitement within her.

He used her arm to pull her so close she could see the thin film of sweat on his taut neck just inside his open collar. She felt the warmth of his body pressing in on her.

"Really, Adam." She tried to sound aloof, but the crack in her voice betrayed her. "I demand that you tell me what's going on here."

"You," he said in a coarse whisper that was pure Adam and no act. "You, dear Ginny, are going on. On my shoulder."

He bent low and fit his shoulder neatly into her midsection.

She gasped and fell helplessly forward, her feet lifting from the floor. The physical sensation was disconcerting yet exhilarating.

"If you won't give me a few minutes of your time, then I guess I'll just have to steal them," Adam whispered for only her to hear. He clamped his arms over her legs and clutched them tightly to his body.

"Adam, are you insane?" Her hands flailed about trying to find something to hold on to. "I demand you put me down this instant."

"I don't think you're exactly in a position to make demands, darlin'." He chuckled.

"Put me down, I said." Her fist came down to land a soft thud on his broad back.

He laughed at the feeble attack, then turned to face the class, giving them a less-than-flattering view of their professor.

The brim of his hat rasped against her skirt as he nodded to her students. "Pardon the intrusion, folks. Don't worry about Dr. Sanborn; she's in good hands."

Laughter from the class rang in Ginny's ears as she struggled again to right herself. Her heart hammered in her chest. The blood running to her head coupled with the unwelcome thrill of his nearness made it hard to think as she wriggled in Adam's iron grasp.

"Now, if you'll excuse us," Adam addressed her students as though it were the most natural thing in the world to have their teacher slung over his shoulder. "We've got to hit the trail. Class dismissed."

He spun on his boot heel and strode toward the

door through the squawk of chairs pushing back, papers shuffling, and chatter.

With considerable effort, Ginny managed to lift her head and nail her students with an icy glare. "Class is most certainly not dismissed. Anyone leaving will be counted absent. I'll be right back as soon as I take care of this."

"What are we supposed to do, Dr. Sanborn?" a young man called out from the classroom chaos.

"Should I call for help?" a female student chimed in.

"No thanks, honey." Adam swung open the door. "She's hefty, but it ain't nothing I can't handle."

"Hefty?" Ginny gasped. "That's surprising talk coming from a man who looks all muscle—"

Adam's stiff spine pulled even straighter with pride.

"All muscle from the neck up!" Ginny propped herself up on Adam's taut back and called out to her class, "You all stay seated. I'll be back in a few minutes to discuss this little demonstration of the wildly differing approaches the sexes take to the bonding ritual."

Then Adam stepped across the threshold and let the heavy door fall shut behind them with a thunderous bang.

Two

"IF YOUR GOAL, ADAM BUCKMAN, WAS TO EMBARRASS ME, then congratulations, buddy-boy, you've accomplished it. Now put me down."

"Not so fast, Dr. Sanborn." He wrung her title and name through his teeth slowly, as if squeezing every ounce of propriety from them.

Holding her like this—in fact, just seeing her again—had his heart thumping like the thrashing hooves of a wild bronc. But he didn't dare let Ginny know that, not if he wanted his plan to work, and a man didn't go to this much trouble for a plan *not* to work.

He strode down the deserted hallway with the only woman capable of making him this loco hoisted high on his shoulder. "I can't put you down until you promise not to retaliate."

She writhed in his grasp, trying to jab his chest with her knee.

He wound his arm more tightly across her legs, commanding, "Promise."

She sniffed, indignant.

He came to a stop beside the glass doors that led outside the building. Afternoon sunlight streamed in over both of them, highlighting the plump feminine curves of her body. Suddenly a moving shadow on the floor behind him snagged his attention.

"Ah, ah, ah," he warned. "I didn't think you were the type to resort to violence to solve a problem, Gin."

He watched the silhouette of her raised fist until it

relaxed and fell limply against his back.

"Now promise you'll behave, and I'll let you down."

"I'll do no such thing."

That figured. Compromise was never this lady's strong suit in the past. But he believed she had it in her, and with the right coaxing...

His chest tightened at the thought of just how he'd like to coax Ginny. Long, slow kisses in front of a blazing fire in his home just outside Tulsa would be nice for starters. Of course, time and circumstances did not allow that at present, so a more aggressive style of attitude enhancement seemed in order. "Looks like I'll have to resort to drastic measures to protect myself from your feminine fury."

"From my—" Her hand flattened to his back. "What are you talking about?"

A bright flash of light answered her question before Adam could. He struck a pose for a second picture, then turned to put Ginny's face to the camera and its owner.

"Billy Owens!" Ginny's tone mixed delight with disbelief. "I should have known you'd be in on this."

"Ma'am." Billy tipped his chocolate brown cowboy hat to her and grinned like a sly bobcat. "You knew the big guy couldn't have pulled off something this asinine all on his lonesome, didn't you?"

Adam chuckled, jostling Ginny to keep a secure grip on her. "As I recall, when we were all in college together at Oklahoma State, I pulled off a lot of things more asinine than this without any help from you, Billyboy."

"Do yourself a favor, Buckman," Billy said with a laugh. "Quit while you're ahead."

"You can apply that advice double to your manhandling of me," Ginny added with vehemence. She flexed her warm palm over the muscles of his back.

Her touch sent a ripple of gooseflesh down his back, and a shudder rattled him to the pit of his stomach. He had to get away from her before he lost the presence of mind to carry out his plan. Stiffly, he bent to set her feet on the floor.

"Wait. One more picture," Billy called out.

Ginny protested, "What do you need a picture for?"

"We want a picture that captures more than your posterior for posterity." Adam twisted his head to peer at her over the curve of her back.

"Or for the college newspaper."

"Billy, you wouldn't!" she gasped.

"We might. But we won't if you don't call security and have us thrown off campus. Deal?"

She drew in a deep breath.

Adam gritted his teeth and waited, wanting nothing more than to release her. Or to hold her in his arms for a long overdue kiss.

In one sigh that captured her pure exasperation, she relented. "Okay, no security. But you don't need another picture. You have one already."

"Not one that shows your face," Billy said. "Now say 'Cheese.'"

"Sleaze," she accused through gritted teeth.

"Close enough." He snapped the photo.

Adam shut his eyes and clenched his teeth as he lowered Ginny to the ground. He didn't know whether he felt more relief from being rid of the weight of her or from being freed of her nearness. He dug his fingers into the aching muscles along his neck. "Have you put on weight? What? Not taking Ralphie for those long walks anymore? Or maybe that's what comes from not having a man to chase you around, huh?"

"Ralphie and I both get plenty of exercise, thank you. And for your information, I am not the type to allow a man to chase me around, even to keep me in shape." She skimmed both hands down her skirt, then crossed her arms at waist level.

"Does that mean you don't have a man, or you've got one but he won't chase you?" Adam raised an eyebrow.

"It means..." She shook her head hard. "What difference does that make? The real question is, what are you doing here, and why did you disrupt my class?"

"He's staying in town all week long," Billy said.

"For spring break?"

Adam grunted. "There's a whole world beyond this university, Ginny, where not everything is measured in quarters, semesters, and winter and spring breaks, you know."

Ginny blinked. "I...I know."

"Naw, Adam didn't come to Enid for spring break. He came to get fitted for a tux and to move furniture. Not to mention the bachelor party." Billy stepped up and clapped Adam hard on the back.

"Bachelor party?" Her face suddenly went pale as she faced Adam. "You mean you're...you're getting... married?"

Her last word broke into a whisper. Her lower lip trembled. Was it wishful thinking, or did the thought of him marrying another really affect her so?

"Him?" Billy barked out with a sharp laugh. "Who'd

marry that old stubborn lunkhead?"

She straightened up and rolled her gaze down the length of Adam, as though sizing up a good-for-nothing ranch hand wanting a bonus in his paycheck. Her smile, about as welcoming as a cactus kiss, was not reflected in her eyes. "Yes, who indeed?"

Adam watched her reaction and had to wonder if he had vastly miscalculated his chances of winning Ginny back. Here they were, away from the prying eyes of her students, and yet she greeted his arrival with more annoyance than interest. Sure, he'd known better than to expect her to fling herself at him, but she could at least seem happy to see him again.

Maybe two months of dreaming of this reunion had caused him to romanticize their whole relationship. Maybe the impending wedding of his best friend had put him in a far too sentimental frame of mind. Maybe he was just a big old mush-headed mule for hoping this demonstration of affection would show her he had changed, that he could now flaunt his emotions for her in front of the whole world.

He folded his arms over his chest. "Billy and Lisa are getting married on Friday, a week from today."

Ginny placed one neatly manicured hand to her cheek. Her green eyes grew wide behind the thin lenses of her glasses. "A week from *today?*"

"It sure is," Billy said with a sappy grin as he tucked his small camera into his shirt pocket.

Adam raised his chin. "I'm the best man."

For the first time since he'd invaded her classroom, she smiled, her eyes sparkling. "You mean *you're* the best man they could get?"

"There's none better, darlin'," he half growled, his senses suddenly awash with hope again. If he could get her to smile and joke, then maybe…

"I'll bet Lisa would argue with you about that," she teased in a sweet, vaguely flirty purr. She turned to Billy. "So, this is it, huh? After all these years, you're finally taking the plunge."

"Right into the deep end." Billy placed his hands together and pantomimed diving. "Which reminds me, I told Lisa I'd meet her in a few minutes, so I gotta scoot. Oh, and Ginny, Lisa asked me to tell you she's looking forward to y'all getting together tomorrow."

"Tomorrow?"

"You know, the bridal shower."

"The shower!" She winced. "I'd completely forgotten it. Luckily, I still have time to get her a gift."

Billy's dark brows angled down over his eyes as he shifted a look from Ginny to Adam to Ginny again. "Don't let me influence you or anything, but I wouldn't complain if you got her something slinky."

"Billy Owens!" Ginny took a step back. "I can't believe you said that."

"He's in love and going to get married in a week, Gin." Adam leaned so close he could see her eyes dilate as he finished in a gruff whisper. "Believe it."

A faint flush brightened her cheeks. "Oh, Adam, really."

"Really." He raised his eyebrows to punctuate the word.

She met his gaze, and her breath caught in a quiet gasp that turned the knife of tension tighter in his gut.

Billy pushed open the door, then paused to touch

his hat to bid them farewell. "Just another seven days and five hours, and we'll be an old married couple off on our honeymoon."

Ginny shifted her attention to Billy and, as subtly as a drowning man grasps for a lifesaver, seized the change of subject. "And where are you going on your honeymoon, Bill?"

The man shrugged and headed out the door, calling back, "Who cares? Ain't like we plan on leavin' the room anytime that week."

Ginny swallowed so hard it made Adam wince and do the same.

He cleared his throat to chase away any huskiness as he showed her some mercy and redirected the conversation in earnest. "I'm sorry about making a scene in the classroom, Gin—"

"Sorry doesn't change anything, Adam. Actions, not empty words, change things."

"I thundered into your room and hauled you off on my shoulder!" He shook his head. "How much more action do you want, girl?"

She glared at him.

"Okay, all joking aside. I was trying to make a point, and I *am* sorry if I used the wrong method." He held out his hand to her. "Apology accepted?"

She glanced at his offered hand, then slowly shook her head. "This was our problem all along, your thinking that you could do whatever you wanted—or not do anything at all—as long as you said the right things to appease me."

"But I—"

"Well, never again." She put her hands to her hips.

"I don't know what on earth you could say that could make up for your humiliating antics in my classroom today."

"Well, then maybe there's something I can *do*."

She narrowed her eyes at him. "Pardon me?"

He whisked his black hat from his head and raked his fingers back through his wavy brown hair. "I said maybe there is something I can do to make up for everything I've put you through."

"I don't understand."

He stepped toward her, his boots echoing in the cool, dim hallway. "That's why I came here today. I've done a lot of thinking since we broke up."

She tipped up her chin. "I can only imagine how taxing *that* was for you."

He smiled. "I deserved that, I'm sure."

She didn't contradict him.

"But I also deserve something else from you, Gin."

"What?"

"A second chance."

A second chance? She took one step backward, then stepped back again until her spine was pressed flat against the unyielding wall. *Fool me once, shame on you...*

"A second chance at what?" she asked.

"At us. At our relationship."

Fool me twice, shame on me.

"Go away, Adam. If I had wanted to see you, I would have returned your call." Her heels skidded easily over the slick floor as she pivoted away from him. "Now if you'll excuse me, I have to find some way to restore order to my class."

"Losing you made me reexamine my priorities, my methods of handling things, my goals in life." He moved directly into her path.

She sidestepped him without missing a beat and continued toward her classroom.

"What are you afraid of, Gin?"

She jerked to a halt. *Everything, you big idiot,* she wanted to cry out. *I'm afraid of everything, afraid of what you make me feel and want, afraid that if I let you near me, you'll break my heart again.*

"I'm busy, Adam. I'm in the middle of a lecture you'd do well to listen to."

"I've changed, Ginny. And the way I see it, I have the next week to prove to you just how much."

"Starting with this little stunt, I suppose?"

"You *are* the one who wanted me to do more than just talk about my feelings. You wanted a demonstration."

"Bursting in on my lecture wasn't exactly what I had in mind, Adam."

Or was it? What better way to save face and also prove her point to both Adam and her class than to use a little creative visual aid?

She peered at him over her shoulder. *Why not?* "Are you serious about wanting to find ways to demonstrate how you've changed?"

He strummed his fingers over the brim of the hat in his hands. "The one thing you know about me is that I don't say a thing unless I mean it."

"Good. Come with me." She motioned for him to follow as she started back toward her classroom.

"What have you got in mind? You don't plan on dissecting me, do you?"

A wistful smile tugged at her lips at the thought. "No, I don't plan on dissecting you. I plan on using you to save my lecture on male-female relationships."

"I don't know about *that*." His footsteps slowed. Only someone who had known the man as long as she had could have picked up on the gentle jest in his tone as he asked, "You don't plan on offering me up as a bad example of manhood, do you?"

"I am going to make an example out of you, Adam. And you may learn something in the process."

"I look forward to it, then." He fit his hat down so low she couldn't help but focus on his deep, calm gaze. "Just what is it I'm to be an example of, by the way?"

"You, Dr. Adam Buckman, are the strong silent type, the stuff of western legends."

His chest puffed up a bit at what he perceived to be a compliment.

Ginny narrowed her eyes and smiled like a kid with a pin ready to prick an overinflated balloon. "You are a walking example of why men and women can never let their hearts rule their minds in matters of romance."

"If that's what it takes." He followed behind her, then found a seat in the classroom.

"And in conclusion, nothing better illustrates the vast differences in the way men and women communicate emotions than the demonstration so thoughtfully provided by Dr. Buckman." Ginny raised her head, straightened her note cards, and removed her glasses. "If there are no questions, then…"

Hands shot up throughout the room.

"I'll take two or three questions, and then class is dismissed." Ginny gripped the sides of the podium.

Adam leaned forward in the chair he'd taken at the back of the room and studied the woman he hoped to take back to Tulsa as his wife. She had a lot of nervous energy. Always did have. In fact, during their years together, he'd taken great pleasure in teasing her about creative ways to vent that pent-up energy. He'd enjoyed that almost as much as he enjoyed knowing he still spurred that kind of reaction in her.

Ginny's gaze flitted over the room but managed to avoid making eye contact with Adam. She settled on a mousy-haired girl in a dress that looked like it had been stolen from someone's granny. "You have a question?"

"I have a question." Adam stood.

Heads turned. Chairs shifted.

Ginny slipped her glasses back on and blinked her enormous eyes at him. "Dr. Buckman, this discussion is limited to students of mine."

"I understand that." He placed his hands on his hips.

"That's nice to know." Only the tremble in her hand betrayed any emotion as she whisked back an imaginary stray lock of golden hair. She drew in a deep breath and focused on the granny-girl again, but Adam didn't give either the chance to speak.

"I'm not afraid to admit that over the years we've known one another," he ran his thumb and forefinger along the rim of his black hat and dipped his head to her, "you've taught me a thing or two."

Laughter erupted in the room.

Ginny raised her head and nailed him with a look as

steady as any bull about to charge. One fist planted on her hip, she spoke above the students' laughter. "That may well be, Dr. Buckman, but no matter how hard I tried, I don't seem to have taught you a thing about manners."

That-a-gal. Stand up to me. Show me that the old Ginny hasn't been completely swallowed up by this prim school-marm with the doesn't-believe-in-love act. "If you're talking about my hat, ma'am—" and he knew good and well she wasn't—"I'd take it off, but there's no place to put it."

"Oh, really?" Her shoes clicked as she rounded the podium, raring for a fight. "Well, may I suggest you take that classic example of a grown man's pathetic need to act out his adolescent bad-boy fantasies and put it…"

Granny-girl gasped.

"…under your seat." Ginny cocked her head and raised one eyebrow.

"Thank you, ma'am, but I think I'll cling to my adolescent fantasies a little while longer, if you don't mind." He hooked his thumbs into his belt loops and lowered his eyelids and his voice. "And I'll keep my hat on, too."

She forced a long blast of air through her clenched teeth.

Adam smiled. "Now about that question, ma'am."

Ginny glanced down at her naked wrist and shook her head. "My, my, look at the time. I think we'd better—"

"Can you really stand there and in good conscience try to convince these people that men and women have such different views, goals, and needs from a relationship? That unless they look at it from an objective vantage point they are doomed to difficulties?"

"I'm only teaching what I learned from—" Her gaze

locked with his for one moment. She bowed her head and walked to the safety of the podium before finishing. "I'm not teaching anything that my research doesn't support."

"You mean your personal research." In other words, he'd done this to her. And he'd have felt like a first-class jerk about it, too, except that he'd come back now to put everything right. He couldn't afford the luxury of wasting time wallowing in regret. Ginny needed him to show her how he felt, and she needed that now.

He stepped from the row of chairs into the aisle. "I'm afraid your research may be flawed, Dr. Sanborn."

She stepped back. "I don't think it is. And I don't think you can convince me otherwise."

"Even if I say that I've come here this week to sweep you totally off your feet? And that I hope that by the end of this week, you'll not only have forgiven me my hard-headed male mistakes, but you'll have agreed to become my wife?"

Three

THE METAL HOOKS OF HEAVY HANGERS SCRAPED ATOP THEIR
rods and were moved along by someone pushing
through a too-narrow gap between peignoirs and
panties. The illuminated curves of a stocking display
wobbled.

Ginny tensed. Even without looking, she realized
that slipping into the least likely place on earth to find a
cowboy—the women's intimate apparel section of a
crowded department store—had not kept Adam from
following her.

After class yesterday she had managed to dodge his
eager invitation to dinner. She had refused to answer her
phone last night or return the messages left on her
machine. She'd even kept Ralphie inside for fear that
he'd get one look at Adam, lope over to him with his
tongue hanging out the side of his mouth, and drape his
paws on the big man's shoulders in a welcoming hug
that would do any lovestruck idiot proud. Then how
would she be able to look Adam in the eye and con-
vincingly argue that making a big fool of himself was not
the same as demonstrating his love for her?

If it was good enough for one of the oldest and
noblest breeds of man's best friend to show the depths of
his affection, how could she ask more from a hound dog
like him? That's what Adam would say. And Ginny
would laugh, and all her hardened defenses would begin
to crumble. She just could not risk that.

Clever words now did not absolve him of the past.

If he had changed, he'd have to prove it over time, not by blurting out some groundless claim. She'd been burned by his words before, and now she needed more than words.

She supposed he thought that was what he was giving her with this dogged display of determination. This morning when she had hopped into her car and headed out to the town's only shopping mall, she had noticed his gleaming black pickup on her tail.

Ignore him, she had told herself. She'd had six months of practice at not thinking about that man; surely she could get through another week.

Still, she could not so easily blot out the bold proclamation he'd made in her class yesterday. She had gone to sleep hearing his words. He'd said he'd come to sweep her off her feet and to get her to agree to become his wife. Her heart thrashed out a faster and faster rhythm in her chest as those words and his unmistakable presence closed in on her.

Sheer stubborn pride kept her head bowed over the selection of lace and satin on the rack in front of her. She had come here, after all, to pick out a present for Lisa's shower this afternoon, and she would not let Adam distract her from even one more of her responsibilities.

She pulled a purple satin, black-feather-trimmed teddy from the rack and held it up. A pair of melt-your-heart brown eyes met her gaze just above the deep vee of the neckline.

"Nice," he said.

She shoved the garment back onto the rack so fast the hangers clattered, and other flimsy pieces fluttered in flashes of silk and lace. She felt the sting of a blush on her cheeks, neck, even the tip of her nose. Still, she held her composure as tightly and neatly as the French braid at the back of her head.

"Why, Adam Buckman. Imagine seeing you in women's lingerie."

Whether it was her calm or her remark that knocked the smirk right off his face, Ginny didn't know, and she didn't care. She just turned her back and made a show of interest in a rack of chiffon-and-lace nighties. "Really, Adam, following me here is too much. I told you I didn't want to spend time with you while you're here for the wedding. Can't you take no for an answer?"

"Not unless no is the answer I want to hear."

She felt his gaze, but she could not meet it. "You're the last person who should be lecturing someone about getting the answer he wants to hear."

"I don't think I've strung together enough words in my entire lifetime to make a lecture." Strain underscored the jest. "That's your department."

"Bringing up yesterday's disastrous lecture situation is hardly the way to ingratiate yourself to me."

"Even if I promise to remove my adolescent fantasy symbol as I do?" He straightened and whisked two fingers along the brim of his black Stetson.

She rolled her eyes and toyed with the top button on her starched white blouse. "I guess I should apologize for making that remark in class. I know you have every legitimate cause to have a trusty black Stetson, and I shouldn't have impugned your reasons for wearing it."

"Well, you know how a cowboy feels about his hat, ma'am." He adjusted it lower on his head, unwittingly emphasizing the deep, hungry look in his warm eyes. "It's second only to his horse and his woman in his heart."

"In that order?" she murmured.

"You know better than that."

"Do I?" She folded her arms over her chest. "I guess if I did, we wouldn't be standing in a public department store arguing."

"We're not arguing, are we, Ginny?"

She put one hand up. "No, you're right. We're not. I'm shopping, and you're leaving."

She pivoted on her heel and focused every ounce of her attention on the rack of silky nightgowns before her.

"You're making this very difficult for me, you know."

"I'm not doing anything but shopping for a gift." She pulled out a sheer pink gown. It shimmied with a telltale tremor of her hand. "If this is difficult for you, you have no one but yourself to blame."

Adam opened his mouth to say something, but just then a small woman with steel blue hair and a designer suit approached them. "May I help you?"

"No, thank—"

"We're looking for something special, ma'am." Adam spoke to the salesclerk, but his gaze never wandered from Ginny's face. "It's for a honeymoon."

Honeymoon. Despite her anger, the very notion of a honeymoon with Adam made Ginny's breath catch in the back of her throat.

"Oh, how delightful. When is the big day?"

"Oh no." Ginny shook her head, slammed back into reality by the question. "It's not—"

"Soon, I hope."

"Soon?" The salesclerk's pencil-thin brows rose in surprise.

"This is a gift *for a friend*." Ginny hammered home the last words to make herself perfectly clear. "I think this will do nicely, thank you."

There, she thought as she handed the chosen gown to the clerk. That was that. She'd made her selection; now she could get out of here. Alone.

Throwing back her shoulders with more dignity than she really felt, she marched to the sales counter, trying not to notice the huge cowboy-shaped shadow at her heels.

Every sound from the cash register grated on Ginny's nerves. The growling rip of her check being torn from the book, the crackle of the receipt, even the voices of busy shoppers all around them ruffled her already agitated state. No wonder her tone came out harsh and impatient when she flattened her hand on the gown to keep the clerk from sliding it into a bag and said, "May I get this gift wrapped?"

"Yes, certainly, dear. But it will take a while. If you have some more shopping to do in the mall or want to go get some lunch—"

"Now there's an idea." Adam curved his hand around Ginny's arm.

At his touch, every muscle in her body tightened. Her thoughts flew back to the incident in her classroom and her unceremonious ride on this man's shoulder. She glanced around at the sedate setting. Enid was not a tiny town, but it was small enough that in any given place—and especially at Oakwood Mall—there was someone you knew around or, at the very least, someone who knew someone you knew.

Ginny gulped. She simply could not have a repeat

of yesterday's indignity here. All her senses went on full alert.

"C'mon, Gin." Adam's fingers wound around her upper arm. "Let's get some lunch; then we can come back for the present."

"Lunch?" She jerked her arm away, seizing the first thing that came to mind to fend off any further contact. "I'm surprised you'd even suggest it, considering how fat you think I've grown since we broke up."

"Fat? I never said that." His expression told her he honestly didn't know what she meant. "You look great to me, Ginny. And if you took anything I said yesterday to mean otherwise, I am truly sorry."

He looked and sounded sorry, but Ginny felt that this tack was her only defense mechanism to keep him at bay physically and emotionally. That revelation hit her hard.

Had she really softened enough toward Adam that she needed contrived annoyance at a nonissue to keep from letting her guard down around him? Her near panic at the grain of truth in that thought edged her tone louder as she adjusted her glasses and said, "You say you're sorry now, Adam, but what does that change? It doesn't erase the things you've done. It doesn't give me back all the wasted time I spent waiting for you to decide you wanted to make a life with me. It doesn't make me—"

She pressed her hand hard against her chest. Here she'd thought to stop him from making a scene in public, and then she had gone and shouted out her frustrations for everyone to hear.

"I get the feeling we aren't talking about my clumsy

jokes about your weight anymore, are we?"

She bit her lip and shook her head, well aware that gazes from every direction in the store remained riveted on her.

"Maybe we should talk about it." He offered her his arm. "Over lunch?"

She swallowed hard—she had to swallow hard to push down her last shred of pride—and accepted his arm.

"All right. I'll go to lunch with you." She collected the receipt she'd need to reclaim Lisa's wrapped present and lifted her head high. She paid no attention to the gawks and smiles of the other shoppers until she and Adam reached the store's outside door. Only then did she steal a quick peek to see if anyone was still watching them.

She dropped his arm, her chin, and her voice to let him know that he may have won the battle, but she was still at war. "I'll go to lunch with you, Adam. I'll even offer to pick up the check since I plan to decide where we'll be eating. But there's one thing you should know."

"What's that?"

"All the *talking* in the world won't make any difference. I have no intention of letting you break my heart again."

He never should have let Ginny pick the place for lunch. But she had demanded they take separate vehicles, asking him to follow her. She led him to a fast-food drive through, then down a back road alongside the mall, and farther still until they stopped near the edge of town.

Adam stared at the hamburger and french fries on rumpled paper atop a badly weathered picnic table. Even with his back to the fenced-off airfield of Vance Air Force Base, he was still keenly aware each time a jet took off or landed.

"There are plenty of nice restaurants around town, Ginny. Even more than one park we could have gone to if you insisted we eat outdoors. Why did you have to choose a roadside table beside a busy runway?"

She shrugged and smiled from behind her raised hamburger. "It's close to the mall. I still have to go back there and pick up Lisa's gift, you know. It just seemed like the most convenient spot."

"Yeah, convenience." He snorted. "I suspect that's exactly what brought us to a place this noisy and distracting when I want to have a serious talk with you."

"What was that?" She put her hand to her ear.

"I said—" The whine of a jet engine blistered his ears.

She sat there, all smiles, showing no distress at the nerve-racking sound.

The glaring late March sun reflected off the aircraft over his shoulder and the still yellow grass all around them, stinging Adam's eyes despite the shade of his hat. The wind had quickly cooled the food until it was distinguishable more by shape and texture than by its flat taste. None of the discomfort mattered, of course, if it afforded him another chance to reach his Ginny, to make her understand she meant the world to him.

He stretched his arm across the battered tabletop to take her hand in his. She drew her hand back until only her chilly fingers remained in his grasp.

The jet engine growled louder.

Adam winced but would not be deterred. "Clearly, you don't want to hear what I have to say, but you can't stop me from saying it."

The set of her jaw, the spark in the depths of her lovely eyes, the way she churned her plastic straw in the crushed ice of her soda all told him she had heard him.

"What do I have to do to convince you of my feelings? Of my sincerity? Just tell me, and I'll do it."

The wind whipped through the shaded area, but not a single hair on her head ruffled. She fixed a gaze on him almost as unyielding as her tight braid.

Low in his gut he felt a wrenching at her response, but he had to press on. "I love you, Ginny. Our being apart these last few months proved to me just how much. I want us to be married. I thought you wanted the same thing."

"When?"

His brow pushed down. "Six months ago, that's when. You broke up with me because I was taking too long to make the commitment."

Behind him another plane roared to life, forcing him to shout. "Some of my friends told me it was a gamble, a tried-and-true woman's trick to force the marriage issue. Well, your gamble paid off, Ginny, and here I am."

She rose slowly from her side of the picnic table, her face pale. "I meant *when* did you want to get married? Not because I was thinking of doing it, but to see if you could actually name a date."

"Name a date? Gin, I'm ready—honest, I am." He stood, too, disregarding the food now entirely cold on the table. "You name the date."

"All right, I will." She leaned forward, bracing both arms, her palms flat against the splintered wood of the table. "I'll tell you precisely when I'm going to marry you, Adam. Never, that's when!"

She struggled to extract herself with some shred of dignity from the bench seat. When she succeeded, she pivoted, her braid slapping the back of her neck as she did.

Adam clenched his teeth. "Why are you doing this?"

She twisted her head to look over her shoulder and blinked at him. "Doing what?"

He strode the few feet to her side. "Acting so stubborn and unwilling to compromise—to even listen to me, much less allow yourself to be open to the idea of our marrying."

"Stubborn? Unwilling to compromise?" She laced her arms over her chest, her eyes shooting little darts of accusation. "Why is it that six months ago when *you* didn't want to marry *me* you were just being cautious and levelheaded, but now that the tables are turned and *I* don't want to marry *you*, I'm stubborn and unwilling to compromise?"

"I never said I didn't want to marry you six months ago," he corrected as gently as the surrounding noise would allow.

"You didn't?" For the first time her features softened toward him.

"I just said we should wait until the time was right."

"In other words, until *you* were good and ready." She rolled her eyes. "And now that *that* time has finally come, I guess I'm supposed to jump at the chance to be your wife?"

He started to say something but stopped. He realized that whatever he managed to sputter out right now would only be used against him, so he clamped his mouth shut again.

"The only place I'm jumping, mister, is back in my car. I still have to pick up my gift and get ready for the shower this afternoon." She walked stiff-backed to her car.

"And what am I supposed to do?"

"Well, for starters, you can clear away our lunch trash. Then after that, may I suggest a little Bible study? Start with 1 Peter, chapter 3, verse 7. I referenced it in my lecture yesterday." She put one hand to her eyes to shade them, standing beside her modest little car, all prim and proper.

Maybe he was some kind of fool to think it, but he felt she was giving him some hope, some direction. And he needed whatever direction she could offer. That gave his squashed spirits, if not his ego, a lift.

Those spirits buoyed even higher when she let a bit of playfulness slip into her tone as she added, "Oh, wait, I made the Bible references before you made your entrance."

"So, if I read this passage, will it give me some clue as to what I'm doing wrong with you?" He put his hands on his hips.

"It should help." She opened the driver's door and started to get inside, then stopped and popped her head up again. "But, Adam."

"What?"

"If the verses don't paint the whole picture, maybe you should try listening to a little old Aretha Franklin.

You want to know what a woman wants from a man, what I need from you before I can even imagine patching things up with you, much less making a lifetime commitment? First Peter outlines it, and Aretha spells it right out for you."

Four

"Oooohhh." Billy's fiancée, Lisa, drew a long silk robe from a white gift box. "How perfect! Just like something I've seen in the movies!"

"Did you get that?" Lisa's future mother-in-law whispered to Ginny.

"Got it." She dutifully wrote down what Lisa had said according to her assignment from the shower's host, Lisa's aunt.

"Okay, that's the last of the presents, ladies." Lisa's Aunt Pat clapped her hands together to get everyone's attention.

Aunt Pat, as everyone who knew her called the woman, shared her elderly years with Aunt Nana, her sister-in-law. Some said the two were a few noodles short of a casserole, and no one argued that their home was about three cats over minimum health standards. But generally they were, as one native to the area had observed, "a hoot."

"Bow Lady? Bow Lady?" Aunt Pat placed one hand to the side of her mouth and called out. "Where are you, Bow Lady?"

"Here I am!" Aunt Nana sang out in an operatic voice. She floated into the room waving a paper plate with all the ribbons and bows from Lisa's gifts taped to it.

"Oh, Nana, what have you done now?"

"I made a hat like you told me to." She showed the riot of color to the gathering of women seated on the couch and folding chairs.

"You were supposed to make a ribbon *bouquet*." Aunt Pat sighed to make sure everyone in the room understood her everlasting frustration.

Ginny used this moment to slip away quietly. She tried to hand the notepad she'd used to record Lisa's responses to the woman seated to her right. No luck.

"Who ever heard of a ribbon bouquet?" Aunt Nana demanded of Aunt Pat.

"Listen to it, Nana, *bow*-quet. It just makes sense. Who ever heard of a ribbon hat?"

"I have. Haven't you ever heard of a *bow*-ler?" Aunt Nana rolled out a deep, contagious laugh.

Ginny turned to the woman on her left, Lisa's future mother-in-law. She thrust the pad toward the woman. "This has been fun, but I have to——"

Aunt Nana swept past just then, knocking into Ginny on her way to plunk her weird creation on Lisa's head.

"Now, where's our note taker?"

Ginny cringed. It was just a little cringe, but one she suspected those seated near her saw. To save face, she felt she had to stay and play along. Sneaking out now would be the height of rudeness.

"You there, with the glasses." Aunt Pat pointed right at Ginny. "Madam Professor, isn't it?"

Not to mention impossible. Ginny opened her mouth to speak but never got the chance.

"We're going to recount for everyone a few details of the love story of Lisa and Billy," Aunt Pat announced. "When Nana points to you, Madam Professor, you go down the list of things you've written and read what Lisa said when she opened her gifts. But skip any repeats or just simple thank-yous. Got that?"

Everyone in the room focused on Ginny. She squirmed in the hard folding chair. "Got it."

Aunt Pat waved her arms as she spoke, making sure everyone followed along as she told a little bit about how much everyone loved the engaged couple, and then told the real story of how they met and fell in love.

Maybe it was the romantic mood of the afternoon or the fact that Adam had suddenly charged back into her life, but Ginny couldn't help thinking back over her own love story as the woman spoke. She'd been so enthralled by Adam, by his larger-than-life good humor, his dedication to making his new veterinary practice thrive, and his deep-seated faith. Those feelings had not died with time, not even with the breakup. But he had been unable to commit, and she had been unable to keep living with the sense that she was the last priority of his life. If that had truly changed now…

Aunt Pat summed up her story, then turned the floor over to Aunt Nana, who launched full steam into the shower game.

"Of course, you've all heard of love at first sight," Nana said. "But when Lisa laid eyes on her Billy for the very first time, she told everyone within earshot—" She cued Ginny with a flourish.

"Um—" Ginny glanced down at her notes. "She said, 'I can't wait to get some use out of that.'"

The group laughed.

Ginny recalled the first time she saw Adam. She'd spent the summer at a church camp as a counselor. Adam had volunteered to do some work with a group that rescued racing greyhounds that weren't winning races from a certain death. He had an arrangement to bring the new dogs out to the camp to expose them to things they never would have experienced living entirely on racetracks and kennels. The kids loved the dogs, and Ginny had loved watching Adam handle both the trembling animals and the rowdy children with ease.

She could still see the summer sun on his broad back. She recalled the way her stomach fluttered at the compelling mix of cowboy brawn and extreme tenderness he showed. She knew then that despite his sometimes monumental macho persona, he was a kind and special man.

"Then, when Billy first asked Lisa out on a date, all she could say was—"

Ginny snapped back to the present, wet her lips, and read eagerly, "'Terrific! Another of these and I'll have a different one for every day of the week!'"

Adam, Ginny remembered even as she put on a cheery face for the group, had asked her out the very day they'd met. And she'd accepted.

"The first time Billy ever stole a kiss, our Lisa cried out—"

"'Thank you! Thank you! It's just what I wanted. You read my mind.'" Ginny surprised herself with her own enthusiastic rendition of Lisa's comments.

Maybe that's because she couldn't help thinking of the first kiss she had shared with Adam on a summer night in the Oklahoma countryside with just about a billion of God's gorgeous stars shining down on them.

"Now, if this tradition holds true," Aunt Nana surmised, her round face beaming, "it won't be difficult to predict what Lisa will say to Billy on their honeymoon."

There was that word again. That big event that she
and Adam might never share. She and Adam as honey-
mooners, imagine that!

"When they're all alone," Nana purred.

She *could* imagine it.

"As he holds her close for the very first time as man
and wife, she'll tell him exactly what she's thinking when
she whispers—"

"'Oooohhh. How perfect! Just like something I've
seen in the movies!'" Even as she got the words out,
Ginny felt the tinge of blush on her cheeks. Of course,
only she knew that the heat tinging her face came from
her own thoughts of being alone with Adam, not from
the silly game.

Around her, however, the group joked and teased.

"Why, Ginny," Lisa said, "I do believe you're blushing!"

Ginny hammed it up with a phony look of chagrin
at her own response. "What can I say? I guess I'm just
one of those icy academics—easily shocked, easily
embarrassed."

"Embarrassed? You?" Lisa sputtered out a disbelieving huff. "After what happened Friday, I didn't think
anything could embarrass you!"

Ginny's heart sank as the guests scooted to the edges
of their seats, murmuring, "What? What happened
Friday? Tell us, Lisa."

Ginny felt like dissolving into the floor when Lisa
relayed the story to the entire shower gathering.

The women surrounding Ginny giggled and gasped.

"How romantic!"

"Can you believe it?"

"What would you do?"

"And he ended the whole thing," Lisa said above the hubbub, her expression that of one totally in the know, "with a marriage proposal, right there, in front of the entire class!"

Someone squealed in delight. Another person clapped her hands.

Ginny pursed her lips, her head shaking as she hurried to issue a correction. "It wasn't actually a proposal. Not technically."

"Then what was it?" Aunt Pat demanded, as if she were the only one sensible enough to sort the whole situation out. "Just what did he say?"

"Well, he said that he wanted to sweep me off my feet." Ginny pushed her glasses up by touching her fingers to the nosepiece. "And that he wanted me to forgive him for all his mistakes and agree to be his wife."

"Sounds like a marriage proposal to me!" Aunt Nana announced. "You *are* going to accept, aren't you?"

Accept? Until now, Ginny hadn't really given the prospect serious thought. She'd been too angry. But as she recalled her relationship with Adam and remembered the man beneath the black-hat image, her heart filled with hope and excitement. "Well, I…"

"Oh, c'mon, Ginny." Lisa gave her arm a gentle shove. "The man put his big old cowboy ego on the line. He's actively pursuing you and is obviously willing to do whatever it takes to win you back."

That remains to be seen. But if Lisa's observation did prove true, if Adam were willing to do whatever it took to win her, she might just be won over to his way of thinking as well.

Lisa grinned at Ginny, giving her a friendly nudge. "Honestly, now, how could you *not* marry a man like that?"

"Oh, I never said I wasn't going to marry him." Ginny smiled for the first time in a long time. "But only if and when he proves to me he's learned a few very important lessons."

"Husbands, in the same way be considerate as you live with your wives, and treat them with respect as the weaker partner and as heirs with you of the gracious gift of life, so that nothing will hinder your prayers."

His answer was in that verse. Adam rubbed his eyes and tucked the small pocket-sized edition of the New Testament into the glove compartment of his truck. A grateful farmer had given him the leather copy with Adam's name stamped on it in small gold letters. Since his work often demanded he get into mud and muck and all manner of things, he didn't carry the gift in a pocket but instead kept it in his truck for reference.

It had come in handy today as he'd waited in his truck outside the tuxedo rental shop. Billy and the other groomsmen were supposed to meet him here to get measured for their tuxes at one o'clock, but since Adam's lunch date had ended early—and miserably—he had come on ahead. He made use of the time by looking up 1 Peter, chapter 3, as Ginny had suggested.

Adam read the whole chapter starting with the admonition to wives. He noted, as Ginny had in her lecture, that these Scriptures came in pairs, with one recommendation to men and another to women. God obviously knows us better than we do when it comes down to relationships.

Adam snapped shut the glove compartment and leaned back against the sun-warmed upholstery of his truck. Neither the small store nor the streets around it were busy, and the quiet only forced Adam deeper into his own thoughts. Thoughts of Ginny.

He'd forgotten until he'd laid eyes on her again yesterday what a contradiction she could be. All harsh and businesslike on the outside, with proper clothes and her hair arranged to such perfection that one might not suspect how soft and naturally wavy it really was.

But Adam remembered. He remembered the feel of her hair like silk through his fingers and the warm softness of her skin. He remembered the gentle spirit that hid beneath the outward severity and the tender soul that anyone might see if he looked past the glasses perched on her nose and into the depths of her wonderful eyes.

He'd seen it the very first day they met, in the way she felt such fierce and sudden compassion for the greyhounds he brought out to the camp. The first time he saw her, he knew. She was the woman for him.

She had only confirmed that to him when she made the decision and filled out the long, detailed forms to adopt a former racer even before he returned that night to pick her up for their first date.

He smiled to himself. They had dated every night that summer and made plans for their relationship to continue when she went back to her teaching job in Enid. They talked of marriage on the last night before they parted that summer, the night he gave her a hand-picked brindle greyhound with a torn ear, a lousy track record, and a heart as big as the summer sky they'd fallen in love beneath.

Adam thought she understood that he wanted to postpone the big event until after he'd established his practice. He didn't want either his work or his family to suffer because he did not have time to devote himself enough to both.

They had maintained a terrific long-distance relationship. At least he thought it had been terrific until the last few months before they broke up.

Then suddenly Ginny lost all patience with his need to wait. He shook his head and, in doing so, caught a glimpse of his own eyes in the rearview mirror.

"Who are you kidding?" he growled to his own image. "There was nothing sudden about it."

He'd known, if he admitted it to himself, that the showdown was on its way for quite a while. Still, he thought that if he could hold off through breeding season, he'd find the time to start his marriage properly. But breeding season turned into birthing season, then preparations for livestock fairs, then getting ready for winter, and then…

And then Ginny had had enough.

Adam pounded his fist against the steering wheel and looked into the blinding glare of the sunlight glinting off the truck's hood. It stung his eyes, but that was nothing compared to the throbbing ache in his chest.

If these last few months without Ginny had taught him anything it was that he'd had a lot more time than he'd ever realized—long, lonely hours from dinnertime until he made himself go to sleep, Saturday afternoons,

Sunday mornings after church. And he'd spent most of that time missing Ginny.

Now he was ready to make the commitment, to *make* the time so that their relationship and marriage would work. If only he knew what to do to bring her around.

His thoughts went back to the verse she had recommended: *"Be considerate."* The phrase rattled through Adam's mind and made him wince at his own behavior.

"Considerate!" He huffed. Barging in on Gin's lecture and hauling her out like that. No wonder she hardly spoke to him. What he'd thought a grand romantic gesture, the kind of show of commitment he thought she'd wanted, had been the exact opposite.

He squinted, looking at the quiet buildings around him and spotted a small, neat little florist just across the way. He'd been a top-notch jerk up until now, first in the way he neglected Ginny's feelings and now in the way he tried to woo her again.

Five

RALPHIE DIDN'T MOVE A MUSCLE FROM THE COUCH WHERE HIS lean, athletic body lay sprawled, but he did cock his tattered ear just a bit and followed her movements with intense interest. For a comfy old couch potato like Ralphie, that was quite the show of curiosity. Ginny belted out another round of one of Aretha Franklin's signature songs as she leaned over to take a big, long whiff of the gorgeous flowers Adam had sent yesterday with, of all things, a hand-written apology.

"I'm sorry I disrupted your class and acted in general like a knuckle-dragging macho moron. Can you forgive me?" she read again.

"I can and I will forgive you, Adam Buckman, *if* this is an indication of things to come. And I mean the apology, not the flowers." She brushed her thumb along the velvety petal of one perfect rose and drew in the mellow fragrance of the arrangement. "Not that we mind the flowers, of course, do we, Ralphie?"

Ralphie let out something between a "woof" and a sigh, then his tongue poked out the side of his mouth, and he gave her a look that seemed to say he'd have preferred food to flowers.

A sharp rap at her front door told her that Adam was a few minutes early. Ralphie's ear pricked up, but he didn't move so much as a paw to get up and go to the door and see what was up—that's what he considered his owner was for, no doubt. Ginny shook her head. "You'd show a little more excitement if you knew who was waiting behind that door. Though, I may be excited enough for both of us." Her heels clicked on the highly polished hardwood floor as she rushed to the mirror over the fireplace. "I don't know who was more surprised when I accepted Adam's offer for a ride to church this morning and lunch after. Well, I did issue the man a challenge to show he had changed. At the very least, I owe him the opportunity to prove it."

At the second knock, Ralphie deigned to lift his head, more seeming to say, "Aren't you going to get that?" than as an offer to rush the door ready to protect her from any would-be intruder. She pushed at the smooth French twist at the back of her head and pulled free a few wispy curls here and there to frame her face. Then she swept the back of her hand down her pink suit's lapel. "I'll be there in a minute, Adam."

She rushed to the door, stopped, took a deep breath, and concentrated on keeping a pleasant but detached expression on her face.

"Hello, Adam." The door swinging inward blessedly fanned her in the heat of her excitement. "You're just a bit earl—" One deep bark, a scramble of long, powerful legs, and suddenly a cold pointed nose poked past Ginny's hand.

"Ralphie! How you doing, boy?"

"Wait, he—"

It was too late. Ralphie went up on his hind legs and, with his whip of a tail slapping at Ginny's shins, flopped his front paws on Adam's chest. Two huge adoring brown eyes gazed up at the man as if to ask him where he'd been for so long.

"Hey there, fella." Adam scrubbed his curled fingers

over the greyhound's graceful neck. "Good to know that at least *someone* around here missed me."

Ginny's stomach knotted at that. She reached out to drag down the dog as a distraction to keep herself from blurting out that just because she didn't throw herself at him and lick his face didn't mean she hadn't missed Adam, too. She pushed Ralphie back inside the threshold, then looked out the door and blinked. "Adam, where is your truck?"

The morning sun shimmered over a dark blue sedan in her driveway. She glanced from the car to Adam and gave a tiny gasp.

"And where is your hat?"

He just grinned down at her like the cat who ate the canary.

"All right." She plunked her hands on her hips and narrowed one eye. "Who are you and what have you done with Adam Buckman, the pickup-driving, Stetson-wearing, throwing-women-over-his-shoulder, cowboy vet?"

Adam laughed as he gave Ralphie a parting pat and walked with Ginny to the car.

But even as she slid into the car he explained he'd borrowed to make her "more comfortable than riding in the pickup," suddenly she had to wonder if maybe her urging had changed the man into someone she would no longer recognize.

"If you don't mind, Ginny, since you chose where we ate yesterday, I think I'll pick a place today." Adam glanced across the car to give her a wink.

"Please do." She gave a stiff nod.

He started the car, then twisted around to check behind them before backing out. Streams of church-goers blocked his path for a moment, so he used the time to study Ginny, sitting prim and proper in the bucket seat beside his.

There was a new softness about her, he decided, nothing he could pinpoint, but something had smoothed down the hard edges of her perpetually ruffled feathers around him. He smiled to himself. *It had to be the flowers.* He'd gotten it right this time.

She sat in silence, her hands curling the Sunday bulletin into a tight tube.

Still, there was a sense of reserve he thought they would have moved past by now, especially when she agreed to accompany him to church and out to lunch.

She tapped the rolled bulletin against the side of the door, her gaze fixed ahead.

Definitely reserved. He wanted to ask her if he'd assumed too much or perhaps been inconsiderate in some way he did not realize. Instead, he said, "Of course, I'd like your suggestions about where to eat. You probably have a much better idea about what is or isn't crowded on a Sunday."

"You sound like it's been years since you were in town on a Sunday." She cocked her head, her eyes narrowed.

She hadn't worn her glasses this morning. If she were acting any less prickly toward him, he might have suspected she kept them off for his sake, both to look pretty and to have an excuse to stand close to him as they sang from the hymnal. She did look pretty, Adam thought, with or without glasses.

Of course, she'd look prettier if she'd just lighten up and smile at him.

"Well, it has been a good six months since I've made the Sunday lunch scene in Enid." He eased the car backward, then guided it slowly into the line of cars departing the parking lot. "Things change."

"Yes, they most certainly do, but not that much. Not in that short a time." Accusation rang in her tone.

He got the idea they weren't talking about places to eat on Sunday, but he played along. "You mean things don't change that much in that short a time in a town like Enid?"

"Oh, Enid has changed." She settled in her seat and leaned back. "Enid has changed tremendously since I was a girl here. For instance, when I was younger, Mom and Dad would take us kids out to eat after church at the Holland House Buffet. We'd listen to the folks talk, and we'd fill up on fried chicken and potatoes and chocolate pudding. Then we'd all go home and get into our comfortable clothes and enjoy a quiet Sunday."

"Sounds nice." He guided the car out of the Central Christian Church parking lot onto West Main Street.

"It was," she murmured, gazing out the window.

It wasn't hard to imagine the peaceful Sundays of Ginny's childhood as they drove down the residential street under a green canopy of old trees. Large old homes lined their way and spoke of a kind of tranquillity of small town life that he supposed he rarely experienced anymore living on the edge of Tulsa.

Suddenly it dawned on him that if he and Ginny were to work things out, he would be asking her to leave the life she had always known. As he pulled up to a stop sign, he frowned and turned to her.

"I guess it would be hard for you ever to leave Enid, your family, your friends, your work, your memories."

"Well, I think I could bring my *memories* with me." The warmth of her genuine smile gave Adam renewed hope.

"But it would be hard to leave?"

"Not really. Not for the right reasons."

"Or the right man?"

She looked at him and said nothing.

A car rolled up behind them, and Adam had to move on. "So, you want to go to this Holland House place?"

She shut her eyes. "It isn't open anymore. And that wasn't the point of my telling you about it, Adam."

"I knew it." Not for the first time in their relationship, he and Ginny were talking about one thing while she meant something altogether different. "Well?"

She twisted the bright white bulletin in her hands tighter and tighter. She started to speak, then closed her mouth, her jaw clenching.

Adam swerved gently to the side of the narrow street and parked. He cut the engine and positioned himself to face her. The fabric of his good suit chafed the upholstery in the tense silence between them.

"So, Ginny." There was a rasp in his voice. "What was your point?"

"That things do change, Adam. Certainly they do." She placed the bulletin in her lap and folded her hands. "The seasons, the places around us, the way we spend our time, they all change. But the things that matter don't fade away or totally transform. Family, home, who we are inside, God's presence in our lives, those essential things remain."

"Why do I have the feeling we're not talking about Enid?"

She broke into a hesitant grin. "I'm just trying to let you know that I never meant for you to reinvent yourself for me. I wouldn't ask that of you."

"I wouldn't ask it of you, either. I respect you too much for that, Ginny, and I love who you are, just as you are, with the possible exception of your stubborn refusal to give in to my cowboy charm and agree to marry me immediately." Adam watched her reaction to his words. It appeared to be exactly what she wanted to hear, and he meant every bit of it.

"I *have* changed, Gin," he assured her for good measure.

"I really think you have. Your apology note went a long way toward convincing me how much."

"As for this car and me showing up on your doorstep 'topless'—" he pointed to his hatless head— "well, I just wanted to illustrate to you how far I'd go to be the man you need me to be as your husband."

She shifted in the seat, putting her back to the door. "Did you ever stop to think that if you just worked on being the man God needs you to be, you'd be more than acceptable husband material for any woman?"

"I read that verse you suggested. It gave me something to think about, something to act on."

"I can tell." Sunlight shone over her pale hair.

"I only wish I had more time to spend with you this week, to show you that I am learning."

She stretched her hand out but didn't quite touch

his arm. "I thought you'd be in town all week."

"It's true I took the week off, but I won't be in Enid the whole time." Suddenly he regretted the plans he'd made half out of friendship, half as a backup plan to keep him from running into Ginny too often if she decided not to give him his second chance. "I promised Billy I'd help him move. He rented a fourteen-foot truck, and we're driving down to Oklahoma City tomorrow to pick up a bedroom suite his grandmother is giving him."

"But that's just one day."

"Actually, we're staying in the city to catch up with some friends from college. Then we'll stay long enough to pick up Billy's cousin who's flying in for the wedding. We won't be back in Enid until late Wednesday."

"Oh." Disappointment clouded her eyes.

"Then on Thursday a bunch of us are helping Lisa and Billy move their stuff into their new house."

The clouds broke, and her face brightened. "I don't suppose they could use another pair of hands to help, could they?"

"Are you kidding?" He knew he was grinning like a wolf in a chicken coop, but he couldn't contain it. This offer meant Ginny wanted to find a way to spend more time with him. "I'm sure Lisa and Billy would love to have your help."

"Good. I'll call Lisa and let her know."

"And until then, we have the rest of today to spend with each other." He rubbed his hands together like a rich man contemplating his wealth. "Starting with lunch."

"So, does this also mean you'll respect my recommendations for a place to eat?" She folded her arms over the front of her delicate pink suit.

He ran one hand back to loosen his smoothed-down hair and growled, "As long as it involves steak and potatoes or anything smothered in hot salsa, I'm listening."

"Now, that's the Adam I know and—"

Love? She didn't say it, but his heart filled in the blank for her.

"Appreciate," she finished.

He felt let down, but, gazing into her now relaxed and twinkling eyes, not *too* let down. He reached out to stroke her cheek, uncertain at first if she would pull away.

When she tilted her face into his caress, he let out a long breath he hadn't realized he'd been holding. His gaze dipped to her parted lips.

She wet them in an entirely innocent and unconscious gesture.

Adam's response came without conscious effort as well, but he couldn't classify it as innocent.

It had been so long since he had kissed Ginny. Really kissed her. Eyes closed. Senses open to the unbelievable softness of her hair, the warmth of her skin, the scent of her perfume.

He half expected her to push him away, but when she wound her fingers around his neck and kissed him back, he lost himself in the moment. When decency demanded that he end the kiss, he moved back fully into his seat and let out a long, low breath.

She cast her gaze downward, a pinkish tinge on her cheek.

Adam smiled as he tipped her chin up and angled it so that he could look into her eyes again. "Does this mean we're making some progress?"

"Yes." She smiled, too. "I do believe it does."

Six

"LOOKING FOR SOMEONE?"

Ginny jumped as she let the curtain fall back across Lisa's kitchen window. Ginny had come over to Lisa and Billy's future home early Thursday morning to help with cleaning and preparations for the furniture. "I...um...it's just that, Adam was awfully tired when he called last night, and since he needed his rest so he could work today, I didn't get to see him, and—"

"And you can't wait to throw yourself into his loving arms again," Lisa finished for her.

"Well, I—"

Lisa shook her head, a knowing expression on her face. "You just let me know if you need any motion sickness pills, girl."

"Motion sickness? What for?"

"For that wild ride you're on." Lisa broke into an impish grin. "Less than a week ago he carted you off on his shoulder and you loathed him, last Saturday you were talking about teaching him a lesson, and today—"

"Today I am simply looking forward to seeing the man again. After all, we shared a very nice Sunday together, lunch and a matinee, a stroll around campus."

"A good-night kiss?"

"No."

"Really?"

A smile eased over Ginny's lips. Her ponytail bounced behind her head as she ducked her chin. "We didn't wait until night."

"Yep, talk about your wild rides." Lisa laughed. "I just want to know what changed."

"Adam did." Ginny wadded up the hem of her over-sized T-shirt in one fist. "Or at least I hope he did."

"He sure seems like the same guy to me."

"Oh, he's basically the same Adam, the same man I fell in love with, but it's how he treats me that's different."

"How's that?"

"With respect. Not that he didn't *act* respectful before," she rushed to add. "But he didn't really respect my feelings before. Otherwise, he never would have put off making a commitment for so long."

"So now he's ready to make a commitment?"

"Oh, it's not just that. He seems to be trying to appreciate my point of view in all this. I can't tell you how much that means to me."

Lisa smiled and put her hand on Ginny's shoulder. "You don't have to. I know exactly what you're talking about."

The sound of a moving truck rattled the nearly empty house.

Ginny snatched at the curtain and swept it aside. "It's them."

Lisa turned and hurried toward the door, calling back as she went, "I hope it all works out for you and Adam, and if it does, be sure to bring a catcher's mitt to the wedding."

"A catcher's mitt? Why?"

"For the bouquet, silly. I'll be aiming it right at you!"

As Ginny watched Lisa fling herself into Billy's open arms, she wished she had the nerve to do the same with Adam. Instead, she stood on the front porch, shifting her weight from one foot to the other as she waited for Adam to get out of the truck and saunter across the small, neatly cropped lawn.

Adam came to the foot of the porch steps and stopped. He said nothing, just stood with his hands tucked into his pockets. Everything from his posture to his expression told her that the next move was hers.

Ginny drew in the sweet smell of freshly mowed grass and the hint of Adam's aftershave. After spending three days with him again and then three days missing him, she felt ready to make that move. She opened her arms and stepped forward, all her senses focused on her happiness and the hope that Adam would reciprocate her emotions.

It would have been a lovely gesture, one of those memorable, tell-the-grandkids-about-it moments. *Would have been.* If Ginny had paid a little less attention to Adam's reaction and a little more to her feet.

She stepped down, but instead of meeting the stairs, her foot just kept going down.

Adam rushed forward.

The heel of her foot pounded to the edge of the second step from the porch, jarring her to her teeth. She reached for the banister.

Adam reached for her.

Just when she thought she'd saved herself from falling, Adam's hand on her arm twisted her just enough to slide her heel from the step.

It only took seconds, but it seemed to play out in agonizing slow motion.

Ginny lunged forward.

Adam half chuckled, half barked, "Whoa!"

Her nose met his hard chest.

His chin bounced off the top of her head.

He staggered backward.

She put out her hands to brace herself, which actually only pushed Adam farther off balance.

She heard him groan just seconds before she heard his body make contact with the sidewalk.

Then she fell on top of him, scraping one knee on the rough concrete as she did.

It took her a few stunned seconds to gather the strength to take a deep breath and push up onto her knees.

When she pulled away, Adam propped himself up on his elbows and looked at her, his hat knocked as lopsided as his grin. "Well, I've heard of falling for someone, but until now I've never actually experienced the phenomenon."

"What can I say?" She rubbed her smarting palm over her jeans. "Looks like when it comes to me, Buckman, you're just a regular pushover."

"You always did knock me off my feet, Gin." He sat up, bringing his face just inches from hers. Her eyes glittered with sincerity and longing as he took her injured hand in his, brushing it gently. "The question is, what are we going to do about it?"

She thought about Lisa's offer to toss her the bouquet, about Adam's apology note that showed her that he valued her feelings, and about his boast that he would sweep her off her feet so she'd want to be his wife.

A small flutter started in Ginny's belly, then worked its way up to put a tremor in her voice. "I guess we get up and get on with the rest of our lives."

His brow tightened.

"Together," she added.

His face lit up. He leaned forward to give her a quick kiss.

No sooner had his lips met hers than Lisa and Billy approached them.

"Wow," Billy said. "Are you two hurt?"

"Yeah." Adam lifted his mouth from hers just long enough to make himself understood. "Ginny is, and I'm kissing it to make it all better."

Billy hooted. "That'd make sense if she fell on her face, Buckman."

Busted, Adam drew away, his eyes sparkling. He picked up Ginny's hand and placed one tender kiss on her chafed palm.

A shiver tingled down her spine.

"I guess this means you two are okay?" Lisa asked.

Without taking his gaze from Ginny's, Adam nodded. "We're just fine. In fact, we're better than fine. Wouldn't you say, Gin?"

"Much, much better," she whispered to him, her heart filling with the hope that they had come so far and now could start thinking about the future and all it held for them.

Maybe a June wedding, she thought as Adam helped her stand up. *Or July.* Now that they both wanted the same things from their relationship, why rush? She'd have to finish out the school year and make so many plans for moving and finding another job near Tulsa.

She took Adam's arm and gave it a squeeze. Now that she knew he truly respected her feelings and would listen to her side of things before making any decisions, Ginny felt she had all the time in the world.

Adam couldn't take his eyes off Ginny. All afternoon he'd found excuses to linger in the same room she was working in. Watching her perform the simple tasks that helped Lisa turn the house into a home played on his male pride as he imagined her transforming his own sparsely furnished place into their home.

"What do you think?" She cocked her head, sending her ponytail swinging as she took a step away from the golden oval frame she'd just hung.

"Perfect," he murmured, his gaze pointedly on Ginny.

"The mirror, cowboy." She jerked her thumb over her shoulder. "Is it the right height?"

"How would *I* know?"

"Well, can you see yourself?"

He moved in on her in swift silence. When he had his arms wound around her small waist, he pulled her close and bent his head to look deep into her eyes. "Yes, I can. I can see myself doing this exact kind of thing with you."

"*This* kind of thing?" She looped her arms around his neck and stole a peck on the cheek.

"Yeah, that." He smiled, tightening his grip to bring her closer still. "And all this domestic type stuff, too. Hanging your favorite pictures over my fireplace, your college degrees next to mine in the den. A special place just for Ralphie to lounge around all day waiting for us to spoil him, then, in time, having some kids to spoil as well. So what about you? Can you see yourself doing that, too?"

"Ginny? I need the hammer," Lisa called from another room.

"Gotta go." Ginny pushed away from his chest.

Adam snagged her back to him, refusing to let her leave just yet. "You haven't answered my question, Gin. Can you see yourself making your home with me? As soon as we're married, of course?"

"Yes, I can." She gave him a fleeting kiss, then slipped from his arms.

"Good," he told her as she picked up the hammer and scooted out the door.

Billy strolled in. "What's good?"

"God is good, my friend." Adam tossed his arm over his friend's shoulders.

"Have to agree with you there."

"While you're being agreeable, then, how about letting me borrow the moving truck now that you're done with it?"

"Sure, but what for?"

"I'm cooking up a little surprise for Ginny."

"And you need a fourteen-foot truck for it? You're scaring me, buddy."

Adam slapped his friend on the back. "I just want the truck to move her belongings to my house."

"Uh, Adam, that doesn't exactly sound like the kind of thing you want to do as a surprise." Billy shook his head.

Adam laughed off his friend's concern. "She just told me it's what she wants. How much of a surprise can it be?"

Seven

"YOU WANT TO WHAT?" GINNY GRITTED HER TEETH, FEELING her face grow hot.

"Load up your stuff to take to my house." Adam tipped his hat to the back of his head. He shifted his big boots on her porch step and folded his arms across his chest. "I know it's rushing things a little, but we have all day free until the wedding rehearsal and dinner tonight, so why not make good use of it and the truck?"

"The truck?" She felt her head shake but could not honestly say she'd meant to move it. She felt too stunned to connect to anything, even Adam's words.

"Yeah, the truck." He glanced over his shoulder at his pickup parked in her driveway. "Not *my* truck. The one Billy rented. We can go over and get it anytime we want. He doesn't have to have it back until five o'clock today."

She blinked; then a flood of relief washed over her. "Oh, Adam, you really had me going."

"What?"

She threw up both hands up. "April Fools!"

"April what?"

"April Fools!" She forced a laugh. "I get it. You can stop the charade now."

He scowled.

"It *is* a charade, Adam." It had to be. "You couldn't possibly have come over here thinking you would load up my furniture to haul it off to your house *today*."

"But you said you wanted…" Adam paused. "Did

you or did you not say that you wanted us to get married and set up our own home?"

"Well, yes." Her hands gripped her hips, the soft fabric of her flowing print dress crinkling under the pads of her fingertips. "But I didn't mean today!"

"Why not?"

Why not? She still wanted to believe he would break into a big grin and yell "April Fools!" any minute. When he didn't, she groaned. "It's happening too fast, that's why not."

"Too fast? We only dated for three years, more than half of which you spent wanting us to get married."

He had her there. If he'd have shown up with this very same truck a day, a week, even one month after their breakup, she'd have run him over trying to get her things loaded in before he changed his mind again. Suddenly she remembered the source of her hesitation.

Adam reached out and grasped her shoulders. "Look, Gin, I told you when I showed up in your class that I expected you to agree to be my wife before the end of the week. You did and—hey, is that what's bugging you? That I didn't make a formal proposal?"

"No, Adam."

"It is!" He bent at the knees to level his gaze with hers. "I can tell it is."

"If you really think that, if you haven't learned any more about what I want, what I need, from a husband than that, then—"

"Ginny, I read the verse you suggested. I am making every effort to be more considerate like it says and to show how ready I am to commit to this, just like you wanted when we broke up six months ago." His hands dropped from her shoulders. The morning sun glinted off his truck. "That's why I arranged to use the truck, to show you, not just tell you, how much I want you in my life. And to be considerate and take care of your needs without having to be asked."

"Oh, Adam." Part of her wanted to pull him into an embrace and laugh over the miscommunication. But she just couldn't do it, not with something this important at stake. "I do appreciate the effort, but don't you see?"

He set his jaw and stared straight at her.

"Your doing this, making these plans without even talking to me about them, is just the flip side of the same old coin." A flash of pain strangled her voice and made her catch her breath as the truth of what she was saying sank into her own heart. "It's all about you, isn't it? First our relationship was guided by your timetable and now…"

Warm tears washed her vision, but she angled her chin up to keep them from falling. She would not allow this moment to be reduced to a crying jag. "This shows me that nothing has really changed. You still don't really have respect for my feelings in our relationship."

She turned on her heel, needing desperately to get away.

Adam snatched at her arm. "Ginny, I don't understand. That is, I understand that you don't want to move your belongings right now, but I *don't* understand what you're saying about us."

"Us?" She peeled his fingers from her arm. "There is no 'us.' I was a fool to think that there ever could be."

She went inside, trying to slam the door, but Adam caught the closing door in one hand.

"I have nothing more to say to you, Adam."

"Good. Then maybe you can listen for a change."

She started to protest, but he spoke before she could. "I've tried, Ginny. Sure, maybe my attempts have been clumsy and off track, but they've been sincere. I wonder if you can say the same about yours."

"My what?"

"I read the verse you suggested, Gin. And I can't get that Aretha Franklin song 'Respect' out of my head," he said. "When I saw the subtle changes in you, I took that to mean we were both trying."

"Changes? In me?" She flicked her loose hair from her shoulder and crossed her arms over the soft bodice of her dress. "What changes?"

He opened his mouth to speak, then shut it. He glared at her a moment. Finally, he shifted his gaze to Ralphie, hunkered down at their feet like a rabbit about to either spring up and give one of them a big hug or to take off running through the house in a burst of nervous speed.

Ginny wanted to caress the animal's velvet soft ears and coo to him that everything was all right, but she wasn't sure she could give that assurance with any conviction right now. "If I've made any changes, Adam, I'm not aware of them."

"Oh." He shifted his lean hips. "Now I get it. It was one-sided all along, wasn't it, Ginny?"

"Get what? *What* was one-sided all along?" She stepped forward. "I have no idea what you're talking about."

"It's not what *I'm* talking about but what *you* were talking about that's the problem here."

She looked at him, perplexed.

"Your lecture." His gaze met hers dead-on. "The demands of me, the verse you suggested, even that song. You didn't share any of them in a spirit of compromise, did you?"

"Well, yes, that is, I intended—"

"Your intentions shine through pretty clearly, Ginny. You intended that I do all the changing and make all the sacrifices in order to keep this relationship alive. You dished out the very same thing you accused me of doing six months ago."

She blinked, unable to process this accusation even as some part of her grasped the truth of his words.

"I admit," he continued, "I am guilty as charged. But when I came to terms with my selfishness and knew that our love, what we had, was worth changing for, I made the effort."

"Oh, Adam, I didn't mean to—" She put her fingertips to her throbbing temple. "I—I need a few minutes to sort all this through."

"I'll be in town until tomorrow after the wedding. If I don't hear from you by then, well, I hope God gives you what you're looking for. Good-bye." He cupped Ralphie's narrow head in his large hand so gently that Ginny couldn't help but think he meant some of that tenderness for her but could not bring himself to share it under the circumstances.

Then Adam turned and was out the door.

She rushed to the threshold, and the door fell against her shoulder.

"Adam, please!" But he climbed into his truck and revved the engine. As she watched him drive away, she realized she had spent far too much time dwelling on his part of the relationship and not enough dwelling on hers. And if she ever hoped to redeem that relationship, she'd better get to work rectifying that immediately.

Fortunately, she knew just where to start.

"Your beauty should not come from outward adornment, such as braided hair and the wearing of gold jewelry and fine clothes. Instead, it should be that of your inner self, the unfading beauty of a gentle and quiet spirit, which is of great worth in God's sight. For this is the way the holy women of the past who put their hope in God used to make themselves beautiful. They were submissive to their own husbands…."

"Submissive." Ginny lifted her gaze from 1 Peter. That word had always been a sticking point for her. It was probably the very reason she'd concentrated more on the instructions given to men than on those given to women. She cradled the Bible to her chest for a moment. If men behaved as they should, using consideration and respect for women, maybe the idea of trusting, of giving over to a more gentle nature might not be so…so…frightening.

"But then," she said to the dog she was using as a sounding board for her thoughts, "this isn't some abstract study in the behavior between men and women we're dealing with here, is it Ralphie? This is Adam."

At the sound of the name, the greyhound raised his head. That much effort from the forty-mile-an-hour couch potato spoke pretty highly of the animal's opinion of the man in question.

"Adam *has* changed, *has* become the kind of man

the verses admonished him to be. Or at least he's tried, hasn't he, boy?" She understood now that as she had unwittingly softened her appearance and her behavior toward Adam these last few days, he had responded, just as the verses said he would.

Now the man she loved and her own faith called her to do more.

She went back to the third chapter of 1 Peter, where she had left off at verse 6, the reference to Sarah. Smiling, she knew what she must do. *"You are her daughters if you do what is right and do not give way to fear."*

"If I do the right thing and don't give in to fear, Adam and I might still make a life together."

Ralphie's ears went straight up like radar tuning in, as if he understood the significance of her words and wanted to add, "Me, too! Don't forget me."

Ginny laughed, her heart suddenly light. "We'll all make a new life together, boy. That is, if Adam hasn't given up on me completely."

Eight

A GUSH OF COOL AIR SWEPT OVER GINNY AS SHE PUSHED OPEN the doors of Faith Lutheran Church. She turned on her heel to the right and tried not to let her shoes click too loudly on the hard floor before she reached the carpeted entryway outside the sanctuary.

The main double doors were shut, but one of the side doors stood propped open. Ginny peeked inside. There was a reverent hush in the room. Lisa, her two attendants, and her mother sat whispering in the front pew. Adam, Billy, the pastor, and the other groomsmen huddled a few feet away in front of the altar.

What now? Ginny had seen movies where someone had burst into a wedding scene just as the minister asked if anyone knew why the couple could not marry. It hardly fit this situation, though she wished she had some equally dramatic and convenient opportunity to announce both her presence and her motivations for showing up.

She hesitated, lingering at the back of the sanctuary with her hand on the piano.

The minister looked up and straight at her. "Oh, good, your accompanist is here."

"Me?" Ginny clutched at her neckline. "I—I'm not—"

"Ginny!" Adam stepped forward, annoyance in his tone and expression. "What are you doing here?"

She shouldn't have come. Adam wasn't glad to see her. The realization brought tears to her eyes and a knot to her stomach. "I came to—that is, I hoped—"

What had she hoped? That he'd break into a huge smile and come running down the aisle to take her into his arms and make a loving reconciliation? She thought of her own overused motto, Fool me once, shame on you, but fool me twice, shame on me, and wondered if there was a third option: Fool me three times, it's a shame I can't melt into the floorboards and ooze out of here.

She wanted to leave, to do anything but come face-to-face with Adam and his still-fresh anger. Ignoring the ache in her heart and the burning in her cheeks, Ginny tossed her head back. "Maybe I shouldn't have come here at all."

Adam set his jaw and did not reply.

Ginny swallowed hard and took a step back.

"Oh, no, no." Lisa stood and rushed into the aisle at the front of the church. "I'm glad you came. I can really use your help."

"You can?" Ginny, Adam, and Billy spoke simultaneously.

"For what?" Adam then demanded.

"A stand-in bride," Lisa said.

"A what?" Ginny, not too obviously, leaned on the piano for support.

"A stand-in for me, you know, so I can see how it's going to look." When Ginny looked skeptical, Lisa continued. "Besides, it's bad luck for the bride and groom to stand at the altar together before the actual ceremony. Not that I'm superstitious, mind you, but, well, what do you say, Ginny? Will you help me out?"

What an awkward situation. But what could Ginny do? It was either give in to Lisa's request and put up a gracious front or go back to trying to explain why she'd just shown up uninvited to try to reach a man who seemed to have no interest in her anymore.

"Um, sure, Lisa, I'll do whatever I can to help." She felt Adam's gaze on her face but decided she must avoid eye contact with him at all costs.

"All right, then." The pastor clapped his hands.

Ginny flinched.

"If you'll just come down here, young lady, we might as well go over that part of the ceremony while we wait for the pianist to arrive."

"Okay." Ginny started down the side aisle.

"Wait, Ginny, come this way." Lisa made a broad gesture to indicate she should come down the center aisle.

Ginny froze.

"I want to see if these candle holders block out the attendants when they come down the aisle." Lisa put her hand on the brass fixtures attached to the two front rows. Her request made sense. Not good sense. But it was not the kind of thing she felt prepared to argue over in front of the wedding party in general and Adam in particular.

She scooted around the piano and over to the center aisle. Despite the fact that she took long, confident strides in silence instead of the slow, timed-to-grand-music pace, Ginny couldn't help feeling like a real bride heading toward her groom. It didn't help matters that every time she glanced up, she found Adam's intent gaze on her.

The irony of it all might have made her laugh out loud if not for the profound sense that her own foolish pride had cost her the trust and respect of a good man.

By the time she reached the front of the church, a flurry of activity had already begun. The attendants hurried forward, the groomsmen, likewise, and Lisa gave a crisp nod and a thumbs-up. Ginny supposed that affirmation meant either the candlesticks were fine or perhaps Lisa felt they'd fooled everyone with this last-ditch cover-up.

"Now, young lady, if you'll stand here." The pastor pointed to a spot directly in front of him. "Bridesmaids here, and groomsmen over there." He waved his hands like an orchestra leader directing a symphony, and everyone obeyed.

"There." He held his hands palms down to signal all was settled. "Now, let's go over the vows."

"Excuse me, Pastor." Lisa stood, her arms folded and her head tipped to one side. "I hate to interrupt, but if I could talk to Billy for just one second…"

"You're not going to back out, are you?" The grin stretched over Billy's face indicated he didn't suspect any such thing.

"Just come here and don't argue," Lisa said with feigned agitation.

Billy rolled his eyes and sighed. "Already she's giving orders."

"And already you're following them." Adam laughed.

Billy paid the comment the due it deserved by turning his back on his friend and going to Lisa. The couple put their heads together to whisper for a moment; then Lisa looked up. "Pastor, since we're going to have these candles up front, can we see how it will look with them lit and the overhead lights dimmed just a tiny bit?"

"Certainly, my dear. Let me see if I can find the switches." He hurried off, muttering to himself.

"Patrick, why don't you help Pastor?" Billy called out to his younger brother, the other groomsman.

The young man made himself scarce in an instant, and Ginny realized that Lisa had motioned away the bridesmaids. Ginny and Adam had been left alone at the church's altar.

"Imagine meeting you here." It sounded harder than Adam intended, but he couldn't really help it. She'd caught him off guard just appearing at the church like this. Not that she hadn't been on his mind constantly since he'd left her this morning, but for her to come here now, well, he just wasn't sure how to handle it. He would not be made a fool of again, that much he did know.

But when his eyes met hers, his resolve went out the stained-glass window. He studied her in the warm, glowing light of the sanctuary.

She bowed her head, but before she did he saw regret and pain flash over her face.

His heart leapt in an erratic rhythm. She loved him. He knew it. And he loved her. Maybe neither of them knew how to love perfectly or exactly as the other had always dreamed of being loved. But they loved each other all the same. And he knew now that they were both willing to sacrifice to make that love work.

He watched her stand beside him before the altar with its gleaming cross, the reminder of the greatest love of all. He prayed that she would see that if they both gave in just a little and worked together, they could have a wonderful marriage.

Adam cleared his throat, then jerked his head in the direction in which the wedding party had last been seen slipping quietly away. "They aren't exactly subtle, are they?"

"Says the man who burst into my classroom and threw me over his shoulder." Only the hint of a smile softened her wary expression.

"I am really, truly, absolutely sorry for that, Gin."

She held up one hand. "You've already made your apologies for that, Adam. Now it's my turn."

"Your turn?" *If we both gave in just a little...*

She nodded.

"To apologize?" He wondered if that sounded as eager as he felt.

"Yes."

"For what?"

"Let's see. For being bossy and demanding." She held her fingers up to tick off the reasons, her eyes fixed on his. "Inconsiderate, selfish, narrow-minded...Aren't you going to jump in and stop me at some point here?"

"What? And have you accuse me of not respecting your opinion?" He grinned, though still testing her.

"Okay, I guess I deserved that." She glanced away. "And you deserve an apology. I was wrong to place all our problems on your shoulders. Relationships need work from both partners."

Adam took her hand in his. "When you say 'relationships,' do you mean marriage?"

Ginny lifted her gaze to meet his as she whispered, "I do."

The simple words rattled through him. He gripped her hand tighter. "Tell me that the next time you stand at an altar and say those words, we'll be taking marriage vows."

"Yes." She barely made a sound. Her beautiful eyes widened, awash with unshed tears.

He leaned down to give her a kiss, but before his lips met hers, she sniffed and added, "On one condition."

"Condition?" His cheek twitched.

"When it's time to carry me across the threshold, promise me you won't sling me over your shoulder."

He fit his hand to the small of her back. "That's your only condition?"

"Well…" Her gaze dipped to his mouth. "If anything else should come up, I'm sure we can work it out together."

He kissed her fully, pulling her tightly to him as if he feared she might get away again. Only the sound of giggles and finally a hearty hoot from Billy jarred Adam and Ginny out of their very sweet celebration.

Keeping her in his arms, Adam put his forehead to Ginny's. "Is it just me or do you feel like we've been set up?"

"Well, it is April Fools' Day." She wound her arms around his waist. "But I sure don't feel like a fool, do you?"

"Uh-huh."

"You do?" She blinked in surprise.

"Yep. A fool for you."

"Then that's one thing we have in common."

"Really? You're actually saying a man and a woman

can have the same reaction to their loved one?" he teased.

"Man *or* woman, Adam. With the right attitude, the right person, and God's guidance, we can make it all work out."

Annie Jones gives thanks every day for the opportunity to do what she loves—be a wife, a mother, and a full-time writer. A bestselling author, she has crafted over fifteen novels. Reviewers have compared her characters to Tracey and Hepburn and have likened her stories of Southern friendships to *Steel Magnolias*. Jones gives her readers something to reflect upon as well as something to dream about. Annie, her husband, and their two children live in Kentucky.

OTHER BOOKS BY ANNIE JONES:

Deep Dixie

Father by Faith

Irish Eyes

Irish Rogue

The Prayer Tree

Saving Grace

The Route 66 Series:

The Double Heart Diner

Cupid's Corner

BIRDS OF A
FEATHER

DIANE NOBLE

One

PEARL FLYNN STOOD BACK, ADMIRING THE NEARLY COMPLETED canvas. She had been painting in her garden since dawn, and now the brilliant autumn sun hung much higher in the sky.In all her sixty-something years, never had such a wonder happened to her. A year ago, she'd signed up for a painting class at San Francisco City College, and now her life had changed. How she viewed herself had changed. For the first time in her life, she realized that when God had handed out gifts, he hadn't forgotten her after all.

She examined the painting. Her style was an uncomplicated and bright Americana. She smiled. Her painting instructor called it "uniquely Pearl." If she ever were so fortunate to have her own studio and shop, that's exactly what she would call it: Uniquely Pearl.

The snow geese in the background needed a touch more white, so she dipped her brush into the paint on her palette and made the correction. The scene was created from her memory of Annie and Gregory Westbrook's property out by Everlasting. She'd used winter-twilight colors, giving the Queen Anne cottage in the background a warm glow of candlelight spilling from inside, with twinkling white lights around the edge of its steep roof. This painting was one of several Pearl had done of scenes in and around the historic town.

She stepped back and squinted again. The light was rapidly changing in her garden. It would be better to wait until tomorrow morning to touch up the emerald of the pond in the foreground.

Reluctantly, Pearl put away her paints. She had just moved her easel, canvas, and paint box into the house when a car pulled into the driveway. Good timing. She'd told none of her Birds-of-a-Feather friends about her artwork. Some of the other returning students at the college knew and understood the wonder she was feeling, but she didn't want to share her artwork with those who might not understand.

Besides, she knew the Birds-of-a-Feather members believed that beneath that purple-red hair and ever present plastic visor, there was not a serious thought in her head. Maybe she didn't want to destroy that illusion. It was, after all, what she was comfortable with.

Pearl quickly scrubbed her hands with a fragrant strawberry-scented soap in an attempt to cover up the odor of the oils and turpentine, grabbed a dish towel, and headed to the front door.

When she pulled it open, her mouth dropped in amazement. It was Woodrow Hornberger, whom she had thought was still in South Africa doing work for a nonprofit organization. He smiled and removed his Indiana-Jones-type hat.

"Why, Woodrow," she said a moment later when she'd recovered from the surprise. "My goodness, I didn't know you were back."

"Hello, Pearl." The sound of his voice caused a little skitter in her heartbeat. He was watching her, and for the briefest of moments, she thought she saw a hint of something new in his gaze. Tenderness, perhaps? It happened so quickly she was sure it had been her imagination. She looked at him more closely.

He was smiling at her. Not a bit worn from his globe-trotting ways at seventy years of age. Debonair, graceful, and stately, as always. She let out a small sigh. Not her type at all. He was Fred Astaire to her Lucy Ricardo. Water to her oil. His tender look must have been her imagination.

"Well, come in, sit down." She nodded to a wicker chair overflowing with soft cushions and homemade pillows.

"Thank you." Woodrow seated himself. "You're looking well, Pearl."

She patted her hair, wondering how he could think such a thing. But she accepted the compliment anyway, smiling. "What brings you out this way?" They might as well get down to business; she knew he wouldn't drop by just for a social call.

He'd made no bones about how she rubbed him the wrong way. The only thing they had in common was bird watching, and even then, his approach was scientific. Hers was a passion for the bright little critters themselves.

"I received a telephone call this morning," he began. Pearl sighed. She'd been right. "Actually," Woodrow continued, "Annie tried to call you first, but there was no answer."

"I unplugged my phone."

He frowned, too polite to ask why. The time she spent painting was pure joy. Time she felt unzipped of her earthly body. A fresh, young, new creature. As if she were somehow working with God to create something dear. Such a feeling—both joy-filled and sacred—had never happened to her before. And, by jing, she wasn't about to let any cranky, ringing phone distract her.

"Is everything all right with Annie and the twins?" she asked. "And Greg?"

"Oh yes," Woodrow said quickly to dispel her fears. "The Westbrooks are all healthy. Annie sends her love."

"I can tell by your voice that something's wrong. Why did Annie call?"

He settled back in his chair. "I came to you first— just as Annie tried to call you first—because I know how much you love Everlasting."

She nodded. "We all do." She smiled, thinking of her recent obsession with painting it. Of course she loved Everlasting.

"That's why Annie called." He frowned in thought. "Folks around Everlasting are not sure there's anything wrong, but there are rumors flying that aren't too pleasant."

"Rumors? What kind of rumors?" What could be wrong with the sleepy little gold rush village, virtually unchanged for 150 years? It had been turned into a state historic park several years ago, thanks to the efforts of Annie's great-aunt, Sheridan Anne Hartfield, the woman who'd bequeathed her land to Annie and Greg. The whole community cherished Everlasting's roots.

"No one will substantiate them—and Annie says that Greg's even gone all the way to Sacramento to check on it—"

"Woodrow, would you just tell me about the rumors?"

"Everlasting may be sold to some overseas investors."

"What?" She shook her head incredulously.

"That's the rumor," Woodrow said, a sorrowful note to his voice.

"They can't do that," Pearl sputtered. "Everlasting belongs to the people of California. To the people of, well, of Everlasting."

"It gets worse."

She braced herself. "How could it?"

"It's said that it will be turned into a theme park."

Pearl groaned. "With rides?"

Woodrow nodded.

"Panning for gold with pie tins and fake nuggets?"

"Yes."

She closed her eyes for a minute, picturing asphalt parking lots where a forest of pines now grew, a garish neon entrance with ticket booths and souvenir shops, screaming kids on Ferris wheels and roller coasters and log rides. They'd probably call it Goldyland, Digginsville, or maybe Bear Flags over Everlasting.

She opened her eyes, staring hard at Woodrow. "We can't allow this to happen."

A slow smile spread across his face. "That's what Annie was hoping you'd say."

"Shall we get the gang together? Plan our strategy for a bit of undercover work? We do that well." She grinned.

"The sooner the better. Annie said that she doesn't have room to put all of us up, but if we'd like to bring campers and tents, we can stay by the pond."

"An army encampment." She grinned even wider. "The camp will serve as our war room!" Then she lifted a brow, considering when they'd stayed there last. "Just think, we'll be able to listen to my spotted owls at night."

"You'll never let me live that down, will you, Pearl." He'd been the first to discount her identification of the endangered bird when the group was working on

Annie's house. She knew her haphazard identification of birds and mispronunciation of their names irritated him to no end. What he didn't know was that she did it to hear the resonance of his voice as he invariably provided the Latin name. "Go ahead, rub it in." His voice was surprisingly gentle. "I'm sure none of us will ever hear the last of it."

"Do you want to set up the strategy meeting here? If everyone can make it, tomorrow night works for me. By the weekend we can head to Everlasting. Set up camp."

Woodrow nodded. "Sounds good. You want to make the calls?"

"We both can. One of us can use the fax phone."

"Don't tell me you've got a fax."

"Birds of a Feather couldn't run without it. We had a donation come in, and the group decided it was a good idea. When there's a good cause, we can flood offices with faxes stating our feelings."

"You'll be getting computerized next."

"Nothing will ever make me give up my Olivetti." The manual typewriter had faithfully served her for twenty-five years. She owed the old machine something, even if only keeping it safe from some cold typewriter graveyard.

Pearl led Woodrow to the sunroom, which also served as the Birds-of-a-Feather office. She whisked the dustcover off the fax machine, patting it almost reverently.

"Just poke the 'hook' button. You'll get a dial tone— just like a regular phone." Without waiting for Woodrow to follow her instructions, she reached for the receiver and pressed the button for him. "It's what they call a dedicated line," she added with a sense of importance.

They divided the list of members, Woodrow taking Flora, a city librarian, and Theda, her sister, a beautician. Pearl said she'd call Wyatt, a fireman and part-time search-and-rescue volunteer; Gabe Parker, a bestselling romance writer; and Charley Stiles, a burly seventy-something college student Pearl had met at the student center.

Woodrow looked a little surprised when she mentioned Charley, their newest member who'd joined Birds of a Feather while Woodrow was in South Africa. But Pearl, now standing in the doorway, merely smiled and told Woodrow new blood was good for the group.

She headed to the kitchen and picked up the phone by the table. She reached Wyatt and Gabe, who both agreed to attend the meeting.

Next Pearl dialed Charley's number. She liked the man very much. He was a recent widower, and they often met for tea on the days they were both on campus.

"Charley?"

"Ah, me. It's Pearl!" It pleased her that he knew her voice.

She briefly explained about the meeting and gave him directions to her house. She was about to hang up the receiver when Charley stopped her.

"Pearl?"

"Yes, Charley?"

"I'm glad you called. Actually, I was going to call you."

"You were?"

"Yes. I was wondering if you would, ah, join me for dinner tonight."

"Charley, I would love to." Pearl was touched that he'd thought of her. How long had it been since someone actually asked her on a date? Forever. "I really would."

"I'll stop by and collect you. What time is good?" His voice held a smile.

"Seven o'clock would be just about perfect."

"Good. I'll see you then."

"Good-bye, Charley. And thank you." Pearl felt her cheeks flush as she replaced the receiver.

She turned toward the doorway. Woodrow was standing there, looking for all the world like a towering thunderhead. "I assume our new member will be more than happy to attend the meeting."

"Well, yes. Actually, he will be." She patted her hair. "The others can come as well. How about Theda and Flora?"

"Affirmative." He checked his watch. "Well, then, I guess that takes care of that. I'll call Annie and let her know we're on top of things."

"Good," Pearl said.

"And I'll see you tomorrow night."

This time Pearl merely nodded. She searched his face. There was no trace of the earlier tenderness.

The old Woodrow was back, and she wondered why that made her so sad.

Two

THE FALL AIR WAS CRISP THE FOLLOWING NIGHT WHEN
Woodrow pulled his well-worn Land Rover into a parking space in front of Pearl's house. The smell of wood
smoke filled the air, and lights beamed a welcome
through the windows. A single lamppost, an odd-look-
ing sculptured thing with a verdigris finish, stood by the
gate, lighting the yard.

As he strode up the walkway, Woodrow counted the
other vehicles. Seven, including Pearl's yellow '67
Camaro, for which she'd traded her old lavender Buick
a year ago.

All the members were here, apparently even the
newest, Charley Stiles. There was a dark red sports car
in the driveway that Woodrow didn't recognize. Had to
be Charley's, he thought with a grimace.

Woodrow pulled back the screen door and knocked
on the rock-solid oak door. He could hear the easy
camaraderie of the others, their conversations punctu-
ated with spurts of laughter.

A moment later, the door opened. A radiant-looking
Pearl opened the door, her smile widening when she saw
him. "You're here at last. Come in, Woodrow. We've been
waiting for you."

He'd heard that a woman is never more radiant than
when she's in love, and as he moved past Pearl, he took
in the luster of her eyes, her flushed cheeks, and the
glow on her face. With a sinking feeling, he realized his
suspicions must be true. It had to be Charley Stiles. Pearl

looped her arm through Woodrow's and led him across the room. "Come, meet Charley."

From a chair near the fireplace, a big-shouldered man stood and turned. "Did I hear my name?" He smiled and stuck out his hand. "Name's Stiles." His shake was firm, vigorous.

"Woodrow Hornberger." He wished he had a name that spoke of prize fighting or major-league baseball. "It's good to meet you."

"Woody, good to meet you!" Woodrow groaned inwardly at the hated nickname, wondering if Charley had read his mind.

"I've heard so much about you." Charley shot a pleased look at Pearl, and she returned his smile. "And this group is great. I'm so glad that Pearl invited me to join. I'm looking forward to getting to know everyone better."

I bet. Woodrow noticed Pearl smelled of wildflowers and soap and...turpentine?

"We'd better get started," she said to both men. "Woodrow, I'm sure you've already got this planned down to the gnat's eyelash. Do you want to lead off?"

He was surprised. It wasn't often that Pearl relinquished the gavel to someone else in the group. "Of course," he said quickly, before she changed her mind.

"All right, everyone!" Pearl called out to the rest of the group. "Pull some extra chairs from the kitchen. Grab some coffee and cookies, sit down, and listen up. Woodrow's got some good ideas—as always—that we need to listen to. He's also the one who talked with Annie about what's going on in Everlasting. He'll be able to relay the details better than I can."

Woodrow stood to one side of the fireplace, looking down at the intent faces of the members. They took their work seriously. This was a bit out of the ordinary, but after they'd helped to fix up Annie and Greg's house in Everlasting, the history of the place had settled into their spirits. He knew they'd feel as strongly as he and Pearl did about its preservation.

"Here's the information we have so far, folks." He proceeded to tell them of the rumor about the investors and the theme park. There were groans of disapproval. "I really think those of us who have the time could get to the bottom of this. Nose around in Everlasting. Find out what we can. See what we can do to change their minds."

He paused as some members threw out suggestions; then his tone turned serious as he continued. "We're the perfect ones to act. Greg and Annie are too well known in the community. No one knows us. We could fit right in with the surroundings—"

"I've got some ideas about that," Pearl said suddenly. "Everlasting is always in need of docents—volunteers to lead the tours, dress up in period costumes. Musicians to sit on the street corners. Can anyone here play the fiddle or the harmonica?"

"I used to play the harmonica. Probably could pick it up again," Wyatt said.

Charley raised his hand. "I play both, plus banjo. Just name the tune. I play a mean 'Oh, Susannah.'" He chuckled. "Anyone for 'Dueling Banjos?'"

Everyone laughed. Woodrow gritted his teeth, wishing he'd learned how to shoe horses somewhere along the line. "Good, Charley," he said evenly. "You'll be our musician."

"There's also the theater in town," Pearl said. *Phantom of the Opera* is playing. I'm sure they could use help in the ticket office or with ushering."

The discussion turned to who could remain in Everlasting full time and who would have to commute on their days off. It was decided that a camp would be set up at Greg and Annie's. Gabe said he'd bring his camper and his laptop computer and work in the mornings, then help the others in the afternoon. Wyatt planned to stay during his four days off each week, then commute back to San Francisco for work the other three days. He volunteered to bring an extra Airstream if Woodrow would pull it with his Land Rover.

Charley said that because of his class schedule he could only come on weekends. He looked disappointed, then cheered up considerably when Gabe mentioned that the Thanksgiving and Christmas breaks were right around the corner.

It was soon apparent that only Pearl and Woodrow could be in Everlasting full time.

"I have a suggestion," Woodrow said. "Before we gear up for our undercover work, I say that Pearl and I should travel to Everlasting, nose around, and see what we can find out."

Pearl frowned. "How soon?" He was surprised. She usually jumped at the chance to head to the little town.

"Well, I was thinking of tomorrow. But if you, er, have other plans, I can certainly run out alone."

"No, no. I can make arrangements," she said quickly, glancing at Stiles. "Let's go. We can report back. Finalize our plans after that."

A hubbub rose in the room as tasks were assigned.

Flora said she'd call to see when the next classes were scheduled for docents. Charley said he'd find out about auditions for musicians and playhouse actors.

Finally the meeting broke up. After a bit more chatting as the Birds members headed out the door, the only three remaining in the living room were Pearl, Charley, and Woodrow, who wondered if Charley was trying to outwait him so he could be alone with Pearl, too.

Alone with Pearl? The idea was a revelation. When had he begun to care? He thought back over the years he'd known Pearl. Even though she exasperated him no end, he had always taken joy in her free-spirited ways, her love of life. It was during his trip to South Africa that he realized he actually missed her and wished she were with him. While Pearl and Charley chatted, Woodrow gathered the empty cups and carried them into the kitchen. From the corner of his eye, he noticed Pearl showing Charley to the door. But when he returned, instead of being on his merry way, Charley was speaking in low tones to Pearl on the front porch. The door was partly ajar, and Woodrow could see Pearl's animated face in the porch light. As she talked, she gestured with her hands, and he noticed her tapered, artistic fingers, the graceful way she flicked them this way and that to emphasize her point.

I'm turning into a romantic. But why now? Why, when it is obvious Pearl's affections are elsewhere? And why does that bother me? He had loved his late wife dearly, but never, in all their thirty-two years of marriage, had he considered himself a romantic. Quietly, he found his leather jacket and hat and let himself out through the sunporch and the back door.

By the time he'd rounded the house, Charley Stiles and Pearl were no longer on the porch though Charley's car was still parked out front. As Woodrow unlocked the Land Rover and stepped inside, he glanced back toward the house. He could see the two of them sitting before the fire. He turned the ignition, then pressed hard on the accelerator. The Land Rover lurched forward with a squeal of rubber. The sound made Woodrow chuckle. He hadn't felt this way since adolescence.

And to think of it—over Pearl! Pearl Flynn. Beautiful, red-haired, spirited, funny, wonderful Pearl.

Only now it was too late.

Or was it?

He chuckled again. His suggestion that he and Pearl go alone to Everlasting hadn't been just because their schedules were the only two permitting the trip.

He sped through the city, planning to call Pearl as soon as he got home. He needed to let her know when they'd leave and how long they might expect to stay. The sound of a ringing phone might be just the ticket for getting Charley Stiles on his way.

Woodrow pulled into his townhouse garage, quickly shut off the engine, and locked the car. He practically sprinted to the front door and into his den where he picked up the receiver.

He punched in her number from memory. After three rings, Pearl answered the phone.

"Pearl? Woodrow here."

"My goodness," she said with a faint sniffling sound. "It's late. What's up?"

"Pearl, are you all right?" She didn't sound all right.

In fact, he suspected that she'd been crying. He'd never known Pearl to cry before.

"Yes, Woodrow. I'm fine," she finally managed after a couple more sniffles. "Really."

"Do you not want to go tomorrow?" For a moment she didn't answer, and his heart dropped to his shoes. "It's okay, really. I understand. I put you in a difficult spot tonight. I'm sorry."

"No, you *don't* understand." Her spirit was showing again. "I want to go. It's just that, well, there are other, um, circumstances that I can't really go into right now." She sighed. This was not the spunky and direct Pearl he'd always known.

"You can tell me anything." Well, maybe. He really didn't want to hear about her feelings for Mr. Banjo, but he didn't say so. "About tomorrow?"

"I can be ready by dawn." She sounded considerably brighter.

"Why don't we have breakfast on the way?"

"Perfect. It's my favorite time of day. I'll pack a picnic." Her childlike exuberance was back, and he took pleasure in the sound of it.

"I'll squeeze some fresh juice. Is orange okay?"

"What if I said kumquat?" she said, laughing. "You'd have to start right now."

The sweetness in her voice during their phone conversation stayed with him long afterward, as if awakening some strange and wonderful music in his soul.

Through his window, he watched the moon-silvered branches of a pine move in the soft wind. From a distance he heard the lonely call of an owl, an *Otus kennicottii*, judging from the series of single-pitched whistles.

An enormous ivory moon hung low in the sky, reminding him of the radiance he'd seen in Pearl tonight.

And he felt as lonely as the owl sounded.

Three

PEARL WATCHED WOODROW POUR COFFEE INTO TWO DOUBLE paper cups. None of the Birds-of-a-Feather gang used Styrofoam. Pearl made sure each member followed the rules. She also insisted that they snip the plastic six-pack soda pop carriers into little pieces before dropping them into the trash. You had to make sure a raccoon or stray cat wouldn't get his head caught in one at the garbage dump. Or, heaven forbid, if the plastic made its way to the ocean…She shuddered, thinking of the consequences.

She placed a checkered cloth on the tailgate of the Land Rover and laid out the breakfast spread: berry preserves and low fat honey-wheat muffins; her special egg substitute, lite cheese, and bacon bit casserole; and Woodrow's fresh-squeezed orange juice.

Just as the sun began to crown the Sierra Nevadas, Pearl and Woodrow pulled out their folding aluminum chairs and settled into them, facing a golden valley dotted with live oaks and scrub pines. A covey of California quail scattered from beneath a stand of manzanita, calling out "cha-kee-ta" and beating the air with their wings. In some nearby oaks, scrub jays squawked their greetings as they hopped from branch to branch.

"God's creating another beautiful day for us." Pearl sighed contentedly. She'd cried last night, thinking about leaving her painting for even one day. But now her spirits had lifted, and here she sat with Woodrow Hornberger, a man she once thought unbearably stuffy, enjoying the morning. Enjoying him. Enormously.

Woodrow was intent on watching the sunrise, and Pearl turned to watch with him. The eastern sky was filled with clouds, and as the sun rose, they turned to shades of yellow and orange and pink. Soon the valley was awash with golden light, and the oaks and pines and sycamores were now backlit by the sun.

"'I lift up my eyes to the hills,'" Woodrow quoted softly. "'Where does my help come from? My help comes from the Lord, the Maker of heaven and earth.'"

His voice had a pleasant low rumble to it, and it soothed her as he quoted the psalm. Then he turned to Pearl and took her hand. "Lord," he said, "we praise you for the beauty of your creation. How can we doubt your power when we see such glory! We give you this day, and we ask for wisdom and strength for the task ahead. And bless us today, we pray in Jesus' name."

"Amen." Pearl looked up to see Woodrow's gaze on the sunlit valley.

"It is beautiful, isn't it?" he said. "Makes me want to take up painting just to capture it."

She gazed up at him, her eyes widening in surprise.

He saw her look and laughed. "Now *that's* a silly thought! Can you imagine such a thing?" He laughed again, and Pearl turned away.

She handed him a paper plate, and Woodrow helped himself to a scoop of the casserole, a couple of muffins, and some orange juice. Then she served herself, and they sat down together to eat.

He took a bite of the egg dish. "Wonderful!"

Pearl nodded absently. Her gaze swept across the valley, and she took in every detail, savoring the scent of the air, the light, the color. He'd laughed at the thought of painting it. Some people thought of art as frivolous. Perhaps he was one.

"Penny for your thoughts," Woodrow said, almost causing her to jump.

She laughed lightly, shrugged one shoulder, and flicked her fingers toward the sunrise. "You're right. It's a masterpiece. I was taking in the beauty."

He was quiet a moment, lost in thought. "About last night," he said finally. "I noticed that you seemed, well, a bit reluctant to come with me today." He fidgeted with his cup, then stood to scoop up more of the casserole though he hadn't finished with the serving on his plate.

"Well, yes." She took a sip of coffee. "I had some other obligations."

"So you said." His eyes met hers as he seated himself again.

Pearl saw the curiosity on his face and knew that he was waiting to hear her reasons. She wished she hadn't been so transparent when he'd first mentioned the trip. Her first thought, of course, had been one of dismay. Not only would she miss her early morning painting time in her garden, she would also miss today's ten o'clock class. It was weekly, four hours a session, plus lab in the afternoon. It had saddened her to skip, but after Charley said he'd stop by and explain the circumstances to her instructor and pick up any handouts or information she might need, she'd felt better. She sighed as the image of her latest painting came to mind.

Woodrow was still watching her intently. "Is it Charley? Did you not want to leave him today?"

Pearl's mouth dropped open. "Charley?" she croaked.

"Charley?" Then she giggled. Where in the world did Woodrow get such a notion? "Do you mean...our Charley?" By now her face was aflame from holding back an explosion of laughter.

"Yes," he said rather grimly. "*Our* Charley."

"Oh my goodness, Woodrow! How did you ever—"

"Guess?" he finished for her, then went on before she could correct him. "As soon as I saw the two of you together last night, I knew there was a special closeness...." His voice rumbled into a sigh.

Pearl was almost too stunned to speak. She swallowed hard, still fighting to keep the laughter from spilling. Then a slow, amazing realization began to dawn as bright as the sunrise. The man was jealous. Woodrow Hornberger was jealous!

She looked at him with wide eyes, wondering about the quickening of her heart. "Oh, Woodrow," she finally managed. "Surely you didn't think that Charley and I..." Now she blushed in earnest, searching for the right words. "That we are, or shall I say, we've, ah—"

"I'm sorry." Woodrow jumped to his feet. "I can see that I've embarrassed you. I didn't mean to imply any impropriety—"

"Impropriety?" She stood in surprise, her food spilling to the ground. She didn't know whether to be flattered or offended. "Me?"

"Now I can see I've insulted you, Pearl. Please accept my apology. I promise I won't bring up Charley or your relationship again." He turned to place the ceramic cover on the casserole dish.

"Woodrow!" she exclaimed as he twisted the lid onto the jar of preserves. "Woodrow Hornberger!" He turned, opening the lid to the picnic basket as he watched her. "Now you listen here. There is nothing going on between Charley Stiles and me. Absolutely nothing. At least not in the way you're insinuating."

"But last night—" he began, then seemed to think better of it.

"Last night was about a private matter," she said as gently as possible. But she could see the doubt still lurking on his face. She hadn't convinced him. She sighed again and started over. "You see, we share something very special—"

Woodrow looked stricken, and again, she halted. She was making matters worse. What she wanted to say was that she and Charley shared a love of learning and growing. Of being college students—at their ages! Charley understood how dear her painting class was to her, just as she understood the importance of his algebra, English, and geology classes.

She could say none of that, at least not yet. Of all the people she wanted to understand this new love of hers, Woodrow was at the top of the list. No, she needed to wait until the time was right.

"Well," he finally said with a shrug, "I suppose we'd better get going. I told Annie and Greg to expect us at about nine o'clock."

Pearl nodded, wishing she could say something to cheer him. "Then let's be on our way."

Precisely an hour later, Woodrow guided the Land Rover onto the long dirt road leading to the Westbrooks'. The sun was higher now, and when they rounded the last curve before starting down to the house, Pearl caught her breath. Fall had turned the shimmering aspens that bordered the property to the color of liquid gold, and the emerald pond sparkled like a jewel as a breeze ruffled its waters.

"It's prettier than ever in the autumn," she said. "More substantial, somehow, as if the color is bringing it a second life."

"Much like people." Woodrow grinned at her. Whatever had upset him earlier seemed to be gone.

She laughed easily, glad for the change. "Just like us, Woodrow. Colorful. Substantial. Ready to celebrate life afresh."

He threw back his head and laughed. "Well, I don't think anyone would dispute that you're one of God's most colorful creatures." He glanced down at his khaki pants and black shirt, then to her flowing turquoise-and-fuchsia dress.

"I mean our spirits, Woodrow. Not my hair. Or my bright clothes. God doesn't want us to sit back and wait to die. He's given us all kinds of choices."

Smiling his agreement, he slowed the Land Rover as they crossed a small bridge by the pond, then steered around another bend and pressed on the brake for a rabbit that scampered across the road.

She touched his arm. "Look at you, Woodrow. You build houses for Habitat for Humanity. You volunteer your time overseas caring for little children who need medical help, food, and clothing. And you work in the office of the Ornithologists Union." She thought a minute. "How many birds are on your life list now? Have you reached five hundred?"

He nodded, his eyes on the road.

"See? Talk about colorful! You may wear drab

clothes, but you've got one of the most colorful lives I know."

"Drab clothes?" he said, glancing at her. He lifted a teasing brow. "Are you criticizing my clothes?"

She looked him up and down. Again the words *debonair*, *graceful*, and *stately* came to mind. His clothes fit that image perfectly, from his Indiana Jones hat to the leather jacket. He might turn up his nose at artistic endeavors, but he himself was a work of art. "I wouldn't dare, Woodrow. They're fine. Just fine."

He parked the vehicle in the side driveway. Before they opened their car doors, the twins slammed through the front door and raced to meet them.

Mary Beth lifted her arms, and Woodrow swooped her into the air. A peal of giggles followed as she gave him a quick hug then wriggled to get down. Shamus studied Pearl intently for a moment, then a small lop-sided smile appeared. Pearl knelt so she could look him in the face. "How about a hug for Auntie Pearl?"

"Auntie Pearlie," he corrected seriously and went happily into her arms. She held the little boy close, then took his hand, and they walked up the stairs together.

The foursome had just reached the front door when Annie appeared, wiping her hands on a tea towel. "Well, look who's here!" She pulled both Woodrow and Pearl into her arms at once, the twins wiggling into the middle of the hug.

Pearl stood back, assessing her friend. "You've got that glow again, Annie. Is there something you want to tell us?"

"Does it show already?" Annie laughed, tucking a stray lock of hair behind one ear. Then she patted her stomach. "Three months along. We're expecting in the spring."

"Twins again, dear?" Woodrow asked politely.

Annie rolled her eyes heavenward. "We weren't expecting them the first time, and look what happened." She led them into the comfortable, period-decorated parlor. "Please, sit down. Can I get you anything? Tea? Coffee?"

They declined, telling her about their picnic as Woodrow settled into the love seat and Pearl sat across from him in a pine rocker. Annie bustled the children back to the kitchen table where they'd been playing with homemade play dough.

"You've come at a good time," she said when she returned.

"What do you mean?" Woodrow leaned back in his chair.

"There's a meeting tonight at the theater. The new investors are going to explain their position."

"So it's certain, then," Pearl said. "Everlasting's really going to be sold."

Annie nodded slowly. "They hope to dispel all rumors—or so they say. That's why the open meeting. They want to cover all their bases before the close of escrow."

"How about the theme park? Is that still part of their plan?"

Annie looked at Woodrow and shook her head slightly. "They're denying it. They've spread the word that they're going to keep Everlasting just as it is. They say that they're actually saving taxpayers' money by running the historic park as a private enterprise." She paused. "At least that's what was being tossed about until yesterday."

"What happened yesterday?" Pearl asked.

"There was an article in the *Everlasting Gazette* stating that it's a business venture, and the whole community will eventually profit."

Woodrow narrowed his eyes. "The only way to do that is to run it as a business. Maybe charge admission—"

"Build roller coasters—" Pearl's heart sank—"Ferris wheels. The whole kit and caboodle."

Annie nodded. "Exactly what we think. Can you stay for the meeting?"

"We wouldn't miss it." Woodrow glanced at Pearl as if expecting her to say she had other plans.

She met his look and reassured him with a nod and a smile; then they both turned back to Annie.

The twins raced into the room, and Annie pulled them to her lap. "We don't expect them to be up-front about their plans." As the kids settled back, thumbs in mouths, she continued. "Greg suspects there are some state officials involved. Perhaps even organized crime." Annie shook her head. "I didn't know about the organized crime connection when I called you. You must promise me that you'll only nose around for information—that you won't get involved in any other way."

Pearl smiled. "But we have a strategy, dear. We had a meeting just last night, planning it down to the minutest detail." She explained their ideas.

Annie frowned. "We don't know who we're dealing with here. We only know they're in powerful places. There are millions of dollars involved in this transaction. You could be placing yourselves in danger."

Woodrow's nod was firm. "Anything worth doing has risk involved."

"I agree." Pearl looked up at him proudly. He'd worked in war zones feeding starving children, in racially divided communities building houses, in disease-ridden jungles photographing rare birds. He'd met danger head-on. There was no one she'd rather have beside her in this.

Besides, they were simply going to help save a historic park. How dangerous could that be?

"When I called," Annie continued, "I was thinking more of your helping us find out the whos and whats—not jumping in and doing something about it." She paused. "I don't want anything to happen to you—to any of you."

Pearl dismissed her worry with a light laugh and a flick of her fingertips. "Not to worry, dear Annie. We're tough old birds!" She met Woodrow's warm gaze and went on, "These scoundrels—whoever they are—won't know what hit them."

Four

PEARL AND WOODROW SLIPPED INTO THE BACK OF THE PLAYhouse and took their seats. There were maybe fifty to sixty other people seated in the rows in front of them.

Onstage, the set from *Phantom of the Opera* provided a rather bizarre backdrop, especially with its enormous antique chandelier, which hung precariously above an old wooden table. Six folding chairs flanked it, and a podium was center stage with a microphone to one side. Stage lights illuminated the whole affair.

Pearl turned to Woodrow. "Rather dramatic, don't you think?"

"Seems appropriate to me. A phantom orchestrating the action from behind the scenes." He gave her a half smile.

"How true." She turned her attention to the six men who were now strolling across the stage. They seated themselves just as the seventh, a jovial-looking, bespectacled, round-faced man carrying a briefcase, hurried to join them. There was light applause from the audience, and smiling, the man nodded his balding head in acknowledgment. He then took his place at the podium.

"That's state senator Roland Thorpe," whispered Woodrow.

"I know. Champion of the little people."

"That's what he'd like folks to believe."

"Ladies and gentlemen," Thorpe said after the applause died down, "we're so glad you've joined us to talk about Everlasting's future, to clarify any questions, and to finally put to rest the rumors."

Thorpe leaned forward, pulled his eyeglasses from his nose, and rested his arms on the podium. His stance suggested intimacy and honesty—a man you could believe and trust.

Pearl couldn't resist rolling her eyes at Woodrow.

"Folks," Thorpe said, "we have an opportunity here that's greater than any I've seen during all my years of public service. Not only is it a wonderful opportunity for this community, but this model will someday be replicated throughout the state, perhaps even the nation."

Woodrow groaned softly. "Not the universe?" he muttered under his breath.

Pearl stifled a snicker.

"For you see, privatization is the wave of the future," Thorpe continued. "Privatization facilitates growth. It grows the economy of the community. It's more economically viable than any state or federal park system now being used. Privatization cuts through red tape and bureaucracy. The result is a lean-and-mean organization that benefits all. And I believe in my heart of hearts that this is exactly what we all want here in Everlasting—growth in the local economy while maintaining the beauty of the area and keeping intact its glorious history."

There was light clapping, and Thorpe nodded his head, smiling broadly. "You see, there have been rumors that have threatened to derail our project. And that's why we're here tonight—to finally put to rest any more scuttlebutt. This project *must* proceed." He hit the podium with his clenched fist. "And proceed it will!"

Pearl watched the chandelier jiggle as Thorpe struck the podium again.

"Now," he said after a pause, "I want to read to you the legal disclosures pertaining to the purchase of Everlasting by the organization known at the date of this document as Everlasting Enterprises Incorporated, or EEI." He opened his briefcase and pulled out some papers, set them in place on the podium, then put on his glasses. He began to read in a monotone.

"You know what they've done, don't you?" Pearl whispered to Woodrow. He raised a brow, and she went on, "They've succeeded in keeping us from finding out who the investors are by renaming their investment group. EEI is a front for others." Already her mind was exploring ways to find out who was behind the new name.

Thorpe droned on through the legalese. Tapping her foot, Pearl timed the reading of the document. Twenty-seven and a half minutes. Finally, it was time for the other men on stage to take the podium.

The first three were introduced as members of the community who would raise the questions that had been posed to them by Everlasting residents. Several questions were brought up about land usage, environmental impact, and zoning. A younger man, seated at the end of the table, then asked if Everlasting would remain historically correct no matter what improvements were made.

A red flag shot to the top of Pearl's mental flagpole. She had already been feeling that the questions were staged, but the word *improvements* was open to interpretation.

Woodrow nudged her and nodded. He'd caught the same word. Pearl reached for her handbag, pulled out a notepad and pencil, and began to scribble questions of her own.

The three remaining men were introduced as representatives of EEI. There was a quick assurance that the community would remain the quaint, historical village people from all over loved to visit. Then they addressed the questions, answering in such endless, obscure detail that Pearl had forgotten the question by the time the EEI representative finished his lengthy answer. She looked around. Judging by the puzzled expressions, everyone else was just as confused.

Finally, state senator Roland Thorpe stood to thank the participants by name. There was no mention of accepting questions from the floor, and it was apparent that the gathering was about to be dismissed.

Pearl checked her watch. Two and a half hours had passed, and she and Woodrow had discovered nothing they didn't already know. It was time to stir the pot a little.

She stood and waved her hand. Senator Thorpe looked to the back of the theater, but it was obvious he was about to ignore her.

"Yoo-hoo!" Everyone craned to see who was speaking. "Senator! Here in the back row. Yoo-hoo! I've got a question!"

He finally acknowledged her with a nod.

She gave the room an amiable and innocent smile. "May I ask a question that's very important to me?" The men on the podium shuffled their feet and tapped their fingers on the table, anxious to be on their way. She cleared her throat loudly. "May I ask a question?"

The senator took a deep breath. "You must understand, questions were supposed to have been turned in ahead of time—"

"But this is a question no one would have thought of unless they'd been here tonight."

Senator Thorpe picked up his papers from the podium, straightened their edges with a soft thud, and gave her a patronizing smile. "Go ahead. What is it we haven't covered?"

She smiled. "Why aren't there any women on the agenda tonight? I know there's a glass ceiling in the business world, but my goodness, I would've thought you'd have known better."

There were titters of laughter throughout the room, and beside her, Woodrow groaned softly. But the senator's relief at such a question was palpable.

The man grinned broadly. Good. She'd disarmed him, just as she had planned.

"Can you tell me, Senator, why women weren't chosen as representatives? Or at least as consultants? The impact of EEI's wondrous plans are as important to us as to anyone else."

"They are, Miss, er, Mrs...."

"Ms. Flynn. And I say that because we females own 49.2 percent of Everlasting's shops, run 78.2 percent of the businesses, and constitute 95.1 percent of the docents. I say that it's unfair for you to have excluded us from the process."

Still smiling, Senator Thorpe raised his hand to regain the attention of the audience. "Yes, yes, I quite agree—"

"And that's not all," Pearl squared her shoulders. "If there are going to be profits in EEI's running of

Everlasting, I, for one, want to have the chance to invest. I want to know *how* I can do that. I would like to get in on the ground floor, so to speak, and be part of this marvelous, innovative enterprise."

Again, Senator Thorpe started to speak and Pearl interrupted him. "I have some absolutely wonderful ideas I'd like to present to EEI about—"

This time the senator interrupted Pearl. He was still smiling, but if she was reading his expression correctly, he was beginning to get annoyed. "Please, Ms. Flynn, let me tell you how glad I am—and I think EEI will be also—to know of your interest in our project." He paused, seeming to measure the sentiment of the audience before continuing. "And you've brought up a valid point. We do need a female perspective. I'm impressed with your homework. I think you would be quite an asset as a representative on behalf of the ladies of Everlasting."

There was applause from around the room.

"I would be honored."

"You *are* part of the community here?" the senator asked.

"Oh yes, of course." Pearl would have to move here immediately.

"And what is it you do, Ms. Flynn, if I may ask, that's related to Everlasting?" He watched her carefully.

She gave him a wide smile. "I'm an artist. I paint oils of Everlasting and the vicinity." The words seemed to spill forth unbidden. She felt her cheeks flush as Woodrow looked up at her. She avoided his gaze.

Again the audience craned to get a better look at her. "Why, yes," the senator said, "I do believe you'd be perfect, Ms. Flynn. I'll pass on the word to EEI that you're our new committee representative."

"Thank you, Senator."

"Now, as soon as we're dismissed, I want you to come to the front and meet the other committee members. And Ms. Flynn?"

"Yes?"

"I would love to see your oils of Everlasting. The next time I'm out this direction, will you promise to show me some of your work?"

"Of course, Senator. You just look me up in town." Now she'd have to set up shop in Everlasting. She hoped there was available space. She swallowed hard. "You just ask for me. Remember, my name's Pearl. Pearl Flynn."

"All right, Ms. Pearl Flynn. You be expecting me."

Finally the senator dismissed the meeting. Before she could say a word to Woodrow, Pearl was surrounded by audience members. They walked with her to the front of the theater, asking about her ideas, telling her about theirs, asking about her artwork and when they could see it. It seemed she'd become an instant celebrity.

She was met near the stage by the senator, who pumped her hand vigorously. He introduced her to the other committee members. In turn, they shook her hand and offered some bland words of welcome.

After several minutes, she pulled herself away from the group and headed back up the aisle, searching for Woodrow.

She finally found him in the foyer, flipping through old theater programs that were stacked on a table near the exit.

"Woodrow!" She couldn't wait to discuss all that had

happened. "What did you think?"

When he turned, she was surprised by the cold expression in his eyes. It was as if he didn't know her.

"Woodrow?" Her eyes widened.

"What do I think?" He ground out the words between clenched teeth. "You don't know me very well if you have to ask."

She put her hand on his arm, attempting to break through the emotional wall he'd put between them. But Woodrow turned away from her and stormed out of the theater.

Five

THE SUN HAD BARELY RISEN WHEN PEARL PADDED FROM THE guest room to the kitchen in Annie's borrowed robe and slippers.

"Good morning," Annie said with a smile. "How about joining me out on the deck for some coffee?"

She poured the steaming liquid into two mugs and handed one to Pearl. They headed through the kitchen door. Below was an autumn vegetable garden, filled with ripe squashes, pumpkins, and herbs. They pulled chairs to the railing where the view was best and settled into them. Pearl let out a contented sigh.

"Tell me what happened last night," Annie said. "Woodrow seemed grumpy when you two got home. Said we'd talk about it this morning. Then Greg left early for school, and Woodrow left soon afterward to check out something in town. He didn't say what." She took a sip of coffee. "What happened?"

Pearl went over the details of the meeting, how she'd thrown out some statistics, then had been asked to join the committee as a representative.

Annie grinned. "Where did you get those numbers?"

A sheepish smile crept across Pearl's face, and she swallowed hard. "Well, I, ah, made them up from estimates I've seen in the past. I just figured the more precise I sounded, the better. We'll just hope no one double-checks."

Annie laughed. "You're priceless, Pearl!" She took

another sip of coffee, then set down the mug. "But what about the paintings? I don't see how you'll be able to get by that prevarication."

"I wasn't lying about that." Pearl looked out at the forest that ringed the Westbrooks' property.

"You paint?" Annie was watching her carefully. "I mean, really paint?"

Pearl turned back to face her. "Yes, really. I've been taking classes. I've taken to art like a bird to a feeder." She sat forward, suddenly glad to tell a friend who would understand. "The canvas I'm working on right now is of your pond, the wild geese, and your house the way it looked that first Christmas."

Annie touched her arm. "Pearl, that's wonderful!"

"Will you help me get a place in Everlasting—something I could rent as a working studio? Right in the heart of downtown. I've got a little nest egg. Perhaps I could find something that's a lease/option. It would need to be just outside the state park land. And I would need it quickly—within days, if possible."

Annie nodded. "I'll get right on it. Shall I call you tonight? Or better yet, I'll have my realtor friend call you in San Francisco to let you know what she's found."

"Perfect." Pearl looked at the streams of sunlight through the forest. The air smelled of fresh pine mixed with the herbs from Annie's garden. "Who ever would have thought that your great-great-grandmother and grandfather started all of this? Because they picked this very place to live, to build, 150 years ago, you and Greg also landed here."

"Actually, if you mean getting my family to Everlasting Diggins, it was my ancestor Sheridan

O'Brien's twin brother, Shamus, who turned the family toward this part of the country. He came here during the gold rush to seek his fortune. The story is that he hit quite a big strike, then promptly disappeared." She smiled as she related the story. "Sheridan, who was very Irish and very determined, took it upon herself to search for him."

"I assume she found Shamus?"

"Aye, but she did!" Annie said. "At least she traced his whereabouts, and he eventually got himself back to Everlasting Diggins to reclaim his mine. Appropriately enough for an Irish lad, he'd named it Rainbow's End."

"For the pot of gold he thought he'd find there," Pearl said.

"The real gold was the community itself. Sheridan married Marcus Jade, the newspaperman who'd helped her search for her brother. Shamus returned from his adventures, and they all settled here to raise their families."

"What happened to Rainbow's End?"

Annie laughed. "The strike didn't amount to much after all. Shamus gave up mining and instead opened a mercantile. Greg and I tried to find the old mine once, but the area is so overgrown with brush that we gave up." She shrugged. "Maybe someday we'll try again."

Pearl frowned. "I would love to paint it as part of my Everlasting series. Do you have any old maps or a description of where it's located?"

"There was something tucked into the back of Sheridan Jade's journal. We made photocopies so we wouldn't wear out the original. I'll get you one."

Just then two little voices called out from an upstairs window. "Mommy! Mommy!"

Standing, Annie looked at Pearl. "I do believe our moments of reverie are over. This is when my day begins."

A few minutes later, the children were wriggling in their chairs at the breakfast table, and Pearl was studying the map that Annie had handed her. It was crudely drawn, and she had difficulty making out the names, but she folded it and tucked it into her pocket, then turned her attention to the twins.

"Now," she slid into a seat between them, "who's going to say grace?"

"Me, me, me!" Mary Beth shouted. "It's my turn."

Annie poured their cereal, added a touch of milk, and set the bowls before them. Then she sat opposite Pearl and bowed her head.

"Dear Father," chirped Mary Beth, "thank you for this food. Thank you for this day. And please make Auntie Pearlie marry Uncle Woodrow. We want them to be our gramma and grampa. And God bless Mommy and Daddy and our new baby. Amen."

Pearl met Annie's gaze, and they both stifled chuckles as they poured their own bowls of cereal and milk.

Pearl and Woodrow drove back to San Francisco later that morning. Woodrow said he would call the other members of the group to tell them it was time to carry out their plan, to begin their move to Everlasting.

"I won't be staying with everyone else at the Westbrooks'," she said after a few minutes.

He turned to her in surprise. "You won't?"

She shook her head. "I'm going to get a studio in

town—to set up my paintings." There, she'd finally said it. She held her breath and watched his face, awaiting his reaction.

He let out a long sigh. "You know, Pearl, you didn't have to go to such lengths last night."

"What do you mean? What lengths?"

"Lying to get appointed to the committee. You're stooping to their level by pulling such stunts. And now…you've dug yourself into a hole I don't know how you'll get out of."

"You thought I would do that?"

He ignored her question. "You lied about the statistics. I checked those out this morning."

She didn't trust her voice to answer. How could she defend herself? Woodrow still thought of her as silly, frumpy, nary-a-serious-thought-in-the-head Pearl Flynn. No, actually, his assessment of her was obviously worse than that. Dishonest had now been added to his list. She turned her head to look at the passing scenery. But the tears that stung her eyes made everything blurry.

Nothing more was said except a curt good-bye when Woodrow dropped Pearl at her house. As she unlocked her front door and stepped inside, the ringing telephone quickly drew her attention from Woodrow and their uncomfortable ride.

She tossed her handbag onto a wicker chair and hurried to the kitchen.

"Pearl?" said the female voice after Pearl had said hello. "This is Dana—out in Everlasting. Annie's friend."

"Oh, yes, Dana. I just this minute arrived home."

"Well, Annie told me what you're looking for, and I think I've got the ideal place for you."

"Tell me about it." Pearl settled into a chair at her bright yellow chrome-and-Formica kitchen table.

"It's located just down the street from the state park portion of Everlasting but still within the city limits. The lease is less than some of the other centrally located shops, but that's because it's rather small. It's also very rustic—unpainted wood walls, ages old." She told Pearl the lease amount as well as the selling price, should she decide on that option.

Pearl grinned, suddenly feeling better than she had all day. "It sounds perfect. There doesn't happen to be an apartment attached, does there?"

"No, I'm sorry. As I said, it's very small. But when Annie told me what you're up to, I checked with the Candlelight Inn, a bed-and-breakfast up by the old schoolhouse. It's an old Victorian that's been lovingly restored. A beautiful place. The woman who runs it, Bea Blankenship, said because it's off-season, she can give you a good price on a room. Weekly, monthly, whatever you'd like."

"Perfect," Pearl said. "Absolutely, positively perfect. When can I come look at the studio?"

"How about tomorrow?"

"I'll be there," she said without hesitation.

By the time Pearl hung up the phone, she realized that this was something she'd wanted to do for a very long time. Open a studio of her own. Paint right there in front of tourists or anybody else who wandered in. Paint all day and all night if she wanted. Sell her paintings to people who fell in love with Everlasting and wanted to take a bit of it home with them.

She dialed Charley's number, glad when he sounded

so happy to hear from her. She told him of her new dilemma—she needed to get a dozen or so of her paintings framed in just a few days. Not only was he happy for her venture, he said he had a friend in the framing business and would call him immediately. By the time Pearl told him good-bye, she was more thankful than ever for his friendship.

She headed to the sunporch to take inventory of her beloved paintings of Everlasting. She kicked off her shoes and did a little Irish jig—in honor of the young man who started it all, Shamus O'Brian. Everlasting was sure to be her rainbow's end.

Before dawn, Pearl rose to load her Camaro with canvases, easels, art supplies, and clothing. She had no doubt that the studio and the B & B Dana had found would be perfect. She planned to return once a week to attend her painting class and check on the house.

At half past seven, Charley stopped by to pick up the paintings and told her they would be ready in three days. He also gave her the notes and handouts from the class she'd missed.

At eight o'clock she crossed the street with a bag of cat food to ask a neighbor if she could bring in the mail and feed the cat. Then at 8:16, she backed out of the driveway and headed the Camaro toward the highway leading to Everlasting.

At 8:22, Woodrow pulled his Land Rover around the corner leading to Pearl's house.

He'd found out about his mistake when he phoned Annie the night before to let her know when the Birds-of-a-Feather group would arrive in Everlasting. In passing, Annie asked if he'd ever seen Pearl's paintings. When he said no, she proceeded to tell him all that Pearl had said about her newfound love of art and painting.

All night he'd tossed and turned, worried about how to apologize for his terribly rude behavior. The worst part was that he'd accused Pearl of lying—lying about something very dear to her heart.

He pressed on the brake and slowed to turn into Pearl's driveway. Even before he got out of his car, he knew he was too late. The Camaro was gone, the shades were pulled down tight—as if the house would be empty for a very long time.

THREE DAYS LATER, PEARL HAD SIGNED THE LEASE DOCUMENTS and moved into both the B & B and the small studio.

She'd just finished hanging her quickly designed and hand-painted sign above the door of the studio: Uniquely Pearl. When she stood back to admire her handiwork, she heard the clatter of an engine and turned to see Charley leaning out the window of a decades-old truck she'd never seen before. He smiled and waved as the vehicle rattled to a halt in front of her studio. He stepped from the vehicle and slammed the door.

"New truck?" she asked.

"I borrowed it from a neighbor, just to bring your paintings." He grinned as she walked with him to the back of the pickup. "Can't wait for you to see them."

They unpacked the pickup, carrying the paintings one by one into the shop. When they'd finished, Pearl stood back to admire the artistry of the framer. He'd chosen well. The simple wooden frames were perfect for her bright Americana style.

She grinned up at Charley. "Perfect! Absolutely perfect."

"Let's get them hung," he said. "I brought my tools. You just need to say where."

Hands on hips, Pearl surveyed the small shop. "There." She pointed to one of the largest, a painting of Everlasting's famed City Hotel. Years ago, it had been called the Empress, and that's what she'd named the painting. "Hang *Empress* fairly high on the long wall. Okay, then the smaller one, oh, and that one too, beneath the first." Charley did as she said, then the process was repeated again and again, until finally, two hours later, they had finished.

They stood back, looking at their work. The colors seemed deeper and brighter, the balance even better than she'd anticipated. Even her easel, paint table, and high metal stool set up in the side room added to the ambiance of the setting. It was as if this little studio had been designed just for her.

"Uniquely Pearl." Charley was obviously pleased as punch he'd been able to help.

"Now we sit back and wait for customers."

"One can't sit back and wait," Charley said. "We must get out flyers—all around town. If you'll design them, I'll get them printed and hand them out in all the other businesses around Everlasting."

Pearl nodded, frowning slightly. "I can't lose sight of my real reason for being here. The flyers will also let the other shopkeepers know that I'm their EEI representative. In case EEI checks on my community activities, at least people will know I'm here."

She went behind the counter by the door, propped herself up on a stool, and set about designing the flyer. When she was finished, she handed the paper to Charley.

"Why don't we get together for dinner tonight," he said, "and we can discuss how they were received?"

"Good idea." She told him where she was staying. They agreed on a time, then he departed to get the copies of the flyers made.

Charley had just left when she heard another car stop out front. Hoping for her first customer, she hopped on the stool again, looking businesslike, busy, and friendly.

But it was Woodrow Hornberger, the last person she expected to darken the doorway of Uniquely Pearl.

For a moment neither spoke. Finally, Woodrow met her gaze. "I came to apologize," he said in his wonderful rumbling voice. "I had no reason to believe that you were lying. Pearl, I'm sorry." He stepped closer and reached for her hand.

But Pearl slid her fingertips away from his grasp. "Your apology is accepted, Woodrow. How did you find out?"

"Annie told me. I came by to see you a couple of days ago—at home. But you'd already left." He looked around the shop, then stepped closer to a large painting of Everlasting's main street. "This is wonderful." He spent several minutes browsing, looking at each painting carefully, sometimes shaking his head slightly as if in awe. Finally, he turned back to her. "I had no idea, Pearl...."

Pearl laughed. "I hadn't told anyone. Until, well, the other night at the meeting when I had to come up with something fast. It just didn't feel safe."

"But these are wonderful! You've got real talent. You should've been shouting about this from the rooftops." He paused. "You said you didn't feel safe, Pearl. Why?"

She looked at him for a moment before answering. "I saw the look in your eyes the night of the meeting. You'd placed me in a little box filled with only your expectations—not very high expectations, I might add.

You were willing to believe that I'd lied to get my way."

Woodrow reached for her hand, and this time she let him hold it as she continued. "All my life I've been labeled silly and thoughtless. In a way, I lived up to others' expectations. Funny, silly Pearl. An airhead. Life of the party." She shrugged one shoulder.

"Oh, Pearl..."

But she didn't let him finish. "It took me sixty-some years to realize that I'm not that person. That God created me in his image. And this—" she glanced at one of the paintings—"this act of creating something unique is as close as I can come to understanding my own uniqueness in God's sight." She frowned, wondering if Woodrow could possibly understand.

But his expression told her he did.

She brightened. "Enough of all that." She pulled her hand away from his. "My first meeting with the committee is tomorrow night. Beforehand, though, I want to visit the shopkeepers in Everlasting, find out how they feel about EEI."

"You're taking this role seriously, aren't you?"

"Well, of course," she said. "It's a ruse to find out what EEI's up to. Besides, what better place could I be in to fight for the rights of all of us shopkeepers?"

Woodrow nodded. "It occurs to me, Pearl, that God put just the right combination of spunk and fun and leadership abilities in you." He smiled.

Pearl looked up at him in wonder, then shook her head slowly. "I didn't think I'd ever live to see the day that those words would fall from your lips, Woodrow Hornberger."

He grinned. "I'll make you a deal, Pearl." His tone

was half teasing, half tender.

"What kind of deal is that?"

"You just got through saying I'd put you in a little box."

She nodded.

"Well, my dear, I do believe you've done the same with me."

"Now, how's that?"

"You haven't believed that I could see beyond that image you've projected so long—that colorful, delightful creature you've always been to me."

Pearl was so stunned she could have fallen over. "Colorful? Delightful? Me?"

He nodded. "Not only have you guessed how I have seen you—you've also seen me, I daresay, as stuffy and rigid."

Pearl felt her cheeks color a bit.

"Isn't that true?"

"Well, not quite." She wondered how much she should tell. Well, why not? She'd just told him more about herself than she'd ever told anyone. She laughed. "You'd be surprised how I see you."

"Tell me." He looked apprehensive.

"Just the other day—when you came to my door?"

He nodded again.

"Well, I looked up at you, standing there, and the three words that came to mind were *debonair, graceful,* and *stately.*" She smiled into his surprised eyes. "Rigid and stuffy never entered my mind."

He looked enormously pleased. "Well."

"We keep getting off the subject." They were still staring into each other's eyes.

"Ah, well, yes. That's true." Woodrow cleared his throat. "Ah, back to tomorrow night's meeting. Do you suppose there would be any objection to my accompanying you?"

"There wouldn't be from me," Pearl said sweetly, wondering why her heart seemed to be dancing.

"Hmm. You're the creative one of the two of us, Pearl—how do you think we can convince them that I'm needed on the committee?"

"Why don't we form a new organization?"

"What do you have in mind?"

"Listen to this," she said excitedly, as the thought began to take on substance. "I've always thought that it was odd that Everlasting didn't have its own historical society."

"That's true."

"Well, let's form one. All of the Birds-of-a-Feather members will, of course, join immediately. Maybe Annie and Greg can help us with a charter. Print it out on their computer. We'll head around town to see if we can get other shopkeepers, docents, and musicians—anyone who has anything to do with the state park—to join. You'll be president."

"And as president, I'll insist on being part of EEI's committee." He grinned appreciatively.

"But of course, my dear." She resisted the urge to pat him on the cheek. "Um, let's see. A name." She narrowed her eyes in thought. "How about the Everlasting Circle of History? Or since EEI's so fond of acronyms, ECH."

"You've done it again, Pearl." He stared into her eyes, looking for all the world as if he might kiss her. But he touched her cheek gently instead. "How about if I go out and tell the others—they're setting up camp at the Westbrooks', by the way—and sit down with Annie to devise a charter?"

"Perfect."

"Then, my dear, how about joining me for dinner tonight?"

"I would enjoy that," Pearl said, her heart sinking. "But I have other plans. I'm sorry. Charley—"

Just then another shadow fell across the open doorway. "Did I hear my name?" Charley stood there grinning. "Sounds like I arrived just in time to defend myself." He laughed at his own joke and stepped inside to shake hands with Woodrow. "Good to see you, Woody."

Woodrow was cordial as they talked, but there was definitely an air of disappointment about him, Pearl thought sadly. And she knew it had to do with Charley.

A moment later they were interrupted by the sound of tires on gravel as another car slowed, then halted in front of the store.

"Your first customer!" Charley moved to the window and peered out.

A chauffeur stepped out of the black Mercedes, opened the rear passenger door, then stood back as his passenger emerged.

"It's Senator Thorpe," Woodrow said.

Seven

WOODROW'S ADMIRATION FOR PEARL GREW AS HE WATCHED HER give Thorpe a tour of her studio. Her hands seemed almost fluid as she gestured toward her paintings, and her animated face took on a glow of satisfaction and self-confidence as she spoke.

"I'd like to purchase one of your paintings," Thorpe said suddenly. "Which would you recommend for my Sacramento office?"

"Well, my goodness, Senator. I thought you'd come here to talk about EEI—not to look at my work. Not that I'm displeased...."

He laughed. "Actually, I came out of curiosity, but I'm so taken with your paintings that I don't want to leave without one."

"In that case, I would recommend Main Street." She strolled to the wall where the painting hung, and Charley and Woodrow exchanged glances. It appeared Pearl was about to make her first sale. "It will remind you of this charming town after it has become that model you said would be used throughout the country."

Woodrow exchanged another glance with Charley, who raised a brow. She was obviously baiting the senator. Woodrow held his breath.

"Ah yes, Pearl. You're right, of course." Thorpe seemed extremely pleased that she'd remembered his words.

"Why, Senator," she said with a wink, then lowered her voice slightly. "We all know that profit is profit.

Progress is progress. If EEI's running of Everlasting is as successful as it appears, there will be profits to be had, am I right?"

A cold expression appeared in Thorpe's eyes, then quickly disappeared.

"I said at the meeting that I wanted to be in on those profits," she continued calmly. "There's nothing illegal about that, is there?"

"Of course not," he said brusquely.

"Perhaps EEI's been worried about the wrong thing. They've been concerned about all of us making a fuss about the amusement park, when what we really want is to share in the success of the model."

Senator Thorpe looked uncomfortable. "I believe these issues are best left to discussion at the committee meeting tomorrow night."

"That's something else I wanted to talk to you about." Pearl gave him another of her charming smiles.

"What's that?" Thorpe's lips were now in a thin line.

Pearl took him by the arm and led him back to where Woodrow was standing by the counter. "I suppose during your trips here you've heard of the Everlasting Circle of History."

"Ah, no."

"Well, it's a very strong group and getting stronger all the time," she said seriously. "And Woodrow, besides being the lifeblood of the organization, is also its president. As an official part of the committee, I would like to invite him to join us tomorrow night."

Woodrow simply nodded and smiled at the senator, who was looking as if he knew he'd met his match in one Pearl Flynn. Woodrow supposed Thorpe had thought he would sweep in and charm Pearl into becoming his ally. Buying her painting was perhaps a calculated effort to buy her silence—or at least her gratitude.

"It would be an honor, Woodrow, to have you join us. But you must understand that it will be as a silent member only—no voting privileges. We had agreed to a limit of seven members. When I asked Pearl to join us the other night, she made up that final seat on the committee." He laughed lightly. "But don't feel bad—I'm not a voting member either."

Thorpe turned back to Main Street, strolling over to stand beneath it. "I do believe you're right, dear," he said to Pearl. "I'll take it."

She told him the price, and even though the amount was enormous for an unknown artist, Thorpe didn't even blink. "Yes." He pulled out his checkbook. "This will be perfect."

Pearl was so delighted she could only nod as he handed her the check.

"What scenes do you plan to paint next?" he asked her as Charley wrapped the painting in brown paper.

Pearl nodded to the unfinished canvas. "As soon as I complete this work, I'll continue with others of Everlasting. A friend just told me about an ancestor's gold mine. I might try to find it. I think it would make a wonderful subject."

Woodrow, still leaning casually against the counter, noticed that Thorpe's expression changed.

"Gold mine, eh?" He took one end of the wrapped painting to help Charley carry it to the car. "Very interesting. I'd like to hear more about that on our next visit."

Woodrow suddenly felt a chill travel up his spine. There was something in Thorpe's expression that hadn't been there before. It was as if he was looking at Pearl in a different light, and it wasn't one of admiration.

She felt it too because as soon as Senator Thorpe's driver had placed the package in the trunk, helped the senator into the car, and driven away, Pearl turned to Woodrow, her eyes questioning.

"What happened?" she asked. "I thought everything was fine until just before he left."

"Something changed in his attitude. I think he was disgruntled because he came here to sweep you off your feet." He chuckled. "And you obviously weren't about to be swept anywhere. You turned around whatever agenda he had and used it for your advantage."

Looking pleased at his words, Pearl picked up the senator's check again and studied it.

"Your first sale. How does it feel?"

She smiled into Woodrow's eyes, and his heart skipped a beat.

"The best part about it," she said, "is that now we can afford to hire a lawyer."

"A lawyer?" Charley asked. "What for?"

Pearl laughed. "I thought that part would be obvious. We need to have someone go over every legality involved in the pending sale. There may be a loophole. Or a clue as to what's really at stake here."

"My brother-in-law's an attorney," Charley said. "He handles real estate. He's in Sacramento. I can give him a call."

"Good idea," Pearl said, and Woodrow nodded in agreement. "Contact him as soon as you can. If we can get the paperwork we need from the EEI meeting tomorrow night, then he can get started on his search."

Woodrow's brows slanted in a frown. "You've got something else in mind for Birds of a Feather, don't you? I mean, something besides our snooping around here in Everlasting."

"I've had a feeling from the beginning that Nuggetworld isn't the real issue."

"Nuggetworld?" Charley asked, puzzled.

"Goldyland, Digginsville, Bear Flags over Everlasting—whatever EEI decides to call it," Pearl said. "I think all that's a smoke screen they've thrown out to get us off track. I think this little committee is a ruse to give us the idea that they're letting us in on their secrets."

"Why do you think that?" Charley asked.

"Any corporation worth its salt wouldn't let the likes of me jump right into the saltshaker."

"Don't put yourself down, Pearl," Woodrow said gently.

She surprised him by chuckling. "I was about to say—or the likes of you, Mr. ECH president!" Then she paused a moment and frowned. "I wonder if EEI's the source of the theme park and organized crime rumors. Maybe just to send us off on some wild-goose chase." She raised a brow. "Not a bad thing for Birds of a Feather."

But Woodrow didn't laugh. "Even if organized crime has nothing to do with it, I'm still of the opinion that these people are dangerous. Did you catch the look in Thorpe's eyes as he left?"

She nodded. "But he's a well-known state senator. He may be lining his pockets with EEI political-influence money, but he's too public a figure to go beyond that, don't you think?" She looked uncertain.

Woodrow couldn't resist reaching out to touch her shoulder—right there in front of Charley Stiles. "We can't be too careful." By now the afternoon sun was casting long shadows along the street outside. Soon she would head to the B & B—alone. "Pearl, I worry about you staying here in town without the rest of us."

"I'll be with Charley this evening." She said. He let his arm drop from her shoulder.

Woodrow checked his watch, not wanting to be around when the two left together. "I'd better be going myself," he said casually. "As president of ECH, I'm a busy man."

"Give my best to Annie and Greg." Pearl followed him through the door.

He gave her a quick wave as he got into the Land Rover. For a moment she stood on the porch, looking as colorfully Americana as any of her paintings. He waved again as he rounded the corner, and when he looked into the rearview mirror, Pearl surprised him by blowing him a kiss.

The following night's EEI meeting was held in the City Hotel dining room. The participants were seated at one long table. Since the senator was absent, an EEI spokesperson led the proceedings.

The meeting droned on through the evening. Each of the committee members gave a report on topics such as environmental impact, parking issues, and publicity. Finally, Pearl was asked to give a report on behalf of the Everlasting shopkeepers.

"An issue has been raised," she began, "that needs to be handled before it gets blown way out of proportion." She had their attention immediately, just as she'd planned. Smiling sweetly, she continued. "You see, the rumors about the theme park simply will not die." She feigned a sigh. "The only way to dispel them is to circulate a copy of the escrow papers for the sale of Everlasting. The shopkeepers would like a full disclosure. They'd like to see what all was included in the offer."

Joe Horn, one of the EEI reps, a slim man with steel-colored hair, leaned forward across the table. He sat at the end opposite Woodrow and Pearl and seemed to be EEI's choice for leader of the group in the absence of Senator Thorpe.

"That document is confidential," he said calmly. "You can understand why it's not in the best interests of either the state of California or EEI to make that kind of information public."

"You are aware of the rumors?" Pearl said.

"Oh yes," Horn said, and the others around the table nodded their heads.

"As I mentioned the other night, there are many who would like to be in on the profits if there is a business venture included in the sale." Pearl frowned, as if considering a new thought. "They're clamoring for the chance but also worried about things such as, well, for instance, zoning laws."

Woodrow stifled a smile. Pearl was doing it again: throwing out curveballs wild enough to make even the most sophisticated hitters dizzy. She gave them figures and statistics and quotes, wandering everywhere except across home plate until everyone around the table was yawning. Finally, she said, "Now, gentlemen, can anyone tell me if Everlasting is zoned for something as enormous as a theme park—a place that thousands might visit each day?"

The men exchanged glances, then Joe Horn shrugged. "I don't know what this has to do with the sale of the land. We've made our intentions very clear. We are not going to change Everlasting. There would be no reason for zoning to be an issue."

Pearl smiled and nodded happily. "If that's the case," she said, pausing as if a brilliant thought had suddenly occurred, "I've got an even better idea. Since you are adamant about Everlasting continuing as is, why not open the offer for investment to the community? Run the corporation just as some of the more innovative airlines run their companies. Community-owned, but EEI remains in control of the whole operation." She beamed. "What a perfect solution! If there are indeed profits to be made—we all win."

Woodrow watched as the EEI committee members fumbled with their responses, looking at each other, then back to Pearl.

She leaned forward. "The other night Senator Thorpe said that Everlasting would become more efficient and profitable under EEI, that it would serve as a model for other such historic parks around the nation. What better way to show your appreciation for the people who work here? I recommend that you pass on some of those savings, gentlemen. Let everyone get involved. I'll get started immediately with getting the word out."

Again there was hemming and hawing and clearing

of throats. "Well, I do see your point, Ms. Flynn," Joe Horn said. "I'll certainly bring it up to the EEI CEO and board of directors. I would recommend that you, ah, not get the community all riled up over this. The profits are going to be negligible. This is, after all, a state historic park; we are doing this ultimately for the people."

"Well," Pearl said, "there is something else I might mention." Collective sighs rose from around the table. "I do believe if the shopkeepers and others in Everlasting could see all the documents related to this sale, they might not be so inclined to pursue the investment angle."

Again, Woodrow stifled a smile. Pearl was about to blackmail EEI.

"And why is that, Ms. Flynn?" Horn asked.

"If the profits are truly as negligible as you say, well, there really wouldn't be any point, right?" She gave him another of her sweet smiles.

"Yes, well, that's true." This time Joe Horn glared at her. "We'll take the matter into consideration. We'll get back to you, and the, ah, other shopkeepers in Everlasting."

"Thank you," Pearl said. "When?"

His eyes pierced hers. "I said we'd get back to you. The timing is really up to us."

For a moment there was no other sound in the room. Woodrow realized with a stab of fear that Pearl had just made another enemy.

Eight

THE WEEKS RACED BY FOR THE BIRDS-OF-A-FEATHER GANG, and autumn began to creep closer to winter.

Pearl moved down Main Street on her usual morning stroll, talking to shopkeepers and owners, musicians, and vendors. The shops were now decorated for Christmas. Twinkling white lights, Christmas trees, pine boughs, and cedar garlands had turned the town into a Norman Rockwell painting.

Escrow was still in process, due to close a few days after Christmas—only two weeks away. EEI was becoming more closemouthed than ever. Even worse, the community of Everlasting had become complacent, willing to accept that EEI had the best of intentions for keeping the historic town exactly as it was now.

It was a Saturday, so all the Birds members, in gold rush costume, were working in their volunteer positions. Theda, dressed in cranberry red velvet and carrying a fur muff, waved a hello and strolled over to Pearl, her long skirt swishing around her ankles. She drew closer and whispered, "Have you heard that Senator Thorpe will be here today?"

"No, not a word." Pearl frowned. "When was it announced?"

"Someone from Sacramento called the museum. He plans to hold a press conference at the gazebo at noon. I wonder what he's got up his sleeve?" Theda said.

Pearl let out a sigh. She was beginning to lose her patience with EEI, their stonewalling, and especially their obvious ally, Senator Thorpe. "Maybe we should spread the word—raise a bit of a ruckus in front of the press."

Theda grinned. "Exactly what do you have in mind?"

"I don't know yet."

"I'm sure you'll think of something before noon," Theda said with a laugh.

Gabe stepped over to join them. "Think of something for what occasion?"

They told him of the senator's impending visit, and he looked worried. "I don't think we should take this lightly." He glanced around to see who might be listening. "I've heard only this morning that escrow might close early. I wonder if that's why Thorpe is coming today—to make some sort of announcement."

Pearl's heart sank. The three talked for a few more minutes; then she headed out onto Main Street again. Charley was just taking his banjo from its case, and Wyatt was standing, one foot propped on a log bench, warming up his harmonica. They both looked up and smiled as she approached.

"How's Everlasting's most famous artist?" Charley asked with a grin.

"Not very well right now." She told them about the press conference.

"My brother-in-law was planning to stop by this evening with his findings," Charley said. "I called him after classes yesterday, and he said that he'd finally made some progress getting through the web of red tape surrounding this deal. He sounded pretty excited."

"I wonder if he could make it here sooner?" Wyatt

asked. "Maybe we're the ones who need to call the press conference."

Pearl nodded in agreement. "I've got his phone number at the shop. I'll call and see what we can set up."

But Charley looked doubtful. "His appointments are booked weeks, sometimes months, in advance. And, of course, that's not considering his hours in court." He noticed Pearl's crestfallen look and touched her arm. "Maybe he can give you something to go on by phone, then deliver whatever else he's got tonight in person."

She nodded, feeling more hopeful. "Where are we supposed to meet tonight?"

"I suggested Annie and Greg's. They've agreed—especially since most of us are already out there. Woodrow mentioned that it's probably not a good idea for all the Birds to be seen together in town."

"That's fine. Meantime, I'll give your brother-in-law a call and see what he's uncovered. Then I'll see everyone tonight. I plan to keep the shop open late since it's a Saturday so close to Christmas. Don't worry if I'm a bit late."

Main Street was now filled with visitors milling about, and Pearl said her good-byes to Wyatt and Charley, then stepped back to listen to them play. Even in the midst of her worry, she couldn't help smiling. The two men, dressed like mule skinners, played a lively "Oh, Susannah." People gathered nearer to listen, tapping their feet and humming along.

After a few minutes, she gave Wyatt and Charley a small wave and went on her way. Next she stopped by the *Everlasting Gazette* office to look for Woodrow. He'd taken a volunteer position, playing the role of editor in the *Gazette*'s museum and explaining the 150-year-old history of the building and its artifacts to visitors.

Bess, the *Gazette*'s current editor and museum curator, looked up as Pearl entered. "Well, hello, Pearl."

"Is Woodrow here?"

"Downstairs in the museum, dear. He's preparing for our big morning."

Pearl was surprised. Woodrow hadn't said anything about a special group coming in. "Reporters?"

"Yes, dear. How did you know? From some of the biggest newspapers in the region. They're getting together in Sonora for their annual conference. They're usually in bigger cities. First time they've picked a little community."

Pearl nodded. The senator was obviously using their conference for his own press purposes.

"I'll run down and see Woodrow. I promise I won't keep him but a minute."

"He probably needs a break. He's been here helping everyone prepare since dawn."

Pearl headed down the stairs and spotted Woodrow by one of the ancient printing presses. He looked up and smiled a greeting. He looked more handsome than ever in his nineteenth century editor's costume.

"Can I steal you away for a minute?" she asked. "Bess said you need a break."

"Ah, that I do." He took off his green visor. "Let's go next door for some coffee. We can take it out on the terrace."

"Perfect."

A few minutes later, coffees in hand, they rounded the corner of the old Empress Hotel and walked through the iron gate to a brick terrace behind the century-and-a-half-old building. A fountain bubbled a welcome, and some nearly spent winter roses circled the terrace, their light perfume carried on the morning breeze. It was the kind of place Fred Astaire might have danced with Ginger Rogers, Pearl thought with a sigh as she and Woodrow strolled to a cast-iron love seat and sat down.

Pearl told Woodrow about the press conference Senator Thorpe had called, and he nodded solemnly. "EEI's time line's been stepped up whether or not we're prepared," he said.

"I'll call the attorney, but we may be too late to stop the sale—if that's what Thorpe's about to announce."

"Do you have any idea what the attorney's found?"

"No, but I'll let you know as soon as I find out."

"I'm not going to be of much help today—of all days," Woodrow said. "I'm giving a talk to the newspapermen. I really can't get away."

Pearl suddenly smiled and arched a brow. "Newspapermen?"

Woodrow caught her look, threw back his head, and laughed. "No wonder I love you so! I know what you're thinking…that while I've got the media as a captive audience, I can give them some real infor—"

"What did you say?"

"About the captive audience, you mean?" he teased.

"No, before that."

"About knowing what you're thinking?"

"Ah, no. Before that."

Suddenly, he caught her hand and lifted it to his lips. "Oh, you mean the part about loving you?"

She nodded, almost too stunned to speak. No man had ever before uttered those words to her. "Love?" she whispered, just to make sure she hadn't heard him wrong.

He smiled gently. "Haven't you guessed by now, Pearl?" For once she was speechless and waited for him to go on. "For weeks now, I've known. I've wanted to say something. I was waiting until we had some time alone, maybe in a special place." He laughed self-consciously, looking down at his worn costume, the ruffled armband on his sleeve. "I really didn't expect that time to be now. It's just that I've thought so often about the wonder of loving, it just, well, spilled out."

"You love me?" were the only words that Pearl could manage. "Me?"

"I can't hope that you care for me as much as I do you. I'll understand if you never want to see me again—I mean, in a romantic way. I promise, I won't ever speak of love again if you say so." His eyes searched her face.

"Me? You love me?"

He chuckled softly. "Yes, Pearl. You."

"Oh, Woodrow," she said, breathlessly. "I—I don't know what to say." Her heart pounded so hard she thought he might hear it.

"You don't need to say anything, Pearl. Just know that you've been in my heart for a very long time."

She nodded and drew in a very deep breath. "Woodrow, there's so much I want to tell you. I—"

The clamor of footsteps and a voice calling her name drifted from the street side of the terrace. She and Woodrow exchanged puzzled glances, then turned to see who was coming.

"It's Charley Stiles," muttered Woodrow. "I'd know his voice anywhere."

Charley, red-faced, carrying his banjo, galloped around the corner and into sight. "I just heard from my brother-in-law!" he panted. "On the cell phone. He's going to call you at Uniquely Pearl in just a few minutes. I told him you'd be there; then someone said they'd just stopped by and you weren't there, so I came hunting. I hope I didn't interrupt anything."

Woodrow let out a very deep, very long, very noisy sigh.

Pearl stood and gave Woodrow a tender glance, then headed back through the gate with Charley. He returned to his corner, banjo in hand, and she walked to her shop.

She unlocked the door and let herself in, trying to concentrate on the phone call she was about to receive—instead of the heart-thumping words Woodrow had just spoken.

Two steps inside and the telephone rang. Once…twice…three times by the time she'd raced across her studio to reach it. She slid onto the stool behind her counter and reached for the receiver.

"Ben Johnson here. The attorney. Charley's brother-in-law."

"Ah, yes, hello, Mr. Johnson."

"Ms. Flynn, I'm glad I reached you, though I plan to be out there tonight to give you all the details in person."

Pearl explained about the news conference, and when she'd finished, Johnson said, "You can bring up this issue at the conference, but I've got the proof in hand. Without it, what you say is so much innuendo. EEI and Thorpe know that; they could easily turn the tables and make you look very foolish."

"What is it you've found?" Pearl's heart pounded. Then her mouth fell open as he told her. "I need every detail." She grabbed a piece of paper and scribbled wildly as he spoke. She paid no attention to her shaking hand.

"Pearl," Mr. Johnson warned before he hung up, "don't try to handle this alone!"

But she barely heard his warning. She was already planning her next step. "I'll be careful," she said absently. "And I'll see you tonight."

Pearl quickly turned the Closed sign to face the street and locked the door. Minutes later, she was in the Camaro heading to the main highway leading out of town. For the next hour, she wound through the Sierra Nevada foothills. The day had dawned bright and clear, but now there were clouds forming over the mountains, darkening every minute.

She pressed on the accelerator in her hurry to reach a ridge of volcanic rock overlooking the valley. The ridge was mentioned on both the plot map that Johnson described and on the map that Annie had given her. She rounded several hairpin turns, then came to a turnoff.

The road climbed upward now, the car bumping and rattling along the rutted road.

One more rise. She peered ahead. An outcropping of black volcanic rock rose just beyond the next curve. She pointed the Camaro toward it.

The dust that had been trailing behind her billowed and rose into the cloudy skies. She coughed as it covered the car.

By the time she spotted the small boulder in the road, it was already too late. A bump. A sickening crunch.

Nine

WOODROW WRAPPED UP HIS TALK ON THE *Everlasting Gazette* by relating some of its colorful history. Then he took a deep breath. The reporters were still watching him attentively. "What I'm about to tell you cannot be proven, but perhaps you can help us prove our suspicions."

For another several minutes Woodrow proceeded to tell the men and women everything he knew to be true, and what he and others suspected about the pending sale of Everlasting to EEI. The reporters took notes, writing almost furiously.

Finally he asked for questions. Hands shot up and voices called out. Woodrow took one at a time, answering each as best he knew how.

"We can't print any of this without proof," said a young redheaded reporter from the *Bee*.

"No one knows that better than I," Woodrow said. "If you print even our suspicions at this point, we could be sued for libel."

"Do you think the press conference is to make some grand announcement about the sale?" asked another reporter.

"I would bet on it," Woodrow said. "I think, however, that if you bring up some of these allegations, perhaps the senator will become flustered. Maybe give something away."

"And you think EEI's not going to turn Everlasting into a theme park?"

"Again, I can't say for sure. But it does seem to be a

smoke screen for something else. The trouble is, that something else hasn't yet been discovered."

Finally his talk was over, and the reporters, after asking a few more questions, filed from the museum to head over to the gazebo. Woodrow exited right behind them and hurried over to Uniquely Pearl. But Pearl wasn't there.

Frowning, he hurried toward the gazebo where a large crowd was gathering. Just as he threaded his way through the crowd, Senator Thorpe's black Mercedes drove into the gravel parking lot adjacent to the park.

There was a smattering of applause as the senator stepped before a lectern that had been set up for him. He smiled at the crowd and cleared his throat. "Ladies and gentlemen, the announcement I'm about to make is one of vital importance...."

Pearl opened the car door, coughing in the still-rising dust. With a sigh, she stooped and looked under the car. Her worst fears were realized. The oil pan, or whatever it was called, was cracked. She could see a dark liquid dripping onto the rock, then trailing down into the soft, dusty soil.

No one knew her whereabouts, she suddenly thought, her shoulders slumping. She had left no messages for Woodrow, Charley, or any of the other Birds-of-a-Feather gang. It might be days before anyone discovered where she'd gone.

She looked around. Clouds were gathering, and a brisk wind had kicked up. She wrapped her arms across herself and shivered, looking around and trying to decide what to do next. Finally, she trudged up the incline, trying to keep her fears at bay.

Dear Lord, I know you're with me. No one else knows where I am. But you do! Give me strength to endure what's ahead. And courage, too, Lord, for I'm beginning to get a little worried.

She murmured the words of Isaiah 41:13: "For I am the LORD, your God, who takes hold of your right hand and says to you, Do not fear; I will help you." Her pounding heart slowed, and she could breathe again.

After a few more minutes, she reached the top of the ridge. The outcropping of volcanic rock was exactly where it had been described.

She turned back to the south and could now see Everlasting. She smiled. It might be too far to walk, but it was comforting that the little village looked so solid and friendly in the distance. She glanced at her watch and, noting that it was just after noon, wondered what lies Senator Thorpe was about to tell.

She turned, letting her gaze sweep the surrounding area. Though she was standing on a jutting ridge, above her the mountains continued to rise, and to the north, a deep canyon swept downward.

A glint of metal caught her attention near the bottom of the canyon. Pearl stepped to a higher part of the ridge and looked again. It appeared to be the roof of a crude shed, barely visible through the heavy foliage. Small rocks and gravel slid down the path as she hiked into the canyon. Overhead the sky was darker still, and now the wind moaned through the trees. Pearl whispered another prayer and continued on her trek.

A pile of granite blocked her trail about halfway

down. She reached for a small twisted pine growing between the rocks and grabbed onto it for support as she crawled to the highest point on the boulders.

Half kneeling, she halted suddenly. About a hundred yards from her, just feet from the shed she'd seen earlier, two pickup trucks were parked near a narrow canyon to the north. The road followed a small stream that she could hear bubbling along its rocky bed and rushing down small falls.

Several men in hard hats stood talking near the corrugated metal shed. One was unrolling a large, rectangular length of paper, and the others were standing nearby. Their backs were to Pearl.

Pearl drew in a quick breath. So the attorney had been right. She thought about what he'd told her on the phone. The location. The probability of what would be found there. She remembered the old map Annie had given her, the map drawn by Shamus O'Brien 150 years ago.

Of course. It all fit together. Rainbow's End. She smiled. She'd found the missing mine.

Unfortunately, so had the men below her. And they were up to no good. Just as the attorney predicted. But now she was more curious than frightened.

She assessed the distance, wondering if she could sprint from the boulders to the far side of the little building, hide, and listen to their conversation. It was worth the risk, she decided. She slid off the rocks and landed with a soft thud. She peered out to see if the men had heard anything.

They were studying the length of paper, so she held her breath and tiptoed into a small stand of dogwood and pine, creeping forward slowly, one step at a time. She had almost reached the edge of the copse of trees when a gray squirrel, looking down from a sugar pine, barked a warning, then barked again. And again.

Pearl froze, praying for the little animal to shush. But the barking continued. A stellar jay joined the ruckus, squawking without pause. He was joined by others.

First one, then all of the men turned around, their expressions startled, then angry and menacing.

Pearl had seen every one of them before. Heart skittering, she gave them a shaky smile as they started toward her.

Woodrow milled through the crowd at the gazebo, looking for Pearl. Theda, Flora, and Gabe had all told him that Pearl had definitely said she would be there. Charley seemed particularly worried and hovered near Woodrow while Senator Thorpe droned on about the wonderful improvements that would be coming to Everlasting because of EEI's control.

"Do you have any idea what your brother-in-law told Pearl?" Woodrow whispered to Charley.

Charley shook his head. "No."

"Do you still have your cell phone with you?"

"It's back in the car."

"How about giving your brother-in-law a call? Maybe he can help us figure out where Pearl's gone. I can't help but worry." Woodrow frowned. "She was so sure about being here. Something must have come up."

Charley nodded. "You stay here—see what Thorpe's

pulling this time. I'll go call and check back with you in a few minutes."

"Right."

Thorpe had finally indicated he was about to spill his big news when Charley returned. He looked triumphant and worried at the same time.

"The key to this whole thing's been right under our noses!" he whispered. "And from what we can figure, Pearl's gone to check it out."

From the podium, Thorpe's voice rose. "And now, ladies and gentlemen, you who love Everlasting and want to see it thrive—"

"What key?" Woodrow whispered to Charley, though he was still looking at Thorpe.

"He said that EEI's added parcels of land to the original acreage. And that's not all."

Thorpe's voice lifted as he continued. "Those of you who aren't ready to accept the status quo for either Everlasting's historical significance or for its bright and wonderful future—"

"What else?" Woodrow whispered loudly.

"Mineral rights! They've gone after mineral rights for the new parcels. I've got the plot descriptions," Charley whispered back. "From the same plot map my brother-in-law told Pearl about." He handed a sheet from his notepad to Woodrow.

Woodrow's mouth dropped open as Thorpe finally got to his point.

"Because, dear friends," Senator Thorpe cried, "the future is now! As of midnight tonight, Everlasting will officially and legally belong to EEI—Everlasting Enterprises Incorporated."

"It's gold they're after!" Woodrow announced. "And they've found it. They've found gold!"

The melee that followed was akin to what had followed the shout of "Eureka!" during the original gold rush. Hollering and shoving and calling out questions, the reporters jostled Woodrow to the front of the crowd and handed him a microphone.

Out of the corner of his eye, Woodrow saw Senator Thorpe slink off to the safety of his chauffeured Mercedes. There would be time enough to deal with him later. Pearl was what was important now.

"It's not too late to stop the sale!" Woodrow turned to the crowd. "But it's going to take all of us working together."

"There's a gold mine or maybe two out in these hills. EEI—or its parent company—is probably setting up to mine a newly discovered vein as we speak. And I say we stop them now."

"Catch 'em red-handed!" someone called out. "Let's go!"

There were howls of anger at EEI and shouts of willingness to help.

"Listen carefully, now," Woodrow said when he again had their attention. "This is a plot description telling exactly where this vein is located. Some of you are more familiar with the area than we are. I say let's head out together and put a stop to this deception once and for all." He read the description carefully and watched as some of the old-timers scratched their heads, then nodded.

"One more thing," he said. "Someone very courageous already headed out to search for these scoundrels.

And we need to get to her as quickly as we can. Her life may be in danger."

Murmurs of worry rose from the crowd. "Who is it?"

"It's Pearl Flynn." Woodrow paused, thinking of how she had looked that morning, sitting next to him, her eyes aglow with affection. "A very special woman."

"Oh," came the almost collective whisper. "Uniquely Pearl—the artist."

"Let's be on our way!" shouted one of the reporters. The others began grabbing up their camera equipment.

"Hear, hear!" shouted a woman from the back row. "Everyone with four-wheel drives meet at Highway 41 just north of town!" The newspaper reporters took off en masse.

"Eureka!" yelled someone else as the rest of the crowd scrambled in all directions. "Let's be off to find our Uniquely Pearl!"

Ten

PEARL WAS USHERED TOWARD THE SMALL METAL SHED.

"You're going to be very sorry you took it upon yourself to follow us out here," Joe Horn opened the shed door. The open padlock clanged against the metal siding. "You and your so-called Birds-of-a-Feather group should've learned a long time ago to keep your beaks out of places they don't belong."

"I was just scouting out a place to paint. Birds of a Feather doesn't have anything to do with where I choose for the settings of my paintings. This place is a natural for my work."

His laugh was more of a scoff. "We've known what you and your group were up to from the day you rode into town with your white hats."

Narrowing her eyes, Pearl looked hard at the three men who were residents of Everlasting. They had originally been chosen to represent the community. *Some representation*. "So you knew about the mine all along?" All three shrugged and didn't answer. "Shame on you. This is theft, and you're no better than common criminals."

"That's enough," Joe Horn said with a laugh, giving her a shove toward the shed door. "We don't need a lecture. Besides, you're too late to do anything about it." The padlock clicked into the slot outside the door. Pearl drew in a deep, frightened breath as her eyes tried to adjust to the darkness. There didn't seem to be any windows, and the only light was what filtered in through the joints between the sheets of metal siding.

Shivering, she stood as close to the center of the shed as possible so she wouldn't brush up against the spiderwebs or dust that lined the walls. This building was old enough to have years and perhaps decades of dirt and grime and rat droppings. She shuddered again, almost afraid to breathe.

The men didn't seem to care that she could clearly hear their every word. They spoke openly about their plans—the bulldozers that would arrive by dawn the next day, the workers and equipment on their way from San Francisco, the brokers in New York who were already awaiting the "product." Pearl realized that they didn't plan to let her live to tell others what she'd heard.

By now her eyes had adjusted to the shed's dark, dusty interior. She moved around, examining the piles of old mining equipment. They were mostly scraps of old wood and rusted iron implements, picks and shovels and shallow pans.

Suddenly, she spotted a couple of six-foot boards of an old Long Tom at the back of the small room and knelt to rub her hand over the rough wood. These devices had been used for only a few decades beyond the gold rush, and she touched it almost reverently. Despite her fears, Pearl's curiosity got the best of her, and she moved from one piece of equipment to another. She even forgot her concerns about spiders and mice and lifted some of the lighter pieces of equipment to discover what was underneath.

Her eyes had adjusted better now to the darkness, and she noticed something the shape of a window frame at the rear of the old shed. It was so dark she thought it must have been boarded over, but she gingerly stepped over the debris until she was close enough to inspect it.

It was covered with layers of dust and dirt and spiderwebs. Wrinkling her nose, she reached one finger up
to swipe through the grime. She felt the cold, solid surface of glass beneath her touch.

Looking around, she saw an odd cradlelike piece of
equipment, briefly wondered what part of the mining
process it had been used for, and pulled it to the window
and turned it upright. Then she carefully stepped to its
top and began to scrub at the window with her sleeve.
Gradually the small room became filled with light. Not
the bright light of a sunny day, but light nonetheless.

Smiling, she stepped down from the makeshift stool
and brushed off her sweater. Now she could at least
assess what equipment was in the little treasure trove,
especially those pieces that would help in her escape.

But as she stepped back, her gaze fell again on the
piece of mining equipment that so resembled a cradle.
Curious, she knelt beside it, then laid it back down in its
rightful position.

She realized it *was* a cradle. Made for a baby, not for
gold mining. It was filled with webs and dust, and she
gently turned it over to empty it and wipe it out. She ran
her fingers over its still-smooth wood, in awe at such a
find.

Her fingers felt a series of indentations on the
underside of the cradle, as if something had been carved
there. She turned it over, then toward the light from the
window. Precisely spaced, the words were clearly legible:
*To my darling sister Sheridan for your coming blessed bundle.
May the wee babe never forget its Irish blood.*

Pearl was stunned. What a discovery! It was more

precious than any vein of gold. She looked around at the equipment again. Could all this have been Shamus O'Brien's? Perhaps he'd passed it on to members of his family. Only they never came back to claim his equipment—or the mine.

The men outside were speaking in more animated tones now, too low for her to make out. Her knees trembled as she wondered if the discussion was about how and when to take her life.

She needed a plan and looked frantically around, her gaze finally resting on the window. She grinned as a strategy formed.

She moved the Long Tom, the cradle, and other equipment into place. Then she worked out her timing. Finally, she stood on the upended cradle and again reached the window.

She lifted a heavy pick and shattered the glass, poking out the shards so that the entire window was nearly clear. She quickly tossed out a couple of pieces of equipment. They landed with loud thumps and rolled down the hillside.

For a moment there was a stunned silence among the men outside. It was immediately followed by the sounds of fast-moving footsteps and frantic voices.

Pearl scrambled under the Long Tom, letting it down to the floor so that it covered her as completely as an upside down coffin. She held her breath as she heard the padlock click open.

Just as she expected, the men rushed in. "She's gotten away!" Joe Horn shouted. "Quick! Head around back. Find out where she's gone."

"Follow me!" someone shouted.

"Hurry! I think she's gone toward the creek," yelled another.

Pearl waited until their footsteps moved toward the streambed. Then she lifted the Long Tom and very quietly crawled out and tiptoed to the door. She carefully peered out. The area immediately in front of the shed was clear. At least for now.

She ran toward the cover of oaks and pines beyond the shed. When she reached the trees, she felt her heart pounding in her chest and stopped, gasping for breath.

There was an unnatural silence, almost as if the men had been caught up in some net. No voices carried toward her. No chattering of jays or squirrels. She shot up a quick prayer, hoping they were still heading in the opposite direction.

Finally, Pearl's heart calmed, and as the silence continued to reign, a grin of triumph crept across her face. She headed up the hillside.

She had just reached the outcropping of boulders when she heard the ruckus of cars and people heading along the dirt road leading into the canyon. She climbed to the topmost point and peered down, expecting to see the equipment the men had been talking about earlier.

To her amazement, she saw a caravan of cars and four-wheel drives heading up the road, clouds of dust billowing behind. They halted and at least a hundred people spilled out of them.

But one of the last cars to arrive caught her attention. A worn-looking Land Rover pulled off the side of the road, passing all the other parked vehicles until it reached the front and pulled to a stop beside the shed.

Pearl didn't wait to watch Woodrow step out.

She scrambled from her granite perch and ran down the hillside. As she made her way through the milling crowd of reporters, photographers, shopkeepers, street musicians, and even the Birds-of-a-Feather gang, people fell silent and stepped back to let her through.

She heard calls of "It's Pearl Flynn!" and "It's Uniquely Pearl!" as she passed.

"She's safe," someone nearby whispered. "Praise God, Pearl's safe!"

Finally she saw Woodrow. He was watching her, his face filled with relief and love. He held out his arms, and with a small cry, Pearl ran to him.

The crowd sent up a cheer, and she smiled up into his face. "I didn't get to tell you what was in my heart this morning."

He merely arched a brow in that debonair, graceful, and stately way she adored.

"It's you, my dear, dear man. You are in my heart," she said softly. "How I love you!"

The crowd cheered again as Woodrow bent his head and kissed her.

Epilogue

IN THE OLD-FASHIONED BALCONY ROOM OF THE CITY HOTEL, Pearl stood in front of the oval full-length mirror. Sighing, she watched her reflection as a very pregnant Annie Westbrook, the matron of honor, lifted Pearl's tulle veil off its hanger and carried it over.

"You look beautiful, Pearl," Annie whispered, her eyes misty.

Pearl smiled at Annie in the mirror. Her wedding dress was traditional only in its ivory color. Its handkerchief-lace hem and sleeves spoke of a style that was uniquely Pearl. More gypsy than Victorian, certainly more artistic than what one might consider elegant. She'd designed it herself.

Below the balcony, the musicians were already playing: Charley on the banjo, Wyatt on the harmonica.

"Okay, hold still now." Annie placed the veil on Pearl's head. Pearl also had designed the headpiece, with its miniature sunflowers and mix of orange and yellow tiger lilies. "Take a look at you!" Annie stepped back. "Oh, my. You're a vision."

Pearl turned and smiled. She did feel beautiful, perhaps for the first time in her life. To think of it…a bride at her age! She wanted to lift her arms and dance a jig.

"Did you know that my great-great-grandmother prepared herself for her marriage to Marcus Jade in this very room?"

"No, I didn't." Pearl shook her head thoughtfully. She was reminded of her wondrous find in the shed. "Did Greg finish his work on the cradle?"

"He did, and I can't wait for you to see it. He only sanded it lightly—just enough to remove the years of dust and dirt. Then he put on a coat of oil. It's oak, hand carved." She smiled, patting her stomach. "It'll be perfect for the baby."

Pearl nodded.

Annie caught Pearl's hand and squeezed it. "Greg and I are so glad you and Woodrow are going to live near us. You're really part of our family."

Pearl swallowed hard and nodded. "I've never had a family before." She sighed. "So many years I lived alone, content, but not realizing what I was missing. Now here I am, a bride so in love I think I've suddenly set foot in heaven. And now that we're building a place so close to you and Greg and the babies, well—" she gave Annie a hug—"well, my dear Annie, I never knew God's blessings could fill me with such joy."

"What you've done for Everlasting, Pearl, can never be repaid. We're not the only ones who love you."

"What Everlasting's done for me is greater," she said softly, with no need to explain. Annie knew what Uniquely Pearl, her paintings, and the townspeople all meant to her. Oh yes. She'd been blessed beyond all measure.

A few minutes later, Annie helped Pearl down the stairs, through the parlor, and out onto the rock path leading to the gazebo. Every inch of it was covered with tiny lights, cutout valentines, and flowers of every color and description, compliments of the Birds-of-a-Feather gang, who must have cleaned out the supplies of every florist in a twenty-five-mile radius.

The gazebo and lawn were filled to overflowing with friends from Everlasting and San Francisco. The instruments played softly as the minister walked to the center of the small bandstand; Woodrow took his place beside him, and Greg, his best man, stood beside Woodrow, grinning at Annie and Pearl.

Mary Beth and Shamus, skipping and jumping, started down the center path, dropping flower petals from baskets as they walked. Then it was Annie's turn.

The banjo music rose as Annie moved forward. On the road beside the gazebo, a team of six gray horses whinnied and shook their manes in front of an old stage-coach, decorated with flowers, old shoes, and tin cans.

Annie reached the gazebo and turned to watch as Pearl stepped to the aisle and paused.

The banjo music stopped, and a single flute began to play some lively Irish music in honor of Shamus O'Brien and his Rainbow's End, deeded to the people of Everlasting.

A hush of expectancy fell over the guests as they stood and turned toward the bride.

Pearl began to walk down the aisle, a bit faster than most brides might have, she knew. But this was a joyous occasion and, by jing, she was going to look like she was having fun.

As she moved closer, Woodrow's eyes met hers. Pearl's heart danced, and she fought to keep her feet from following suit. Now that would be a trip down the aisle folks would remember, she thought, her gaze locked on Woodrow's face.

It would also be uniquely Pearl.

So she hiked her skirts just a tad above the ankle, danced a few quick steps of an Irish jig, then grinning at her groom, let herself be gathered into his arms.

 Award-winning author **Diane Noble** has penned more than a dozen novels, novellas, and non-fiction works for women. She is the recent recipient of the Silver Angel Award for Excellence in Media and has been nominated for the 1998 *Romantic Times* Career Achievement Award for Inspirational Romance. Diane and her husband live in the picturesque mountain village of Idyllwild, California. Visit Diane's little corner of the web at www.dianenoble.com.

OTHER BOOKS BY DIANE NOBLE:
Distant Bells
Tangled Vines
The Veil
When the Far Hills Bloom

WRITTEN AS AMANDA MACLEAN:
Everlasting
Kingdom Come
Promise Me the Dawn
Stonehaven
Westward

NOVELLAS:
"Gift of Love" in *A Christmas Joy*
"Legacy of Love" in *A Mother's Love*

NONFICTION FOR WOMEN:
It's Time!: Explore Your Dreams and Discover Your Gifts

A SEASON
FOR LOVE

LINDA WINDSOR

One

"DOES THIS MEAN WHAT I THINK IT MEANS?"

Nurse Audra Anderson couldn't believe the giant hunk of diamond surrounded by a cluster of smaller precious gems nestled in its satin lined case. With a wry twist of her lips, she glanced up at the handsome doctor who presented it to her. It was best to make a joke of it, just in case.

She and Mark had been dating six months. Their colleagues said they were the perfect couple. Audra *almost* felt that way, save one twinge of insecurity. Dr. Mark Chadwick was from an old Southern Maryland family—blue bloods; Audra was an orphan who'd changed bedpans to support herself through medical school.

"Well, it's phase one of what I think you think it is. I am asking you to marry me, Audra." Mark's smile stretched white against his golf course tanned face, revealing a perfect row of teeth. Dr. G, the nurses called him behind his back, short for Dr. Gorgeous. He was sure of himself, sure of the ring, and knew her answer.

Well, not quite. Audra gave him a quizzical look. *"Phase one?"*

Mark slipped a reassuring arm about her waist as they stood on the balcony of her apartment, surrounded by the glittering lights of the city. "This is a *pre*engagement ring," he explained. "According to Chadwick tradition, my sweet, sealing the agreement between the prospective bride and groom. You don't get the official one until it's been formally announced by our families."

"Oh. For a minute I was afraid I'd have to get a blood test," she teased.

Must be nice to have old family traditions. If Audra had them, she knew nothing of them, even though her father had come from an old Virginia family as prestigious as Mark's. His family, who had disowned him for marrying beneath his station, had never accepted his orphan as anything more than a burden. Audra's blood was tainted with that of a New York soap actress.

Mark lifted one brow and gave a wounded grunt. "This isn't exactly the reaction I expected."

Audra shook off the invasion of past insecurity, determined to savor the joy of the present. She'd come a long way from being an unwanted burden to her father's family. Wasn't the fact that Mark wanted her ample proof of that?

"Yes! Yes! A thousand times *yes!*"

Throwing her arms about him, Audra gave Mark an enthusiastic kiss. When she would have lingered, however, he pushed her away.

"Wait, put on the ring first. Then we'll seal this deal properly."

"Sounds like a contract." Audra snickered.

"It is." Mark slipped the ring on her finger. It fit perfectly.

"Well, *half* a contract," she amended.

Mark put aside the empty box and turned her into his arms. "Don't worry. My folks adore you. The fact that you hail from the Harvest Home Andersons doesn't hurt, but they'd love you anyway…just like me."

His whisper died as he drew Audra fully into his embrace and sealed the agreement with fervent affection. Audra's discomfiture at the reference to her being of the "right" family melted. Dr. Mark Chadwick loved her, with or without her *pedigree*. This was what she'd prayed for on many a lonely, abandoned night—acceptance for who she was and, in later years, the perfect man for her. Love was good. Life was good. God was good.

So what was that annoying noise bleeping in the background of her rush of happiness?

Mark pulled away abruptly with a muttered oath. Reaching inside his designer dinner jacket, he withdrew his beeper and read the bright red numbers flashing across the miniscreen.

"Of all the nights!"

Ah, the beeper. The curse of private life for anyone in the medical profession. Yet, not even that could dim the light shining in Audra's gaze. She pointed toward the telephone hanging in the kitchenette, which was part of her living room, and noticed for the first time since their arrival from the osteopathic department's dinner party that Mark was not the only one with a blinking red light demanding attention. Her answering machine signaled she had waiting calls.

Mark was needed at the ER for a pedestrian versus compact car case requiring surgery. With a reluctant smile and gallant kiss on the hand now boasting the expensive cluster of jewels, he took his leave.

It wasn't until Audra closed and bolted the door that she floated over to the answering machine and pushed the button. The weight of the ring felt foreign to her left hand. Next time she exercised, she could leave the wrist weights off that one, she thought, grinning from ear to ear. God was *so* good!

"Audra, this is Margaret Anderson Morrow."

Audra's smile froze in unison with her heartbeat at the sound of her aunt's voice. *Margaret Anderson Morrow.* Her father's sister. Audra's joy was doused like a light at the flick of a switch. Only dark news could come from the aunt who'd raised her after her parents' death.

Stricken by the sudden rush of insecurities from the past, she rewound the message and played it again, for it had been lost upon her the moment she'd heard Aunt Margaret's name.

"My regular nurse has had a family emergency, and I need you to come home and take up her position until she can return. I would not have called you if I'd had other options, but that is not the case. Call me as soon as possible, and we'll make the arrangements. Our number hasn't changed."

Before the sudden roller-coaster drop in her stomach got the best of her, Audra sank onto one of the bar stools next to the counter. Was it possible to die from such a crash of joy? Of course, she was still in shock. Maybe she *was* dying, sinking into memories of the dark days of Margaret Anderson Morrow's rejection and tyranny. *God in heaven, how can this be happening? It isn't fair!*

The shuttle flight to Richmond from Baltimore was short, too short for Audra's peace of mind. The more she dreaded returning to her childhood home, the smoother the trip went. There was no doubt in her mind as to why she was going home after being on her own for six years. No matter how she tried to rationalize a way out of this, she owed her aunt for giving her a home. It was time to own up to the debt, even if it was with the same reluctance as it had been given. Except this time, instead of going to Harvest Home an impressionable, easily hurt orphan with hat in hand, Audra was returning as a professional caregiver. This time it was her aunt who was in need. Life did have its ironic twists.

Audra slung her carry-on bag over her shoulder as she debarked from the plane and walked toward the terminal. Her fair shoulder length hair whipped about an attractive face, which boasted William Anderson's Swedish ancestry. She might have been a model, considering her inherited height as well, or even an actress, as her mother had been, but Audra's dream was to care for people. Faith, the small insurance policy her father had left her, and hard work had made it come true.

Faith had pulled her through harder times than this, she thought, heading for the baggage claim area. There was no doubt in her mind that God could somehow salvage something out of even this; although how was beyond her understanding at the moment. At least Mark would be visiting her in a few weeks to meet Aunt Marge. That gave Audra something to look forward to.

As she walked through the crowd and followed the signs, Audra caught a glimpse of a tall man sporting a Stetson half an escalator's length behind her. He'd been at the terminal entrance, scanning the passengers as they entered and had stared at her, even after she looked away and walked past him. Living in the city, not to mention having been mugged once by a purse snatcher, had made her very much aware of her surroundings and the people in them. Why on earth had she worn her preengagement ring! It practically screamed *Take me!*

She scanned the busy baggage claim area, looking for a uniformed guard. If the man was still looking at her and following her after she retrieved her luggage, she would report him. For now, safe here in the crowd, she pretended to ignore him until curiosity got the best of her. Casually, she glanced around to see if he was still by the turnstile where she'd last seen him. To her astonishment, he stood behind her, a tentative smile on his lips.

"Oh!"

So much for her self-defense course! No loud *hee-yah* for her, just a strangled gasp. No sharply delivered blows or kicks, just a desperate grope to keep her heart in her chest.

The cowboy took a step back at her start, nearly tripping over someone's overnight case. "Sorry! I didn't mean to scare you. You're Audra Anderson, aren't you?"

He knew her name! Her throat still constricted, she nodded hesitantly.

"Well, hey there, Sunshine! It's me...Jake. Jake Turner."

"Jake?" Audra looked in disbelief into the deep chestnut brown eyes of the handsome stranger. That was impossible. This guy couldn't be the timid, gangly son of Harvest Home's late head trainer, another parentless kid who grew up at Harvest Home under Margaret Anderson Morrow's care. His glasses were gone! In fact, so was his slight body. This man looked like he'd just walked off of a poster selling mineral water from the Rockies.

"I almost didn't recognize you, either. You let your hair grow."

"You've got contacts!"

Their simultaneous observations made them both laugh. Braces had done wonders for Jake's smile, white and even against sun-bronzed skin that was developing a deeper tint by the moment. At least she wasn't the only one blushing! It had been years since Jake went away to college and then she in turn did the same. Their only contact since had been cards at Christmas.

Jake! The big brother figure who'd made life bearable for her at Harvest Home, in spite of the fact that her aunt favored him hands down over her. Better an employee's orphan than a relative's.

"Yes, I did." Jake glanced at the moving ramp and then back at Audra. He hadn't lost all his shyness.

"Yes, what?" she asked, pulled back from musings by his soft Virginia drawl.

"Yes, I did get contacts. It was cheaper than replacing all the missing and broken glasses."

"You should have done it long ago. You've got beautiful eyes! I'll bet you have girls lined up to the highway."

"Not hardly." He glanced again at the luggage ramp. "I stay pretty busy with the farm and horses. What color are your bags?"

"A tapestry of mauves trimmed in taupe."

He cut her a bemused look. "What?"

"Pink flowers with a gray brownish trim."

"Mauves and taupe, huh?" He smiled again. It was teasing, infectious, and warming. Her dread eroded beneath it. Audra pointed to the chute where the first bag shot out catawampus and slid onto the moving belt.

"Mauve and taupe!" she announced as he snatched the weekender off. "There's a matching Pullman and a hanging garment bag."

Jake's dark eyebrows arched. "You moving in?"

"Not in this lifetime!"

The teasing twinkle in his eyes sobered, and the lines etched by the sun about them relaxed. "Can't say that I blame you. Things are pretty sorry around here."

"There's the Pullman. The garment bag's right behind it."

Jake turned to fetch the other two bags. His long arms, revealed by the roll of his shirtsleeve, bulged with the strength it took to bear their weight, but it was the only sign of strain. As Audra leaned over to pick up the weekender, he protested.

"I'll get it! I need it to balance this traveling trunk, or I'll be walking lopsided for days." After tucking the rolled garment bag under his arm, he picked up the weekender, leaving the Pullman for his other hand. His broad shoulders shifted up and down like a seesaw as he measured the weight, then he nodded.

"Ready to go, Sunshine?" He'd called her that from the first day she'd come to Harvest Home. Except this time he didn't ruffle her hair. But then, his hands *were* full.

Audra wondered if that was all that would stop him. Jake always had a way of making her laugh. She hadn't been expecting anyone to meet her as she'd told her aunt that she would get a taxi. Whatever God's purpose for returning her to Harvest Home, he had to have had a hand in sending Jake.

Just like in the old days, he was making it easier for her. Funny he'd never told her how he'd been hired to run Harvest Home after the accident that killed Aunt Margaret's husband and left her an invalid.

"So tell me," Audra asked later over a shake purchased at a fast-food restaurant. "What am I in for?"

They turned off the interstate and now traveled along a familiar state highway. Fast food was a new convenience to the home setting Audra remembered.

"Not much nursing," Jake answered, with a crook in his grin. "Aunt Marge had a girl come in each morning to bathe and dress her for the day. That and companionship is really all she provided. She's qualified to do more, but Aunt Marge doesn't need anything else. At least, according to the doctor she doesn't."

Audra stared at her companion across the leather seat of the newer model red pickup. "Then why did she send for me?"

Her aunt had presented a dark picture of a dependent invalid at the mercy of the medical world. The nurse in Audra was touched by the plea for help beneath the brusque request. Her decision came after much prayer and soul-searching. Even though reluctantly, her aunt had raised her. Audra had become a nurse to help others and the woman needed help. How could she refuse? To do so was to disobey God's command to forgive as one wanted to be forgiven.

The result? She'd taken her accrued vacation to return to Harvest Home, time she'd hoped to set aside for a honeymoon! God *had* to have known this! How could he let that woman jerk the strings of obligation and duty and get away with it?

Jake shrugged, no wiser than Audra. "Maybe she misses you."

"Right! The only thing she misses is the opportunity to rub my nose into the fact that I owe her and will owe her forever!"

"I let that go in one ear and out the other."

That was a familiar line, an irritating one that he'd delivered to Audra too many times to count.

"Jake Matthew Turner, you *do* have a college degree, don't you?"

"Four years at Purdue in agriculture and husbandry."

"Well, I hope you learned more about animals in those four years than you have about people in your lifetime! That woman is a harbinger of bitterness, and she's so miserable, her only relief is to inflict it on others." Audra exhaled in exasperation. "I can't believe she lied about needing me so desperately! You don't know what I've been through, wrestling with duty versus a reluctance to submit to her constant slams against my mother and me, and bearing the blame for everything bad that has ever happened to her!"

"I think being confined to that wheelchair has given her a lot of time to rethink her life."

"You saying she's changed?"

Her straw slurped up the last of the shake. Jake pointed to a trash bag. His truck was as well groomed as the garden he'd kept for as long as Audra had known him. Some men were meticulous regarding their looks, their abodes, and their work. Jake Turner was one of them. He could fall in a mud hole and come up clean. But then, Margaret Anderson would tolerate nothing to the contrary in her home. The woman would have made an excellent drill sergeant.

"People are always changing, just like the seasons."

And Jake was just as slick at evading questions. He stared at the dull, gray-ribbon road ahead, which rose and fell with the contours of the green and yellow fields to either side of it. Audra had to admit, he was right about that. He'd certainly changed, at least physically. Jake had wholesome, rugged good looks, as opposed to her doctor's polished, pampered ones—and she found herself drawn to Jake in ways she didn't understand. Maybe it was because she knew Mark's tan and well-developed physique were the result of a health spa and recreation, where Jake's were the product of hard work in the raw elements—manicured versus natural.

Goodness, just listen to me! Jake is family, not a man—at least not in the hunkadoodledoo sense!

Astonished by the runaway tangent of her mind, Audra focused instead on the scenery unfolding around them of spacious pastures, white fences, and grain ready for harvest. Here she was, almost an engaged woman, all but drooling over, of all people, Jake Turner! Sure, he's drop-dead gorgeous in a rugged sort of way, but she had no right to feel school girl giddy inside. It was just nerves.

"That ring for real, or did you hit the jackpot with a gumball machine?"

Audra stilled the fingers rapidly tapping the purse on her lap and glanced down to where the sunlight was split into shards of brilliance by the diamond Dr. Mark Chadwick had given her only a few nights ago.

"Oh, it's real." She flicked at it with her finger. "And this is the *preengagement* ring. Protocol demands that I pass approval of his family before I get the official one."

Jake smirked. "What do you have to do, pass a medical test?"

Odd. That was the first thing she thought when Mark explained the process to her. "It's just tradition. It means a lot to the Chadwicks. Preengagement means he and I have accepted each other. The engagement ring means our families approve. Then the wedding ring means..."

"I get the picture. Much ado about something that's nobody's business but the bride and groom's, to my way of thinking."

The mention of family approval reminded Audra of the rest of her quandary. It was foolish, but earlier in their relationship, she'd wanted to make a good impression on Mark and his riding circuit family. It seemed harmless at the time to say that she was at ease around horses and could ride. Who could have guessed Mark would get so fired up to see the horses at Harvest Home and go riding with her when he came to meet Aunt Margaret during the Founder's Day festival. He'd been so happy to hear Audra knew her way around a horse that she'd been reluctant to rectify the situation.

"Well, that's just the way people like the Chadwicks are. We lowborn types have to accept that if we're going to ride in their circuits."

She cleared her throat, uncomfortable when Jake didn't agree. From the jut of his jaw, it appeared just the opposite.

"Not that I mean you're lowborn, Jake!" She suddenly realized how she'd sounded. Heavens, she was making a muck of this. "I meant..."

"I know what you meant, Sunshine. Don't sweat it."

He reached across the seat and ruffled her hair, flashing a devilish grin.

Some things never change. Audra tucked her hair back into place, warmed by the attention. "Well, I *am* sweating one thing."

"The Chadwicks meeting Aunt Marge?"

"No, I imagine they can hold their own there." The pleasing thought was not enough to diminish the frown furrowing her brow. "The thing is, I told Mark I could ride, that I liked horses."

"You *what?*"

Jake hit the brakes, slowing the vehicle to an abrupt stop before they passed the long white-fenced lane leading up to Harvest Home. Audra continued forward but was checked by the seat belt. Her purse flew to the floor, abandoned by the hands that were now pressed against the dash. Apparently Jake hadn't been paying attention to where they were headed.

"Come here often?" she managed shakily. Rather than look him in the eye, Audra focused on a beautiful thoroughbred racing across the pasture toward them, as if it recognized the truck.

"Sorry." Jake sharply turned the wheel and the pick-up eased around the red and gold lettered white sign that marked the entrance to the Anderson's home. "I could have sworn you said you'd told your fiancé that you were at ease in the saddle!"

"I did."

The way the horse frolicked and kicked up its stockinged feet caused Audra's stomach to shrivel and twist. Her heart was in her throat, partly from the sudden stop and partly from the realization that the journey was over and the two things she feared most awaited her—her aunt and the horses she'd professed to love.

"Me," Jake mumbled, lost in his own thought. "I wouldn't want any man tending to any of my ills who would base his decision to marry a gal on whether or not she could ride a horse!"

He gunned the engine for emphasis. Audra leaned back against the seat, her bravado draining like the color from the fist she'd inadvertently made. If her aunt hadn't made her feel so unworthy, maybe Audra wouldn't have resorted to lying about something so insignificant. The way Jake made it sound, it was silly. She knew it was. But knowing and feeling were worlds apart at the moment.

It was déjà vu. Once again Audra was an eight-year-old orphan, making the same trip up that same road, to the same house—every bit as scared and just as unhappy.

Two

"Miss Audra, as I live and breathe, just look at you!"

"Maynie!" Audra was engulfed in the arms of the housekeeper at the front entrance of Harvest Home's crisp white manor house while Jake unloaded the pickup parked at the end of the colorful mum-bordered walk.

"I got a jar full of snickerdoodles with sprinkles on 'em, just the way a certain little girl likes them."

"You are too sweet!"

"And your room is aired out and ready. 'Twouldn't surprise me to find a cookie or two in there too."

Your room. It had a deceiving hint of welcome home to it. Of course, Maynie's reception was real. If anything, the housekeeper had served more as her mother than her aunt.

"You haven't changed a bit!"

Audra meant it. Maynie Mackenzie was as solidly built as she'd been years ago, thick like a good tree in the center, she'd often remark proudly.

"Well, you have, child! You've grown into a beauty of a girl. Am I not right, Jake?"

"You're always right, Maynie."

Jake stopped and gave Audra a head-to-toe inspection, as if to make sure. Audra felt the heat from the color rising in her face. Goodness! Why didn't she just giggle and complete the giddy school girl impression!

"And look at you." Maynie noticed Jake's armload for the first time. "Showin' off for the missy, eh?" The housekeeper pulled the garment bag out from under

Jake's arm and nearly cost him his hold on the weekender, which she took next.

"Keep that up and the missus won't be the only one needin' a nurse and a wheelchair!" Maynie turned her attention to Audra next. "And speakin' of Miss Margaret, she's waitin' to see you in the family room."

"*Was* waiting! That is, until you saw fit to detain the children with all your blathering." Audra spun around at the sound of Margaret Anderson Morrow's voice. The electronic wheelchair had been so silent, she'd not heard the woman's approach. Accusation had not left her aunt's voice, nor had she lost the imperial carriage so carefully schooled before her debut into society. Neither smile nor welcome graced her lips. They were as noncommittal as the impassive gray gaze studying Audra from head to toe and back.

"Your taste in clothing has improved."

Audra's blazer and matching skirt were a department store special, washable, which was imperative on a nurse's schedule and salary. "Thank you, Aunt Margaret. It's been serviceable."

"Classic styles always are. You've learned well."

"I've got work to do, so I'll put your things upstairs and split," Jake told Audra. "You two gals have some catching up to do."

Audra mumbled a "Thanks" while her aunt gave the young man no more than a cursory glance.

"And I'll have some tea and cookies ready before you even get started!" Maynie called over her shoulder, heading for the kitchen in the back.

With no other distraction, Audra braced herself. Every day she cared for the ill and dealt with their families.

Every day she offered advice and consolation. People said she had a gift, but suddenly she felt like an insecure little girl again, except that now, she was staring down at the ice queen instead of up. It did not go unnoticed.

"You'll get used to it. I have." Her aunt spun the wheelchair around on the spot. "I'm as good on this contraption as I was on Medallion, except I've yet to win a ribbon with this."

Although she wasn't asked, Audra followed her aunt as expected into the family room, which was bright with the afternoon sun. "It says a lot for you, that you've adapted so well. Some patients never…"

"Never *what?*" The chair made a sharp 180 degree turn. Margaret Anderson Morrow tilted her head, much like a cat waiting for the mouse to error. "Never accept their fate?"

"They never learn to cope with their handicap."

"Is that what you call this? *Coping?*"

"Well, yes, I've seen—"

"I call it resignation…surrender…defeat!"

Her aunt backed the chair to the window so that the light warmed her shoulders and cast a golden glow on her hair, which was now lightly salted with time. Bitterness twisted Margaret's tone and mouth.

"I've never made secret of what I thought about your mother, Audra, but I have to admire her good sense to die with the man she loved, rather than remain a martyr in a chair."

"Fortunately God doesn't give us those choices, Aunt Margaret. We might not choose wisely."

"*God!*" the woman challenged in disdain. "You call this a wise choice? I think not!" She dismissed Audra with a wave of her hand. "What do you know of being left behind by the man you love!"

Pain grazed Margaret's face, scoring lines her expensive makeup had hidden until now. Her anguish was as deep and raw as though newly etched. The skim of ice in her eyes dissolved into a wet glaze, which she struggled valiantly to contain. Compassion rose in Audra despite the wounded child who wanted to cry out that she did indeed know what it was like to be left behind by a loved one. Somehow, she knew exactly what to say.

"God sees the whole picture, Aunt Margaret, not the narrow view we have."

A squaring of the chin and a deep breath squelched the rise of emotion threatening her demeanor and the queen resumed command. "So, that's what they taught you in nursing school?"

Audra shook her head. "That's what I've learned from God's Word. I'd hate to face the challenges of my career without it to lean on."

"Well, don't lean too hard, Audra. He'll let you fall smack on your face. I don't need to tell you the years I've devoted to the church, the hours I've given to charity, and *this*—" Margaret slapped her hands on the cushioned arms of the chair—"is my reward."

"Your *life* is his reward! God has seen fit to give you a second chance." She had argued this point scores of times to many patients who rebelled against their infirmities and the God they blamed for them.

"A second chance at what? I lived a life any churchgoing woman would be proud of. My life is the only thing left I didn't give. *This* is what being good has gotten me."

Audra could almost taste the acrid emotion in her aunt's voice. She'd heard that plaintive cry for help too often to let it go. She knelt by the wheelchair and covered her aunt's clenched hand with her own. It was one thing for her aunt to accuse her of being unworthy of respect and regard, but quite another for the woman to accuse the God who'd spared her.

"God obviously sees more in you than you do in yourself. It's something he considers worth saving. Aunt Margaret…"

Of all the things she expected to be doing at this meeting, this never would have crossed Audra's mind. She heard her words with utter incredulity as they spilled from her lips, straight from her heart.

"Aunt Margaret, I am going to pray for you, that God will show you what he thinks is worth saving."

Where was the girl who was not going to take any of her aunt's imperious attitude, the adult who'd outgrown that?

"It's there, inside you, where only he can see," Audra went on, "but it's there."

The conviction in Audra's heart was jarred by the hand her aunt wrung from her grasp with nothing short of outrage. She balled her fist against her chest as though she'd been assaulted.

"Get out of here! I made a mistake! I should never have sent for you! You think that by being nice to me, I'll leave you my money! Well, I told you the first day you appeared on my doorstep that you'd never see a dime of it, and I haven't changed my mind."

"Hey, what's the ruckus?" Jake stepped through the door and glanced from Margaret to Audra and back to the woman who'd raised him.

"Get this gold digger out of my sight, Jake. Please!"

"I don't want your money, Aunt Margaret." Audra bowed her head. "I want to see you healed."

"At what cost?"

"Aunt Marge!" Jake shot the distraught woman a sharp look.

"She has her mother's blood, Jake. Beware of that before you get taken in by those big brown eyes and that saintlike demeanor. If it comes out of my pocket, it comes out of yours, inevitably."

"You are talking nonsense! Audra...she came here to help you."

"I'll go to my room." Audra wanted to avoid dragging Jake into this. His place here as Anderson heir apparent was becoming clearer by the minute. He deserved it for putting up with her aunt. "But I'll not be going home...not for six weeks, anyway."

Circumstances had changed. Jake had changed. Aunt Margaret had changed. So had she, Audra mused, trying to take it all in. Now she knew the reason God had called her back home. Until she saw the anger and hurt in her aunt, Audra had thought her own resolved. Now it tasted as real and bitter as it had the day she left the horse farm. Healing was the reason—not just Aunt Margaret's, but her own as well.

Three

THE ALARM NEXT TO AUDRA'S BED SOUNDED ENTIRELY TOO early the following morning. Perhaps it was the result of emotional fatigue, but she'd slept soundly as soon as her head hit the pillow—and after some of Maynie's snickerdoodles and milk.

Sleep still pervaded her mind as she dragged on a robe and headed for the bathroom next door.

Breakfast was served at seven-thirty sharp, and Aunt Margaret would need to be showered and dressed by then to preside over the Anderson table. Her mind a sleepy muddle of emotion and thought, Audra rounded the doorjamb of her room into the semidarkness of the upstairs hall and ran into a solid wall of flesh, slightly damp and smelling of a spicy masculine soap. Strong fingers caught her arms and steadied her, while her own lay helplessly plastered against the raw, muscled plane of Jake Turner's chest.

"Whoa, Sunshine! Maybe you ought to wake up before you get out of bed!"

Squinting in the darkness, she looked up at Jake's disheveled hair, a wet tangle obviously combed with a towel. *Rugged* was not a word she'd have used for the old Jake, but it certainly fit the man whose chest hairs tickled her fingertips.

"Sorry," she managed, taken aback once again by the change. If she hadn't been awake, she certainly was now. Every fiber of her being was awake and aware of what it had no business being aware of, her being a preengaged woman.

"You okay?" Jake backed away, as if he, too, had felt the electricity sparking between them.

"Yeah, I…" Audra drew her robe more tightly around her. "Guess we'll have to come up with a schedule." Her nervous smile broke into a yawn, which she shook off as she stepped around Jake and headed for the bathroom door. "I'd better get moving."

"I put out clean towels and wiped down the shower!" Jake called after her.

Now *that* was like the old days. Jake had always been particular to a fault about everything. If either of them had been a slob, it was her. Despite her good intentions, Audra's room was never as neat as Jake's, nor was her appearance in general. Not that he could look sloppy wearing nothing but a pair of cutoff sweatpants slung low on his hip.

"Thanks."

Audra stared at her face in front of the vanity mirror. *Heavens, what's the matter with you? Jake is like your brother, and Mark is your fiancé. End of story!* As if to stop the waywardness of her thoughts, she slapped her face and turned on the shower. She didn't want to make Aunt Margaret late. One, it wasn't professional. Two, *no one* at Harvest Home wanted to start the day on the bad side of Margaret Anderson Morrow.

Punctuality, however, proved as useless in improving her aunt's disposition as Audra's proficiency in helping the woman shower and dress. Because of Margaret's grudging acceptance of her invalid state the day before, Audra fully expected the woman to prove helpless.

Instead, her patient seemed to fight her at every step, as if in open defiance of the help Audra offered.

Audra had seen cases far worse than her aunt's recuperate with therapy. But then, these patients were motivated by the will to improve. Her aunt showed no sign of that. Her husband was gone and she wanted to be. She was bitter that she wasn't. She had no intention of improving, just wallowing in her misery. Somehow, Audra would have to find a way to tempt the woman out of the house, then out of that chair!

"You're pretty strong for being confined to a wheelchair, Aunt Margaret," she observed as the lady rose tentatively on her own effort in order to slip on a pullover knit top.

"Hand me the matching jacket, there on the chair."

Audra picked up the rich silk knit of the three-piece designer pant ensemble her aunt chose to wear for the day. Aunt Margaret always had a flair for dress.

Audra helped her aunt with the jacket, but the moment the woman's arms were in the sleeves, Margaret brushed her away with a wave of her hand and straightened the garment itself until it lay without fold or flaw.

Suddenly, it was Audra who was under inspection. "White isn't a good color for you, normally. If it weren't for your tan, you'd look washed out."

One hour on duty and Audra was starting to feel as though she'd already put in a double shift. "It comes with the job, Aunt Margaret. A chic black wouldn't exactly present an encouraging picture for a health-care professional, now would it?"

The wheelchair pulled away from Audra's guidance

with her aunt's expertise at the controls. She waited, tapping her fingers until Audra opened the bedroom door, although Audra had no doubt in her mind that had she not been there, Aunt Margaret was perfectly capable of doing the job herself. Jake was right. The patient didn't need a nurse, she needed a nanny!

Lips thinned, she followed her aunt to the hall elevator, which had been installed in what used to be the servant's stairwell. As she backed into the small cubicle, Margaret halted Audra from following her in with a frosty steeling of her gaze.

"Well, this is a home, not an institution. Go change into something civilized. I'll hold breakfast for ten minutes, not a second more."

Audra waited until the elevator door closed before she made a juvenile face at it, her professionalism flying out the window. Honestly! What had possessed the woman to send for her? Was she a diversion, someone to sharpen her claws on? Audra stomped off to the opposite wing from the master suite to her room.

"Father, I know you must have some purpose in all this." She snatched off her white pressed uniform and hung it in the closet. "Is it for me to get Aunt Margaret out of that chair? I mean, if I insist on helping her enough, she'll get up and walk just to spite me! Lord, I really need help with this one."

Fifteen minutes later, Audra entered the dining room wearing khakis and a cotton sweater. Aunt Margaret was seated at one end of the long mahogany banquet table, a piece which had been in the family for generations. Jake, now fully dressed in jeans and a chambray shirt, sat next to her. Upon seeing Audra enter the room, he set down his cup of coffee and jumped to his feet, drawing Margaret's attention to her as well.

Audra waved him down. "You don't have to do that. We're family."

"S'cuse me, but I was taught when a lady enters the room to stand. I'm in no mind to get a backhand from Aunt Marge first thing this morning."

"Backhand, indeed!" Margaret Anderson gave him a disparaging look. "As if I've *ever* laid a hand on you, Jake Turner!"

His grin widened as he winked at her. "And I'm not about to give you the chance."

To Audra's shock, the frost on the ice queen's face melted into a reluctant smile.

"Sit down!" she ordered. *"Both* of you!"

Audra was directed to the place opposite Jake. Hands folded, she waited while her aunt poured her coffee from a silver pot, which graced a tray complete with all the matching accoutrements.

"Sugar?"

Audra shook her head. "No thank you. Black is just right."

She took the steaming cup and saucer her aunt handed to her with a steady hand. The light overhead caught the gem in Audra's ring, drawing her aunt's attention instantly.

"Where did you get that? You didn't have it on this morning."

The way her hostess's eyes narrowed, one would think Audra had stolen it.

"I don't wear it when dressing and bathing patients. It could scratch them."

"Audra's got herself a beau," Jake put in. "A doctor...pretty successful by the size of that stone."

"You're engaged?" Margaret asked sharply. "You didn't tell me about this."

"That's *preengaged*, and I haven't exactly had the chance."

Margaret raised a brow. "Preengaged?"

Audra sighed. She was getting tired of explaining this. Especially when she wasn't still completely clear on it herself. "It's a formality. A period of time when Mark's family and I become better acquainted."

Margaret lifted her chin. "I'm familiar with the term. Prestigious families often insist on a preengagment period to ensure the son of the family is marrying the right kind of woman." She gave her a tight-lipped look. "I take it then, that this man's family is well situated...and not one of those *foreign* doctors, I hope!"

"Mark is all American, Aunt Margaret; I assure you."

"When I was in the hospital, half the time I thought I was in a foreign country! Needed an interpreter to get my trash can emptied!"

Audra suppressed a groan. Political correctness was not part of her aunt's vocabulary.

"His name is Dr. Mark Chadwick."

"Who are his parents? What do they do?"

The questions were perfectly natural for a parent or guardian, except that Audra didn't delude herself that her aunt's motive was genuine concern. More likely, it was to find something else to deride. This time, however, Audra held the proverbial ace in the hole with the

Chadwicks of Belle Monde as prospective in-laws. Part of her had been waiting for this moment.

"James and Marian Chadwick. They…"

"Of Belle Monde Farms?" Margaret needed no introduction. Disbelief invaded her expression, as well as her voice.

"Yes. It's also the name of their yacht. They keep it in Annapolis."

"Medallion's dame and I took the Chalfonte Cup from Marian.…" For a brief moment a flush of joy radiated from the older woman's face as she drifted back in time for a taste of glory. "She rode the most magnificent bay.…"

But Margaret wasn't one to dwell in the past too long. It reminded her of all she had lost, and that added an extra dose of bitterness to the present.

"This young doctor, has he introduced you to James and Marian yet?"

"Yes, I've spent a few weekends on their yacht on some bay outings. They're very nice."

Audra gave her aunt time to digest the fact that the daughter of a no-good actress was about to become the wife of one of Margaret's equestrian aristocracy.

"And what do they think of you?"

"Aunt Marge, how could they be anything but happy that their son has chosen your niece as a future bride? Give the girl a congratulations not an interrogation!" Jake chided gently. "Won't that be something, Belle Monde and Harvest Home in the same family, so to speak?"

At that moment, the door opened and Maynie came in carrying a tray with toast and assorted jams and butter.

"Breakfast is comin' right up!" She put them on the

table. "I have fresh whole grain muffins for the missus and a stack of waffles for you children. And—" she took the lid off a small tureen—"hot blueberry topping, someone's favorite, if I remember rightly."

"Maynie, you're going to spoil me and run me up a dress size to boot!"

"A little flesh on the bone doesn't hurt anybody, Miss Audra. Ain't hurt me, and I've carried a little extra since before you was even born."

"Don't argue," Jake reminded Audra as the cook returned to the kitchen for the main dishes. "You can't win."

Audra's mouth watered as she eyed the steaming tureen of cooked blueberry topping. "Well, I don't suppose it would hurt to be spoiled the first day. But after this…"

"I'll speak to Maynie. A young woman must watch her figure, particularly if she wants to keep her beau," Margaret spoke up. "And it does sound as if you've gotten yourself a good one."

Aunt Margaret reached across the table and plucked a muffin from the basket. "I suppose you'll be able to quit working, once the knot is tied. You'll need some advice on what to do with your time, of course."

"No, I love working!" Audra and Mark hadn't gotten that far along in their plans, but she certainly *hoped* he didn't think she'd quit.

"Well, before either of you get to fretting over a bridge some miles away, we have one we need to cross right now."

Audra and Margaret turned in surprise at Jake.

"We have to teach Audra to ride. If she's an

Anderson, we don't want her to embarrass Harvest Home by not being at ease in the saddle."

Audra flinched inwardly, reminded of her foolish claim to Mark. It had been a mistake from the get-go.

Margaret took up the issue instantly. "Absolutely! Child, you are going to have to get over your ridiculous fear of horses. Jake and I will work with you. Why…why we could start this afternoon!"

To say her aunt was animated was an understatement. Audra's stomach knotted at what was unfolding here. A glimpse from her childhood returned—the startled thoroughbred's hooves flying, striking, as she scrambled to retrieve a kitten from the horse's stall. The scar just inside her hairline ached at the memory. At the same time, however, her nurse's instinct took charge, that and a peace that was surely from God's hand. Audra had prayed that he'd show her a way to get Margaret Anderson out of her wheelchair and interested in life again, but this wasn't exactly what she had in mind.

Her aunt covered Audra's hand with her own. "Don't worry, dear. Medallion is trained, and you'll learn quickly…after all, you *are* an Anderson, aren't you?"

For fourteen years, Audra had waited to hear those words from Aunt Margaret's lips, to finally be accepted. A blade lodged in her throat, but it was a double-edged one. Yes, she was being accepted all right, but not as the person she was. It was as the person her aunt wanted her to be. It was a shallow triumph, but one Audra grabbed on to.

"A woman must face her fears sooner or later. And what a wonderful reason to face them!" Margaret tapped the diamond sparkling on Audra's left hand.

Confusion, fear, and anger tumbled in Audra's mind.

"On one condition." She heard the words spill from her lips in absolute astonishment.

"I'll work afternoons learning to ride if you will do therapy in the mornings. With a little earnest effort on your part, you can walk again. And I know you could ride again as well." If her head was going on a chopping block, it wasn't going alone.

"Now *that's* a good deal if I ever heard one," Jake joined in. "I, for one, would love to see you in the show ring again, Aunt Marge. I'll do everything I can to help both my favorite ladies."

Audra saw a hint of her own quandary in her aunt's stricken expression. It wasn't often tables were turned on the ice queen. Time slowed to where seconds seemed like minutes before she finally gave a tentative nod.

"Very well, then. I will...*try.*"

"That's my girl...my *girls!*"

Oblivious to her aggravation with him, Jake was immensely pleased with himself. The fact of the matter was, he had manipulated both of them, the grinning scoundrel! It was hard to discern just what was turning her hot under the collar.

"I guess it's time I started taking my own advice," Margaret said, absorbed in her own thoughts.

A time for every purpose...to heal...perhaps to forgive as well. Again, Audra was struck by the revelation, calm infusing her wildly beating heart and skittering reactions. *But, Lord, what am I getting myself into? Are you sure this is the answer?*

"THAT WAS BLACKMAIL!" AUDRA FUMED LATER THAT AFTERNOON. She stomped her foot next to Jake for emphasis as he cleaned off Medallion's tack. "I'm in deeper than I was before, thanks to you!"

"Don't blame me. I didn't tell my fiancé I was born in the saddle. Little white lies beget more little white lies!"

"Well, you don't have to enjoy it so much." A twinge of guilt flushed Audra's cheeks. "I know it was wrong that I told Mark I could ride, and I feel bad enough without you grinning like a dog passing brambles! All these years I thought you were chicken, but you were just a sneaky fox!"

"Thanks, I was fond of you, too."

Jake snatched the saddle off its rack with one hand and retrieved a matching bridle with the other. It was English, a rich leather one engraved with MAM—Aunt Margaret's initials.

"Wait, I want one with a handle!"

"Medallion is trained for this. If you get scared, you can always slip your fingers under here." He lifted the saddle, indicating the rise where a handle *should* have been.

"And it's a pommel, not a handle."

"Well, pardon me, John Wayne!"

Ignoring the jibe, Jake started down the row of stalls.

"Where's my darlin'?"

As if on cue, the beautiful bay mare Audra had seen

racing across the pasture toward Jake's truck the day before poked its golden head through the opening above the stable door and whinnied. Her lavishly lashed eyes, the same ebony color as her mane and tail, were wide in anticipation. At least they looked big to Audra...almost as big as her own felt.

"Reach in the inside pocket of my jacket and take out a sugar cube."

"What?" Audra was still frozen to the spot where she'd first seen the horse.

Jake stopped and jerked his head, demanding she catch up with him. "I said, reach in my inside pocket and take out a sugar cube. Might as well get on her good side, and she does have a sweet tooth."

Displeased by the fact that Jake stopped short of her stall, Medallion whinnied again.

"I hear you, girl. Jake's got somebody he wants you to meet." He looked back at Audra. "Well, go on!"

Embarrassed by her own cowardice, Audra delved in with her hand. *Jake's chest sure had filled out.* Not that she was ogling or anything. She was a nurse, after all, and trained to notice muscular development.

Of which Jake had plenty.

"Any time now." Jake's chest deflated beneath the pressure of her knuckles with a dour impatience.

"Like I'm supposed to know where a hidden pocket is?"

The moment Audra snagged a sugar cube, she hastily tried to withdraw it from the small pocket, but she couldn't. Her ring had hung up on something, a loose raveling perhaps. She didn't wear it when working for the same reason. It was big and it caught on everything.

"Hey, take it easy! That's flesh and blood you're

shredding between your nails and that stone!" Jake teased her as she tugged harder. "What's going on?"

"My ring is caught."

"And I thought you were being friendly...oops."

Audra lifted one side of her lip in a half snarl. "Stand still!"

"I'm not the one with my hand stuck in a guy's pocket," Jake remarked to no one in particular.

"And stop grinning! This confounded ring has caused more trouble than it's worth!" Audra slipped the fingers of her other hand in to free it, but there was no room. Suddenly she realized how what she'd said must sound.

"I mean, it's always getting caught on things."

Jake lifted one brow. "Sure. I knew what you meant."

There was no way she could free herself from Jake's pocket or his look.

"Oh, just take off your jacket!"

"What?"

At least *that* distracted him.

"The stone setting is hooked on something. I can't get it loose because your pocket is too small. So take it off!" Audra resented the color creeping to her face. It was a perfectly innocent request, but it didn't feel that way.

Jake gave an exaggerated sigh. "Oh, well...follow me."

He walked over to one of the saddle racks mounted by each stall, dragging Audra behind him.

"Like I've got a choice?"

He put the tack on the post. "Look, if you wanted to get into my jacket, you just had to ask!"

"Darn your picture, you're as ornery as you ever were!"

Her frustration more amusing than he could bear,

Jake laughed outright as he shrugged off his jacket.

"You want my shirt, too?"

"Give me a break."

Audra took out the remainder of the sugar cubes and tossed them aside. A few yards away, Medallion snorted, her attention riveted to the two humans delaying her treat.

"We've got more," Jake assured the mare.

Audra cut him a skeptical glance. "Like she knows what you're saying!"

"I swear! She's the most intuitive horse I've ever trained. Is it still caught?"

The strands of denim thread were strong, and Audra was afraid to try to break the ring free in case it damaged the setting. "Got a knife?"

"In my front pant's pocket."

The look she gave Jake this time could have cut off his head.

"Just kidding." He retrieved a buck knife and opened it for her. "Now be careful."

"Then be good," Audra shot back with an evil show of her teeth.

The knife was sharp and freed the ring at its touch. Audra handed it back to Jake and proceeded to pick out the denim strands firmly embedded between the setting and the stone.

"Most girls would be treating a ring like that with adulation," Jake observed skeptically.

"Most girls didn't get it stuck in the pocket of a wise-acre!"

Audra and Jake both broke out in a simultaneous laugh. Taking up the saddle and bridle again in a back-to-business manner, Jake started toward Medallion, who whinnied with impatience, as if to say he'd dawdled entirely too long with this stranger in the barn.

"Sorry, girl, it's her fault."

Audra picked up the sugar cubes and blew them off. The last thing she needed to do was tick off the animal at whose mercy she was about to place herself. She watched Jake put the tack on the rack beside Medallion's stall and seize her large head between his hands.

"Gimme a kiss, darlin'."

To Audra's astonishment, the animal puckered its lips and nuzzled Jake's cheek.

"So tell me, Jake. Have you got someone special in your life? I mean, aside from a horse?"

"Not *that* special," he said, looking at the ring she still fiddled with.

Yes, it was a beautiful ring, expensive and big—too ostentatious to her liking. Maybe that's why it didn't feel natural on her finger, why she didn't wear it more often than she felt obligated to. It also made her feel like she was wearing a second place ribbon, like she was almost qualified for first, but not quite. The blue ribbon came next. Audra quickly buried the insecure uprising of her thoughts. It was nonsense. She loved Mark. His ring simply wasn't her.

But then, getting on a horse's back when she was unreasonably terrified of the beasts wasn't exactly her, either.

"Hey, I didn't mean to depress you."

"Hmm?" Audra's mind drew a blank. "Oh," she laughed nervously. "I was just worried that I'd loosened the setting what with the pulling and all."

Guilt warmed her face and neck at the little white lie. Jake was right about one little white lie compounding and compounding. If only she thought Mark—or anyone for that matter—would love her just as she was. She knew God loved her that way, but that wasn't enough for her human insecurities.

Lord, I know I have to work more on that one. I have so much to work on these days.

"No, I don't."

"Don't what?" Audra was drawn back to the conversation at hand.

"Have a girl…a human one, that is."

Jake took some of the sugar cubes from her hand and fed them to Medallion. "This one's a lot easier to understand."

"But does *she* make you feel warm and fuzzy inside, like she's holding your next breath in the palm of her hand?"

"Nope."

It wasn't what Jake said, as much as what he did that puzzled Audra. He yanked open the stall door and retreated inside like a scalded hound to fetch the horse.

Jake's knees felt like they'd been kicked from behind. The fact of the matter was, Audra had just described how *she* was making him feel, and he had no right to feel that way. When she'd gotten her hand stuck in his pocket, his senses were slammed like a school-boy's with a heavy crush. Warm, kind of belly sick but in a good way, mouth so dry he'd need scissors to spit.

Lord, I don't need this! I don't want what I'm feeling. She's promised to someone else, even if she doesn't seem as sure as she ought to be. I don't want to covet another man's fiancée, but does it count if she's a prefiancée? I mean, I'm going out of my mind down here!

As he walked Medallion out of the stable, a shower of cold water hit his side, startling him from his thoughts. Glancing down, he saw that he'd bumped into the full, flexible water bucket hung by the door, forcing the overflow down his pant leg and into his boot.

"Yuck, horse germs!" Audra made a face and backed away.

Not exactly the help I was expecting, Lord, but a cold shower is a cold shower. Grimacing, Jake led Medallion to the hitching ropes.

"Okay, you're not exactly drop-dead gorgeous," Audra went on with an annoying tenacity, "but I'm surprised some girl hasn't wound you around her little finger by now."

"Gee, thanks." Jake hooked cross ties to Medallion's halter.

"You look great, I just mean…well, *suave and debonair* just don't come to mind."

"I get it. John Wayne."

"Yeah."

A whimsical smile settled on Audra's lips sending a bolt of awareness through him as startling as the douse of water he'd just gotten. Trying to ignore it, he slipped Medallion's bridle on and was about to pull it over her ears when the horse protested loudly.

"Jake, the bit is over her tongue."

"What? Oh, sorry, girl."

He stroked Medallion's neck in apology while his own grew so hot, he half expected to smell singeing hair.

What the devil was he doing?

As if thinking the same thing, Medallion stomped her foot with impatience, her dark tail swishing. "See, she's as temperamental as any female."

Jake turned at Audra's silence to see the young woman backed against the stable wall, her complexion suddenly ashen. All hint of her saucy nature was gone, washed away by fear. While it was silly to have a fear of horses, he knew Audra's was real, nonetheless; put there by a freak accident.

He ran his hand down Medallion's back and over her flanks as he walked toward his stricken companion. "Easy, girl. It's okay."

Audra tried to smile. "Her or me?"

"*Both* of you. When you walk behind a horse or out of its eyesight, you talk. It lets the animal know you're a human and no threat to it."

Audra glanced to where Medallion shifted from foot to foot and tried to look over her shoulder. The ropes held her head forward, however, so she laid back her ears in frustration.

"So, if I'd talked before I darted into King's stall that day, he wouldn't have kicked me?"

"Well, it would have helped. After all, you startled him, and he didn't have time to reason out who or what you were. You see, horses are down on the pecking order in nature as prey, so they have a skittish nature God gave them for their own protection in the wild. Reacting and running is their natural defense until they identify any unexpected company."

Audra swallowed, her gaze fixed on Medallion. "She's so big."

"Yeah, but she doesn't know that. You look big to her."

"So I've heard. But I don't feel so big right now. I feel as little as that kitten I saved."

Jake put his arm around Audra's shoulders and drew her away from the wall.

"Look, Sunshine. Just like God made horses skittish to protect them, he made us look big to them so we could master them. It's all part of his master plan, rather ingenious to my notion."

Jake ushered her toward the horse with a gentle but firm strength. It was tempting to fold her in his arms and give her the protection she cried silently for, but Jake knew that would do neither of them any good. It would only worsen his predicament of wanting another man's woman and enable Audra to cower from a fear she needed to face in order to live up to her deal with Aunt Marge.

"Go on. Run your hand along her back."

It was like prying each footstep from her, but under his arm, Audra stiffly approached Medallion's head.

"She feels like a stiff velvet."

Medallion shuddered at Audra's touch. Jake knew just how the horse felt, but he hid his own tumultuous reaction to Audra's closeness and the scent of her soap. At least, he guessed it was soap. It didn't smell perfumey, just…nice.

Audra moved closer to him as the horse turned its head toward her. His mouth was dry as he spoke.

"She's just looking at you. Like a cat, she's curious. She's already smelled that you're not me.…"

"Considering what you just walked through in that

stable, I'm glad." Audra laughed lightly.

Jake ignored the pitiful attempt at humor. No need to check his boots. It wouldn't be the first time.

"But my voice is reassuring to her. She knows I wouldn't let anything happen to her because she trusts me. Now, go ahead. Give her the rest of the sugar you picked up. Open your hand, palm flat."

Audra's hand shook as she followed his instructions. Jake clasped her wrist to steady it, lest she snatch it away at the touch of the mare's nuzzle and startle her.

"Now that *is* like velvet," she murmured as Medallion nibbled at the treat.

"Hold your hand there and she'll lick it clean for you."

"I don't think so! No horse spit for me, thanks." Audra wrinkled her nose.

He'd always thought it cute, especially when her nose twitched like a bunny's. She stepped away, and an empty sense of cold assaulted where her warm presence had been. It was almost as if part of him had slipped away.

His mind reeled in rebellion. *Father, I have waited on you for the right woman to come along. If this is a test, please spare me!*

He gave himself a mental shake and drew a fortifying breath. "So, are you still game to ride? You've won Medallion's heart, that's for sure."

Audra gave him a soul-baring look, admitting fear, but at the same time, admitting trust. Her look struck Jake with a kick that would put any Medallion could muster to shame. When it came to teaching her to ride, that trust was well founded. Jake prayed God would help him to be worthy of it because he sure as the devil didn't feel that way.

Five

"HEELS DOWN! BACK STRAIGHT! CHIN UP!"

"Aunt Marge, if Audra were any stiffer, she'd fall off!" Jake spoke up in Audra's defense.

Heels down, back straight, chin up! Audra's lips twisted. That was hard to do when one's teeth were being jarred out of their sockets. If she were to relax and concentrate on those instructions, then she'd have to hold on to the saddle, which was also a big no-no. It was like rubbing one's belly and patting the head at the same time—it took coordination, something that was pitifully shattered by fear.

And coordination took time, as she reminded Aunt Margaret that morning when the woman fell back into her chair in exasperation and claimed the exercise was too much for her. Time was something Audra didn't have either. Mark was supposed to arrive this coming weekend.

"Remember, Audra's not competing in a show. She's just riding in the parade...no big deal."

Bless Jake! There was no end to his patience, or his encouragement. He had a way of making her laugh away her nervousness and apprehension. If she showed any signs of panic, he was right there, holding her hand or soothing the horse with the velvet stroke of his hand or voice. If he used that tone with women, he could have any one he wanted, anytime!

"She's representing Harvest Home in front of hundreds, not to mention that she's the heir to Belle Monde stables. I just can't believe Harvest Home is actually in the festivities again. We founded them, you know."

"'Since the Reconstruction,'" Jake quoted, "'which the Andersons survived with heads held high.'"

Margaret gave Jake a reproving look and then laughed. Audra stole a brief glimpse of the woman in the wheelchair at the edge of the practice arena. The change in her expression took years off her face. If only her aunt could warm to *her* in the same way.

"Oh, you! Go ahead and make fun, Jake Turner, but this is the best medicine I've had in a long time."

Audra had to agree with that. The past week, her aunt acted as if she had a new lease on life outside of therapy. Everyone noticed, from Maynie to the trainers, who hadn't seen her down at the stables since the accident. While the smell of fresh manure and hay made Audra wrinkle her nose and sometimes sneeze, it invigorated her aunt.

Of course, Aunt Margaret complained constantly during the morning therapy, but she was gaining strength by the day. The moment Audra insinuated that she didn't need much of an excuse to give up this riding deal, the woman dug in stubbornly and tried harder than before. For an Anderson to be part of Andersonville's founding celebration, even if that Anderson happened to be *that actress's* child, meant more to her aunt than Audra ever dreamed.

"Jake, can I change directions?" Audra ventured as she passed the spot where Jake and Aunt Margaret observed her progress. "I'm getting dizzy!"

She'd been riding in a circle for the past half hour, trying to follow all the instructions and stay atop Medallion.

"I'll do better than that! Today we'll go *outside* for a ride."

Audra started so suddenly at the suggestion, she was nearly bounced from the saddle by Medallion's proud, prancing gait. Immediately she grabbed on to the saddle, slipping her fingers beneath it, and pulled sharply on the reins in her other hand. Medallion tossed her head back and forth in protest.

"Ease up on the reins. She's not going anywhere!" Aunt Margaret snapped out the order. "Your balance is on your knees, not the stirrups, and you can't keep it holding on to the saddle like a ninny."

"Relax, Sunshine."

"I'll never get this in time!" Audra echoed the same tone her aunt had used that morning.

Margaret quoted Audra's response verbatim. "You will if you want to."

Audra wanted to grumble. Okay, so she could give it but couldn't take it! Instead, she reconstructed her riding form. Head up. Heels down. Shoulders back. Now relax...*not!*

Jake took Medallion's reins and held out his arms. "You're doing great, Audra. Come on down. You can walk Medallion a bit and give her some water while I saddle Princeton Magic."

This was her favorite part of riding...getting off the horse. Of course, having Jake lower her to the ground by her waist wasn't exactly distasteful. Sometimes, she could swear his hands lingered a little longer there than was necessary.

Today was no exception, but today, Audra met his gaze. Their eyes connected and it felt like someone had laid crash-cart paddles on her chest. Except there was no "Clear!" to warn her, and she could no more pull away from this than if she held the electrified ends of the wires herself. Awareness pricked at the nape of her neck and at nerve endings throughout her consciousness.

"You're standing on my foot."

The switch was thrown and Audra stepped away thankfully. Jake was smiling now, and the raw current she'd seen was smothered by a sparkling curtain of mischief instead.

Okay, so something was happening between them. It didn't mean anything. It was probably because she was leaning on Jake so much to make truth of that plaguing lie she'd told. She deserved all manner of discomfort for that, except this discomfiture with Jake Turner wasn't exactly unpleasant.

"I'll saddle up," Jake said, breaking the spell, his lips forming a grim line.

Shaking the troubling introspection, Audra took the reins over Medallion's head and started toward the place where her aunt waited. Her legs ached from day one, and while the pain was lessening with each practice, she still felt as though she walked like the horse was still between them.

"I'll probably be bowlegged for life after this!"

"It never affected me, and I was born on a horse, or at least, mother said that about me," Aunt Margaret reassured her. "In fact, in my earlier days, I was told I had the perfect figure for modeling."

"You still do."

Both on and off a horse, Margaret Anderson Morrow possessed a classic grace and beauty, which even her late middle age could not mar.

"Not in this." Her aunt sighed and drifted far off in thought for a moment.

It was a far better reaction than Aunt Margaret had the first time she and Audra had discussed her handicap. Yes, the older woman was improving both physically and spiritually.

"Well, I'd best get back to the house. I'm expecting the parade committee over at three, and I want to get out of these riding togs."

Audra watched her aunt maneuver her wheelchair out of the practice barn with the same rush of emotion she felt the first time one of her patients made a step on her own. *Thank you, Lord, for this miracle in the making! And thank you for making me an instrument in her healing.*

A snicker from her companion drew Audra back to a more present challenge, and she couldn't resist adding, *Although nearly crippling myself on a horse wasn't exactly my idea of how to go about it. You do work in mysterious ways!*

When Jake reentered the area riding Princeton Magic, he was a sight to behold. The western jeans and chambray shirt simply didn't mesh with the English tacked horse almost dancing beneath him. But then, neither did her clothes jive with Medallion's elegance.

"Boy, this is really something." Audra remarked wryly. "We're outclassed by two horses."

"Know what you mean. Every time I take Prince out, he makes me feel like I should have rented a tux."

Without waiting for Jake to dismount and help her, Audra slipped the reins over Medallion's neck and swung up into the saddle like a pro. Well, almost. Pros didn't need to bound up on the count of three.

"Ready?"

Audra took a deep breath and focused on the prospect ahead. No more fences to keep her steed from making off with her. For all the difference it made, she might as well be standing on the edge of one of those high cliffs in Acapulco, ready to plunge hundreds of feet into a swirling ocean. She glanced at the ground for reassurance. Okay, so it wasn't quite as far to fall, and instead of a large wave rolling over her, she'd have a horse.

"I guess we're ready as I'll ever be."

As if in answer, Medallion sidestepped, sandwiching Audra's left leg and Jake's right one between her and Princeton Magic. Their legs brushed as Jake urged Prince ahead. A breath-tripping awareness distracted her momentarily from her riding angst. Suddenly she wasn't certain whether the trails that would force them to ride single file were a blessing or a curse. Having Jake close was reassuring on one hand and nerve-shattering on the other.

Two hours later, when she and Jake emerged from a forest of reds and golds into a cleared field, Audra's confidence had been bolstered considerably, at least where the horses were concerned. Just ahead of her, Jake reined in the spirited stallion and waited for Audra to catch up beside him. His gaze was fixed on the autumnal setting before them with its waving yellow grain waiting anxiously for harvest.

"It's gorgeous, isn't it?"

"I tell God he's outdone himself every year," Jake agreed. "Guess I've never remembered a past season any prettier than the present."

"Like the earth is his coloring book." Audra looked at Jake. "There's a song about that, isn't there?"

"It's one of my favorites. Want me to sing it?"

Audra laughed. "What, and spook the horses?"

As clear and soothing as his voice sounded when he spoke, Jake couldn't carry a tune.

"What say we just canter on back, then, and give the horses a good exercise?"

The recollection of Medallion kicking up her heels as she ran out to greet Jake's pickup the day Audra arrived flashed through her mind.

"It'll be just like you did in the arena, except you'll be going straight ahead, I promise."

"You hear that, Medallion?" Audra patted the bay's neck. "Just like in the arena."

With that she clicked her tongue and urged the easy going bay into a trot. Her teeth slammed together until she coordinated her ups and downs with that of the horse. Audra made a clicking sound once again, and, as if she'd shifted gears, Medallion went out of the prancing trot into a longer, smoother canter.

In a few strides, Jake caught up with her and reined in the eager blue gray roan so its gait matched that of Audra's bay. A few wisps of hair escaped the scrunchie holding up her ponytail. They whipped in the wind about her face. By the time they'd reached the middle of the field, both horse and rider had grown comfortable and moved in unison. Audra marveled at the exhilaration of it all.

"Jake, this is wonderful!" She grinned. "And I *never* thought I'd ever say that!"

"Race you back to the barn, then?" The twinkle in

Jake's gaze betrayed the teasing nature of his challenge and something more.

"Don't push it, cowboy!" Audra glanced over at her companion.

The way he looked at her was enough to curl her toes in the pointed confines of Aunt Margaret's boots. He was obviously proud as punch that he'd done the impossible. That was all it was, Audra told herself, warming in the glow of his open admiration. She had enough problems without inventing more. Besides, she was soon to be engaged to Dr. Mark Chadwick. There was a hunk of diamond on a ring in her jewelry pouch to remind her. She tore away from the embrace of Jake's look, focusing on the open field ahead.

Maybe she ought to wear the reminder more often, at least until Mark was here to remind her himself. Frankly, with the doubts rearing in her mind every time she was with Jake, her fiancé-to-be couldn't come a bit too soon.

Six

FRIDAY EVENING, HARVEST HOME WAS ABLAZE WITH LIGHTS AT twilight, not just the big house, but the barns and arena too. The inaugural party of Founder's Day weekend was always kicked off in the antebellum manor, or had been until the accident that killed Aunt Margaret's husband and left her a cripple. However, when the queen of Andersonville society decided to come out of her self-imposed seclusion, she certainly did so with style.

All manner of staff had been hired to prepare for Margaret Anderson Morrow's reentry into the life of the town, while a solid parade of familiar faces came through the door every day leading up to the big event.

Audra remained strict about therapy and exercise in the morning, but after lunch, she was tossed out of the house and into Jake's care for her part of the *deal*. It was something she anticipated with mixed emotions. She loved riding with Jake and matching his teasing tit for tat. She adored Medallion, who greeted her with a friendly whinny the moment she recognized Audra.

What she didn't love were the questions that plagued her every time she and Jake were together—questions about her engagement.

How could she be in love with Mark Chadwick and feel the way she did when Jake was around? Audra twisted the ring on her finger. Thank goodness Mark was on his way at this very moment to restore some reason to her topsy-turvy world, even if he was running late due to a last minute emergency call.

Audra sat on her bedroom window seat, staring out at the night as if the answers to her quandary lay somewhere among the stars, when a flash of headlights at the end of the drive bought her back to earth. That had to be Mark and Jake now! Her pulses jumping into high gear, she headed for the grand staircase.

"They're here, Aunt Margaret!"

Her aunt appeared in the parlor entrance and stopped her at the top of the steps.

"Get back up there, missy! A proper young lady never appears to be waiting for her beau. Situations like this demand the opposite."

Audra frowned at her aunt's old-fashioned notion. "Aunt Marg—"

"I will not have you panting after this man like some floozy. Now you wait upstairs until I call for you. Go on!"

Margaret waved a silken scarf at her, as if shooing away a worrisome insect, but the mischievous wink she gave Audra dispelled any hint of condescension on the woman's part. If anything, she was more excited than Audra over Mark's visit. The last few days, Aunt Margaret had been advising Audra as if she were her own child, not *that woman's*.

Maybe if Audra had tried a little harder when she was younger to reach out to her aunt, things might not have gone so sour. Evidently that had not been the right season for them. God was working miracles between her and her aunt. Audra still marveled at the way God used their weaknesses for his healing purpose.

At the sound of the front door opening and male voices, Audra shivered. What on earth was wrong with her? She'd heard of wedding jitters, but she and Mark weren't even officially engaged. *Lord, I could use some of your peace where my romantic life is concerned. I just don't know what to think, much less do.*

"Audra?"

She left her room for the second time at her aunt's call, her mouth suddenly dry.

"Audra, are you ready yet, dear? Don't keep this handsome young man waiting!"

This was ridiculous, Audra thought, going to the top of the staircase. At the bottom Mark stood beside Aunt Margaret's wheelchair looking up expectantly. Her aunt was positively aglow with delight.

It was Jake, however, leaning against the closed front door who caught Audra's eye. She could imagine what he was thinking since she'd been ready and dressed before he left the house. She could hear him saying, "One little white lie begets another and another," even if the gaze that followed her down the steps said nothing.

"I'd like to say you were worth waiting for," Mark told her, "but I'm the one who's running late. So sorry, love." He took her hand to help her down the last few steps with the gallantry Aunt Margaret insisted was ingrained in a Southern gentleman's nature.

"You're a doctor. I'm a nurse. I, of all people, understand."

Audra presented her cheek to receive Mark's kiss. She wondered how much the crimson that must be enveloping her face and ears clashed with the bright autumn color of her dress. Here was the moment she'd been waiting for, the chance to flaunt Dr. Mark Chadwick in front of her aunt, to prove her worth in Anderson terms, and she felt like she was going to throw up. That did it. She was going to tell Mark the truth…about Medallion.

"I see you've met Aunt Margaret." The brightness in her tone was as forced as her smile. "And Jake, of course." Audra glanced past Mark to Jake. "Was there much traffic?"

He shrugged. "More than enough for me. Main Street is already blocked off for the parade tomorrow."

"Yeah, they were rolling up the sidewalks when we left," Mark quipped. When no one but Audra laughed, he turned to Aunt Margaret. "I can't tell you how thrilled I was at the offer to ride Princeton Magic in your quaint little celebration. Harvest Home is a familiar name at Beau Monde."

He slipped off his coat and handed it to Jake.

"Here you go, Jim. Take this and my bags to my room. Audra can show me there as soon as we catch up."

Caught off guard, Jake looked at the coat, up at Mark, and back at the coat again. Aunt Margaret straightened in her chair, her face as anxious as Audra felt, waiting for Jake's response.

With a grimace of a smile, he took the coat. "Sure thing, buddy. I can understand your wanting to *catch up* with someone like our Sunshine."

"Jake is like a son to me."

"Jake is family, Mark."

Audra and Margaret spoke together, then both paused. Each waited for the other to speak first before Margaret took command of the situation with characteristic grace.

"Jake and Audra are like my own children. They've grown up together here in this house."

This time embarrassment took its turn with Mark. "Hey, old boy, I'm sorry. I thought you said you worked at Harvest Home."

Jake picked up Mark's engraved leather case. "I do."

"Well, let me help…"

"No problem, doctor man."

"Call me, Mark."

Jake nodded stiffly. "No problem, Mark. You and Sunshine go on and *catch up*."

"What's this *Sunshine* business?"

"Oh, it's just a pet name. Suits her personality." Jake retreated up the steps two at a time with Mark's bag.

Aunt Margaret's gaze turned from the upstairs hall where Jake disappeared to her guest. "I have to go see if everything is in order in the kitchen. Did you eat dinner, Mark?"

"Grabbed something at the airport before my flight left, thanks."

Mark slipped his arm around Audra as Aunt Margaret wheeled away quietly.

"Do we go in here?" He indicated the open parlor filled with its original Victorian furniture.

Audra closed one of the two disappearing panel doors for a little privacy and was pulled straight into Mark's arms. His lips closed over hers, smothering her gasp of surprise with a long, fervent kiss. When he finally released her, he sighed heavily.

"I am one lovesick guy, and my doctor has prescribed a weekend of TLC with a certain nurse."

"Well, if your doctor prescribed it…" Audra's smile was nervous as Mark slipped his hands down over her arms and clasped them behind her back. Somehow her heart wasn't in her words. "I suppose I'll have to do my best to see that his prescription is filled."

He pulled her against him and pressed his forehead to hers. "Have you missed me half as much as I've missed you?"

"Maybe half."

Jake was *so* right about those little lies piling up. She'd been so busy with him and her aunt that the only time she'd thought of Mark was in guilt because of the way she reacted toward Jake. The cowboy had not done one thing out of line, but it hadn't made a lick of difference! Something had happened between them, their bond had changed from a familial one to one far more intimate.

"Kiss me and I might up the ante to missing you *just as much.*"

She moistened her lips in anticipation. This was what she needed, Mark in the flesh, not some cold worrisome stones set in gold. Audra circled Mark's neck with her arms and returned his kiss, determined to rekindle the fire she remembered in their relationship. *Yes. This is more like it.*

Mark wasn't being polite. He wasn't trying to save her from her own clumsiness. Audra was in his arms because he wanted her, he loved her, he needed her…but did she really want, love, and need him?

The sound of footsteps descending on the stairwell broke Audra's concentration, but not in time to pull away from Mark before Jake popped his head in the room. He acted as if he came across couples in passionate embraces every day, or at least he tried to.

"I see Maynie put extra towels on your bed, in case

you want to freshen up from your flight."

Mark forced a smile. "Thanks, but it was just a shuttle."

"Yeah, well…" Jake cleared this throat awkwardly. "You two go on catching up. I've got some chores to do before this shindig gets started." He glanced at Audra then back to Mark. "Nice to meet you, doc."

"You too, Jim…"

"Jake."

"Jake," Mark acknowledged with a grimace. "I'm terrible with names."

Pulling on his hat and tilting it back, Jake grinned. "In that case, I'll answer to Jim. I've been called a lot worse. Catch you two later."

Pivoting abruptly, he retreated to the back of the hall and out the door.

"Jake's a bit on the shy side at first," Audra said, breaking the awkward silence. "Once he gets to know you, he warms up. He has a great sense of humor."

"I'll bet. He was a barrel of laughs on the ride here."

"Well, you should have talked horses!" The snap in her voice took Audra as much by surprise as it did her companion. Mark couldn't have known that. "Jake loves horses. They are his life."

Mark's searching gaze settled on her face. Although she had nothing to hide, it was all Audra could do not to shift uncomfortably beneath it like a guilty child caught in the act of mischief.

Lord, what is wrong with me? Mark's looking at me like I've grown horns. I don't even recognize myself, and it's scary! I need help, I need…

The tinkle of ice in glasses gave Audra the distraction she prayed for.

"Look, Maynie's here with the drinks!"

The house couldn't fill with guests too quickly for Audra. Soon she and Mark were surrounded by well-wishers, saving her another awkward moment alone with the man she was *supposed* to love. Suddenly she'd been grasping at small talk, once she'd gone over her aunt's therapy in detail. What happened to absence makes the heart grow fonder? One of them was a stranger and she feared it was her.

The party was her aunt's moment of triumph, and it should have been Audra's as well. This was what she'd dreamed of all her life, being accepted as an Anderson, a person *worthy* of her aunt's love and attention, not *obliged* for it. Margaret was already consulting her cronies on finding the best wedding consultant.

Audra caught sight of Jake hovering in a quiet corner, ill at ease in a silk suit tailored to fit his lean muscled frame. It smacked of Aunt Margaret's tastes not Jake's. There was a time Audra thought Jake a wimp for letting her aunt run his life, but in the last few weeks she saw who really ran Harvest Home. Who'd have thought it was Jake Turner holding the wheel, allowing Margaret to think she was doing the driving?

As if he sensed he was being watched, Jake met Audra's gaze from across the room and grimaced. He looked positively miserable, but then Jake never was one for show, and, if Aunt Margaret's parties were anything, they were a show.

"So how does it feel to drop the *R.N.* from your

name and add a *Mrs.* instead, Miss Audra?"

Audra turned a blank face back to the conversation at hand between her and Mark and Chester Sigley, the president of the local hunt club. "I'm sorry, Mr. Sigley, what did you say?"

"He said, how does it feel to be giving up nursing to become *Mrs. Mark Chadwick.*" Mark gave her an affectionate squeeze.

"Well, I…" Audra was shocked that Mark would even think she'd give up her career. Sure, they'd never talked about it, but he knew how hard she'd worked to get her position at the hospital and how important it was to her. "I plan to do both, actually."

"No Chadwick bride has *ever* had to work."

"It's not a matter of *having* to work, Mark; it's a matter of *wanting* to."

Aunt Margaret spoke up. "I think Audra is right. Old guard families like ours need to catch up with the times, change our outdated way of thinking." She reached out and took Audra's hand. "It would be criminal to deny some poor crippled soul the gift of healing and encouragement she has. I speak from personal experience."

Audra couldn't believe what she was hearing either from her fiancé *or* her aunt, but at the moment, the latter demanded the most attention. She'd hungered too long for this not to drink her fill. Aunt Margaret had done nothing but complain during every session, so Audra assumed her efforts to build her aunt's strength and coordination stemmed from the deal they'd made, not Audra's encouragement.

Too overwhelmed for words, Audra glanced over to

where Jake had stood. He, of all people, could appreciate what she was feeling. He knew what this meant to her. It should be his arm squeezing her waist in congratulations not Mark's. But Jake was gone. At least Audra couldn't make out his distinctive figure through the emotional mist in her eyes.

"And she's as shy as Jake when it comes to taking credit for her gifts. I'm proud of them both. God's been better to me than I deserve." Once again Margaret squeezed her hand.

Thank you, Lord! There was no high like that of being allowed to glimpse God's plan and one's part in it, nor anything more humbling. Here was the reason God laid it on Audra's heart and conscience to return to the place where she'd felt so unwanted.

"Well, Audra and I certainly have plenty of time to discuss the future without settling it tonight." Mark stifled a yawn. "Goodness! Forgive me. I spent most of last night in emergency surgery, so I'm a little spent today."

"Audra, dear, I think you'd better show your beau to his room. Poor dear was up all night taking a sick colleague's shift and had a full day at his regular practice today," Margaret explained to her guests. "You've been gallant enough, Mark. Go rest up for tomorrow."

Mark leaned over and kissed Aunt Margaret's cheek. "Thank you for your hospitality *and* understanding. Good night, good people. I hope to be more fresh when I see you tomorrow."

A few moments later, outside the guest room door, Mark stopped to say good night. The haggard lines about his eyes betrayed the fatigue he'd managed quite well to hide until now. He backed against the doorjamb and pulled Audra to him.

"She's not nearly the ogre you insinuated."

"No, she isn't. I was so wrong about her." Audra hesitated, aware that that was not the only wrong she needed to address. There was the little white lie.

"Mark, I—"

He interrupted her confession by lowering his lips to hers, taking them as though they were his possession. Audra tried to relax, but with the mounting doubts assaulting her mind, she could not. She was breathless when he pulled away, but only because she'd held her breath, waiting, wishing to escape where she could reason out her quandary.

"The next time we come here, I can pull you in here with me," he whispered, easing his jaw around her chin to nibble at her ear.

It was clear Mark was in no mood for talking, and she didn't share the mood he *was* in. She sidestepped playfully. "In the meantime, rest up, doc. And that's *my* prescription. Princeton Magic can be a handful if he takes a notion."

"If your Jake's the trainer he's reputed to be, I don't think I'll have any trouble at all. Besides, I'm like you, born on a horse."

Audra smiled until the click of Mark's door wiped it away. Okay, so she'd tell him the truth tomorrow.

Seven

TOO MANY THOUGHTS—SOME GOOD, SOME NOT SO PLEASANT— denied Audra rest for yet another night. She should have been sleeping in the clouds, thanks to God's handiwork with Aunt Margaret's change of heart and renewed interest in life. She'd given him the glory and thanks for that all night long. In between, she rode an emotional seesaw apologizing earnestly for her foolish lie and puzzling over her engagement to Mark Chadwick.

A few weeks ago it was like a dream come true. Now…now Audra wasn't so certain. Something was different between them, something she couldn't put her finger on, and it wasn't simply that he expected her to retire from her calling to be his wife.

Audra finally blamed it on the aftermath of all her anxiety these last few weeks as she headed out to the stables in the early morning chill. Jake would be doing his chores, and Jake was exactly the person she needed to talk to right now. He had a way of putting things in perspective. His head was always clear, his feet firmly planted on the ground. She found him combing out Medallion's dark mane and tail.

"Morning!" she called out, more brightly than she really felt.

"Mornin'." Jake never looked up. He kept on working on a snarl in the bay's tail with bit of vengeance, although the horse didn't seem to mind.

"Good morning, Medallion!" Audra took out a handful of sugar cubes and offered them to the mare.

Medallion nibbled them up like a kid with candy and then licked the remains off her hand.

"You are such a pig!" She rubbed the horse's neck.

"You've come a long way, baby," Jake observed over the mare's back.

"Thanks to you...and Aunt Margaret, of course."

When Medallion's tail and mane lay just right, he put the comb on a shelf and wiped his hands on his jeans. His lips were poised, as if about to speak. Audra waited until she thought she'd misread him. Their words came out at the same time.

"I need to talk"

"We gotta talk."

They exchanged apologetic smiles.

"Ladies, first."

Good ole Jake...polite to a fault. Audra once found it annoying. Now she found it endearing. She opened her mouth to speak but somehow couldn't find the right words to explain what she was feeling since she really wasn't sure.

"I'm not sure, Jake."

"'Bout what?" He suddenly looked guarded.

Instead of using the bottle of antibacterial gel she'd carried out for washing her hands after Medallion used them for a snack plate, Audra wiped her hands on her jeans, imitating Jake, and shoved them into the pockets. "About *everything.*"

"That narrows it down." Turning away abruptly, Jake unhitched Medallion from the cross ties.

Who put the burr under his saddle? "Okay, about Mark then."

"What's there to be sure about? He's got it all: money,

career, blue blood…seems like a nice enough guy as well. He goes to church, right?" He opened the stall door and stood back while Medallion entered eagerly, anticipating the grain he dumped into her feed box.

"Well, he has a crazy schedule. He belongs to his family church, but when he's off, he usually golfs or goes sailing. I mean, he needs time off."

Audra asked Mark once to attend Sunday services with her when they were not working at the hospital. His argument worked for him. She wasn't quite as sold, but considering his other qualities…

"I don't know!" Jake's thoughts were the same that kept crossing her mind. "I don't know what's missing, I just know something is. I mean, I *thought* we had it." Then there was her fiancé's cynicism whenever she gave God credit for a blessing. How many times had she heard, "Like you didn't earn it?"

Maybe she'd been avoiding the issue of their faith because she didn't want him to think her one of those television fanatics he disdained. One bad apple and the whole bushel was ruined in his eyes. It wouldn't be the first foolish thing she'd done to impress Mark.

Jake hung the feed dipper up and stood in the frame of the mare's stall, staring down as if looking through her. Clearly, he wasn't in a talking mood, at least about her problems. If anything, she was chewing on a large hunk of cold shoulder.

"So what did you want to say?" she asked, more than a tad exasperated.

"Never mi—"

Jake's answer turned into a startled grunt. He suddenly pitched forward over the stable door sill. Instinctively,

Audra stepped up to catch him, but his weight took them both down to the ground in a sprawl.

"What the—confound it, Medallion!" He propped himself up on his hands. "That animal's gonna push me one time too many! You all right?"

Winded by the fall, Audra nodded, but it was a lie. Her heart was lurching into overdrive, the way Jake was looking at her, as if the sudden riot running in her veins ran rampant through him as well. He licked his lips, and she found herself doing the same. The breath of space between them was a static mingle of excitement, of anxiety...of anticipation.

"Actually..." He seemed to wrestle mentally for words, and then swallowed an oath of exasperation and lowered his mouth to hers.

She didn't hesitate as he slipped his arms beneath her and drew her to him. Nor did she resist the heady kiss that all but consumed them both.

Suddenly she needed Jake as she'd never needed anyone. A dizzying weakness curled from her belly to her extremities in all directions. Audra clung to Jake, praying she wasn't falling into this bright abyss of passion alone.

His fingers were in her hair, his lips caressing her neck, her ear, her forehead, her cheeks, the tip of her nose. Then, still trembling from the staggering tide that swept over them, he pulled back, apparently reining in the spontaneous stampede of passion, his breath ragged.

Audra stared up at him, awed at the change. She wasn't looking at Jake, her buddy, her friend. She was looking at temptation itself, embodied in the man he'd become. Beneath the still waters of his good nature was a roaring fire she'd never suspected. Even now she felt the lick of its flames at the very heart of her being.

"Jake!" she managed in wonder with what little breath it left her, unable to believe what had just happened between them.

The sound of her voice had the effect of dousing the smoldering depths of his gaze. He stiffened and rolled away. In a single motion, Jake was on his feet, reaching down to help her up, his face a mask of cool politeness.

"Sorry. My mistake. It won't happen again…and stop coming to me every time you hit a snag in your life! You're a big girl now. Make your own decisions."

He was another Jake now, withdrawn, guarded, moody. Jake was never moody. He was never—

"There you are!"

Audra dragged her attention from this intriguing stranger in Jake's body as he hauled her up from the dusty stable floor to where Mark stood in the barn entrance.

"Maynie says breakfast is ready." With a rigid smile, Mark looked from Audra to Jake and back to Audra again. "Did I miss something?"

"Not if you don't count clumsiness and an ornery horse." Jake's dourness twisted the lips—the same lips that had awakened and tortured Audra's just moments before. "I warn you now, doc. Grace is *not* Audra's middle name."

"So I didn't see it coming!" Audra snapped at Jake, picking up on his cue. What could she say? She and Jake fell down and were compelled by who knew what to kiss like nothing she'd ever been party to before? With good old mild-mannered, shy *Jake*?

"You never do. A horse'll bump into you in a heartbeat,

especially if she thinks you've got some sugar for her." Jake closed the stable door and called over his shoulder. "Tell Maynie I'll grab something later. I want to make sure the tack is polished to a fair-thee-well, or Aunt Marge'll have my skin."

Once again Audra felt a rise of guilt warming her neck, spawned by the stern look Mark gave her. Not that she could blame him. It certainly looked like something was amiss; and heaven knew, although neither she nor Jake had invited what happened, it sure *felt* like it!

As Jake put away the brushes in the horse trailer at the parade site, he felt his stomach grumble.

Well, that's what he got for skipping breakfast, but he couldn't have eaten, even if he had to, not after making a fool of himself in front of Audra. It was time she stood on her own and stopped running to him every time she got confused by life's little snags, especially this time. He'd proven, both to her and to himself, that he couldn't give her an unbiased opinion.

Not by a long shot.

His knuckles, bruised and skinned from taking out his frustration on an unforgiving hitching post after Audra and Mark left the barn, stung as he drew them into a fist. He'd made up his mind not to do anything to sway Audra because Mark could certainly give her a whole lot more than a horse trainer could, but then she *had* to say she wasn't sure and looked at him with that troubled, helpless gaze!

When the two of them were sprawled on the stable floor, his brain stepped back and let his emotions go unbridled. If looks could kill, they'd be calling the funeral director for him, the way Mark Chadwick glared at him.

"The Lord is good to those who wait for him." It was one of Jake's favorite verses, but he blew it this time.

"Blessed are the meek, for they shall inherit the earth." Jake didn't want the earth. He wanted Audra.

"Thou shalt not covet..." He didn't mean to. It just happened. Coveting had to be bad for the soul because he was misery personified, right smack dab in the middle of a crowd of cheering friends and neighbors. And as for *"thy neighbor's wife,"* well, Audra was practically engaged. *Lord, does that really count?*

"Jake?"

At the sound of Audra's voice, Jake turned to see her step up into the front of the trailer where tack and supplies were stored. She was beautiful, like an angel, the way the sun danced off her hair. Knowing she was someone else's turned an invisible knife in his stomach.

"Are you ready?" Jake took in Audra's outfit from boots to cap.

"About this morning," she began.

"Yeah, well...sorry." Except he wasn't. Jake turned and sorted through the box of brushes and assorted paraphernalia needed to keep a show horse looking its finest. He couldn't look at her, or she'd see his heart slipping right out onto his sleeve.

"Did it mean anything?"

Jake's heart stopped, then lunged into a staccato beat. He stared at the contents of the tack box without really seeing, searching for the right answer.

"That depends on whether you want it to."

"Jake, I just want to know if you were trying to tell me something!" Audra was really annoyed. "For heaven's sake, turn around and look at me!"

Jake tipped back his hat and wallowed in his own pent up emotions. "Okay, Audra, I'm looking at you. Now what do you want me to say? That I think Mark Chad-wick is a good match? That's not up to me to decide. It's up to you! I have my own problems without worrying about yours."

Audra shrank back a step from his outburst, staring at him with wide eyes, misting from the sharp blast. Her lower lip trembled until she seized it with her teeth and summoned her courage.

"Sorry. I didn't realize I was such a bother."

A mix of shame and regret compounded Jake's misery until he could no longer hold back. Heaven forgive him, he had to say something. He couldn't send her off like this.

"Wait!" he said softly as she started to leave. He placed his hands on her shoulders and looked down at her. "*I'm* the one who's sorry. It's not your fault that I get tongue-tied and don't know whether I should speak my mind or keep it to myself. But I just can't. I have to say what I think. And I think that if you have to pretend to be something you're not to impress a man, then that man isn't worth impressing. Any man in his right mind would want you just the way you are."

"*Any* man?" Audra's chin started to quiver.

With a crooked smile, Jake tipped it upward with the tip of his finger. His throat tightened and he prepared to leap for all he was worth with a silent *Lord, help!* as his only net.

"Guess I can only rightly speak for this one."

He drew Audra into his arms and kissed away the storm of emotions glazing her eyes, those beautiful brown eyes that deserved nothing short of sheer delight in them. He inhaled the light scent of her hair, and the effect was as intoxicating as the feel of her petite frame, which swayed against him, as if he could draw away all her fears and doubts. God knew, that's what he wanted to do.

The nurse had worked wonders in healing the invalid, but who would heal the nurse? Jake wanted to, if God would allow it. He'd love Audra with all his soul, all his being. What Jake couldn't say with words, he conveyed with tenderness, underscored by passion. And if Audra didn't understand after this, then—

"Audra, are you in there?"

Mentally, Jake swore at the untimely appearance of Mark Chadwick. Physically, he released Audra as Chadwick appeared in the door of the trailer.

"Gee, I don't see a horse around to lay the blame on this time."

Audra glanced at Jake and then at her disgruntled fiancé. "Mark, I—"

"Later, Audra. The band has started and we're up." Mark disappeared from the entrance as abruptly as he'd arrived. In the background, a Sousa march filled the air, confirming his announcement.

"Maybe you shouldn't ride." Jake put a restraining hand on Audra's shoulder as she started after Mark.

"I can't disappoint Aunt Margaret." She paused at the door and smiled back at him. "I'll be fine, honest!"

Jake followed and helped her up onto Medallion's

back while Chadwick eased Princeton Magic effortlessly around in place beside the mare.

"Be a good man and hand me that riding crop," Mark requested cooly.

Jake took the crop from the trailer and carried it over to the horseman. "Remember, it's just for signal and show. He's not used to a crop for anything else."

Audra sat still as a statue on the bay while it danced in place to the music. Dressed in riding togs, she and the doctor looked like a matched set of dolls, with about as much emotion showing on their faces. Jake wasn't sure if Audra was just scared, upset, or both. He just wanted to ease her anxiety.

"She loves music!" he called out to her. "Of course, she prefers the country CDs I play in the barn when I'm working."

Audra gave Jake a tweak of a smile, but her focus was on Medallion.

"Jake, let's hurry to the grandstand. I want to be in front so I can see them coming," Aunt Margaret called brightly from the sideline, oblivious to the icy undercurrents. "You two look beautiful! We'll see you later."

Although he'd have preferred just to walk alongside Medallion, Jake accompanied Margaret Anderson Morrow through the crowd of familiar, friendly faces toward the grandstand, a decorated flat farm-bed trailer with some folding chairs for the mayor and his judges. While he scanned the street in concern for Audra, his mind raced through the scene in the trailer over and over, as he searched for some sort of commitment in her reaction. There he'd laid his heart bare and Chadwick interrupts! *Lord, did I make a total fool of myself again?*

After what seemed an interminable period of time, the Andersonville middle school band rounded the corner of Main Street from the back lot next to the dime store building. Behind them came Harvest Home's best, coats brushed to a sheen, hooves polished, manes and tails flowing like silk. Both the golden bay and the blue roan pranced to the rhythm of the band, necks arched proudly.

Atop the bay, Audra was statue still, but riding in perfect form, her smile painted on. As they neared the mayor's podium, she sought out Jake in the crowd. Their gazes locked. Jake felt like he'd been kicked in the chest. He forced a smile and waved. He loved her. *Oh, man, he loved her!*

The procession stopped before the grandstand where the horses would do a full turn and stop to bow to the mayor. Jake had gone over the exercise with Audra every day that week.

"Isn't she beautiful?" Aunt Margaret said to no one in particular.

"Sure…"

A sudden succession of crackling explosions erupted on the other side of the street, setting Jake into motion before he had time to even think. People screamed and confusion set in the crowd as to where the noise was coming from. High strung by nature, Princeton Magic let out a startled whinny and reared slightly, trying to back away from the chaos. While Chadwick wrestled to control the panicked horse, Medallion sidestepped into the crowd.

Audra immediately reined her back into the street, soothing her by patting her neck and talking in a low tone, but the young woman's frantic eyes sought out Jake. Although he was already in a half run to where the animals balked, it appeared the situation was getting back under control when another string of firecrackers went off.

"Someone stop those kids before they blow a finger off!" Jake shouted.

Princeton Magic was now rearing on his hindquarters with his rider clinging to the saddle. Jake saw him raise the riding crop and shouted, "Chadwick, no!" but it was too late. Mark lashed the stallion in an attempt to control it.

The blue roan backed into Medallion, who was just barely under Audra's control. Without thought to his own safety, Jake raced between the horses, hoping to pull her off before the bay panicked as well. In the periphery of his vision, he saw the stallion buck fiercely, sending Chadwick, red jacket, riding crop and all, flying through the air and onto the paved street.

"Jake!" Audra's scream alerted him, but Jake never saw to what.

The side of his head exploded in mind-numbing pain and light. The next thing he knew, he was lying on the stone road in a daze. He barely made out the underside of Medallion vaulting over him. He reached up, but all he grasped was a blur of sky. Amid the clatter of horses' hooves and screams of the crowd, he tried to get up, but his limbs were too heavy, as if someone had tied weights to them.

"Dear heaven, Jake!"

He heard Aunt Marge's fear-filled cry and forced his eyes open again to see her leaning over him. *How did she get here?* He glanced about in a daze for the wheelchair.

"Somebody get a doctor!" she ordered, summoning her characteristic control. The silk scarf she wiped Jake's head with came away stained with blood...his blood. "And, Mark, for heaven's sake, help Audra!"

Jake saw a red jacket rising from the ground nearby and heard, "I'm not getting back on that devil. Someone give me some car keys!"

Audra! Jake didn't need to have the situation spelled out for him. It would take Chadwick too much precious time to find a car *and* keys close by. Medallion was a sweetheart, but when she was spooked, it was hard to tell what she might do. Jake pulled himself to his feet and staggered.

"No, Jake!" Aunt Marge tried to detain him. "You need a doctor."

"I'm okay." He pulled away. "Audra needs me!"

Princeton Magic was still quivering, but was nearby, under the control of one of the men in the crowd. Without bothering to see where Chadwick disappeared to, Jake grabbed the stallion's reins from the local feed store owner with a hurried, "Thanks!" and swung up into the saddle. "Which way did she go?"

"That way!" The man pointed toward the park at the end of town.

"Be careful, son!" his aunt called out from where a neighbor helped her upright on wobbly legs.

Praying for Audra's safety, Jake kicked Prince hard and let the animal work out his panic in a full gallop toward the park. *God, I'll give her up, just don't let her be hurt.* He passed the hardware store, the grocery store, and the World War II veterans statue before the street turned toward the river where a city park and picnic area were located. The town was small, but at that moment, it seemed to grow by the second.

He didn't know what to expect when he caught up with Audra, but it certainly wasn't what he saw. Trotting around the pavilion where band concerts were played on summer Sunday afternoons came Medallion, with Audra posting in textbook form toward him. Her cheeks were flushed and her eyes were bright with excitement. Her face brightened even more upon seeing him.

"I did it!" she called out to him excitedly. "I stayed on!"

Thank you, Lord! Relief welled in his throat so thick, Jake couldn't speak. And when he jumped off Princeton Magic's back, his knees didn't want to work right, either. It felt like he was walking on rubber legs as Jake closed the distance between him and Audra, holding out his arms to her.

Jake caught her as she slid off the horse and held her as if he'd never let her go. When he could squeeze her no more, without fear of hurting her, he let go.

"I…" Jake choked on his words, uncertain of what he was going to say anyway.

"Jake, you're bleeding!"

As if her revelation sapped the last ounce of strength from them, Jake's knees gave out. Audra tried to catch him as he crumbled, but his six-foot-plus frame bore the two of them to the leafy autumn carpet of ground.

"You're a slow learner," he mumbled. "Can't hold me…I…I'm just a little woo…oozy." Here he was in an angel's arms, and he was about to throw up…or maybe pass out.

"Prince kicked you, you ninny!"

"Ouch!" he shouted as Audra probed the wound in his hairline with her fingers.

"What are you doin', brain surgery?"

"You might need some stitches."

Jake tried to get up, but the spinning of the treetops overhead nixed that idea. He was supposed to be rescuing *her*, not the other way around!

"Stay still! You probably have a concussion, even with your hard head."

Lord, I love her, warped sense of humor and all! He said as much into the wool of her jacket as she raised on her knees and continued to examine his head for further damage. After the episode in the trailer, he had nothing left to lose.

"I love you, Audra. I don't know how or when it happened. Maybe I've always loved you. I mean, since you came home, everywhere I look, you're there! Even when you're not…and I don't think I could stand it if you ever really weren't there. What I mean to say is…"

In the midst of his bumbling confession, the probing stopped. Jake felt her stiffen and groaned in silent apprehension. *I'm outta my head, Lord, and sure need some help here!*

"I love you too, Jake."

Jake heard her words, but they were just too wonderful to be true. Maybe she meant like a brother, something he felt far from where Audra was concerned.

"And I *thought* you loved me. I mean, that's what I thought your kiss meant, but…well, I just needed to hear you *say* it." Audra went on. "I've been *so* blind, but Jake, you've been just plain dumb! I felt like I was pulling eyeteeth to get it out of you!"

Jake winced as she hugged his head to her with the fervor of her confession. "Okay, I surrender. I love you!"

Despite his dizziness, he reached up and pulled Audra down to his level. "Now *you* say it! I don't want any more misunderstanding."

"I...love...you!" She laughed it out, but it was the sweetest sound he'd ever heard. Then she sobered suddenly. "You were right, Jake. I've been so busy trying to be what others wanted me to be, that I forgot who I was, and...and these last few weeks, you've shown me. The girl I tried to be loved Mark Chadwick, but the girl I really am loves a sweet-tempered, ornery horse trainer with a heart as gentle as his touch...and a cracked skull!"

Jake dragged Audra into his arms and kissed her until his head felt as if it were going to lift off on its own happy flight. He swayed unsteadily, but he refused to let her go. He'd been through too much torment to risk this dream ending too quickly—for it was like a dream, one come true. It wasn't until he heard the screeching of brakes and skidding of tires that he was able to tear his eyes from the china perfect face that had robbed him of sleep too many nights of late.

A black Jeep slid to a stop in a cloud of dust a few yards away from them. With the glare of the sun on the windshield, Jake couldn't make out the driver, but he could guess, even before Chadwick jumped out of the vehicle.

"Well, I see you two are all right after all." Mark slowed as he approached and pointed to the ring shining on Audra's left hand. "I don't think you're going to be needing that, so if you don't mind, I'll take the ring and take my leave."

Audra struggled to her feet. "I'm sorry, Mark. It wasn't intentional on either of our parts. I'm just not the girl I thought I was." She handed him the ring.

"You're not the girl I thought you were, either." He dropped the ring into the pocket of his jacket. "Not to mention, you couldn't ride."

"No, but she busted her butt trying to learn for you." Jake spoke up, trying to assemble enough coordination from his staggered senses to stand on his own without swaying.

"Save it, Jim. I'm leaving."

"Jake!" Jake and Audra said at the same time.

At that moment, another vehicle turned the corner and came rushing toward them. Mark climbed into the Jeep and spun off, throwing gravel and dust in his wake.

Jake had never been so glad to see the back end of someone in his life.

Leaning into Jake's shoulder, that strong, comfortable shoulder that had been there for her from the first day they met, Audra walked with him toward the approaching car as it came to a stop a few feet beyond them. While the driver and another passenger got out and started for the grazing horses, Aunt Margaret threw open the passenger door and swung her legs out. As she struggled to her feet with the support of the door, relief broke in her voice.

"Thank God, you two are all right!" She bolted forward, determined to close the distance between them.

Audra rushed forward, reaching instinctively to steady her aunt, when it dawned on her that the woman had just taken three steps without support! In fact, the wheelchair was nowhere in sight!

"Aunt Margaret, how…?"

"I don't know. When I saw Jake lying on the ground bleeding and that horse running way with you, I *had* to do something! But don't go getting your hopes up too much," her aunt snapped in warning. "If I have to go through *this* every day just to get out of that chair, I'd just as soon be an invalid."

Suddenly, her mask of bravado shattered with a sob. She tried to engulf both Audra and Jake in one embrace. "I thought I'd lost the two of you!"

Audra had read of trauma jarring a patient out of a psychosomatic handicap. The body God created was capable of incredible feats when loved ones were threatened.

"You did lose Mark, Aunt Margaret," she ventured hesitantly. Surely her aunt had seen him tear out of there in a cloud of dust. Audra, however, was totally unprepared for the woman's answer.

"Good riddance! I was wondering when you'd come to your senses!" The lady drew away with a sniff. "And you!" she added, tapping Jake on the chest. "If you were half as good with women as you are with horses, he never would have had the chance to come in the first place! So when is the date?"

"What date?" Jake shifted from one foot to the other, as if ready to evade the matrimonial lasso her aunt was tossing around them.

"Don't waste a minute more of your lives than you have to, Jake Turner. And that goes for you too, miss!" A tremble threatened Aunt Margaret's voice. "I know I'm not going to. I'm going to teach my grandnieces and nephews to ride…. I'm going to cherish every minute of life and love God affords me…."

She pressed her forehead to Audra's, smiling through her tears.

"'Cause you're not going to let me do otherwise, are you, sweetie?"

Sweetie. It was a wonder how a simple endearment could fill one's soul to overflowing, not to mention one's eyes. Audra blinked away a sweep of emotion and, unable to speak for its blade in her throat, shook her head in agreement.

"Hey, you gals aren't going to leave me out of this!"

Recovered from his initial reticence, Jake embraced them both. He planted a kiss on Aunt Margaret's wet cheek and then turned to Audra.

"Especially the grandkids part," he whispered wickedly against her lips.

"Jake Turner, behave yourself!"

He ignored his aunt's reproving swat long enough to make his point. Then, reluctantly, he broke away from the tender, soul-baring kiss.

"You started it, Aunt Marge! I mean, you've all but proposed for me and laid out our future family tree. I'm just trying to keep up."

He gave Audra a wink as he helped her sputtering aunt into the car. Like his kiss, it made her feel all warm and fuzzy inside, like he held her breath in the palm of his hand.

Love was a powerful thing, one of God's greatest gifts. It healed the broken; it bonded a childless widow and two orphans into a family; and it removed the last doubt from Audra's mind, replacing it with unsurpassable joy and peace. It had come in God's time, not her own, but it still had come just as he promised...*a season for love*.

Linda Windsor has written seventeen historical and contemporary romances and has more than 850,000 books in print. Her heroes have won the *Romantic Times* KISS Award and her novels are enjoyed around the world in many languages. Linda and her husband, Jim, are lay ministers in their small country church and also enjoy an active music ministry. They live on the coast of Maryland in a restored, eighteenth-century farmhouse with their son and daughter, not to mention an ever-changing assortment of strays, both human and feline. Over the door hangs a sign that sums it up—Registered Historic Nut House.

OTHER INSPIRATIONAL TITLES BY LINDA WINDSOR:
Hi Honey, I'm Home

The jungle drums are sounding…calling you to an adventure you'll never forget!

Not Exactly Eden
by Linda Windsor
Coming July 2000

When spoiled socialite Jenna Marsten journeys to the wilds of Brazil's Amazon rain forest, she thinks she's going to a beautiful place where she'll find her past—and the father she never knew. But the jungle has a mind of its own, and what Jenna finds there is a world beyond anything she'd ever imagined. A world that is *Not Exactly Eden.* Harsh, untamed, and too frequently savage…this is a world that pushes her to the limits of her faith and endurance—and brings her to the brink of love with Dr. Adam DeSanto…a man she keeps reminding herself she can't stand!

Listen to the drums…let the sounds and feel of the jungle sweep you away, teach you lessons you never knew you needed, and change your life forever.

A BATH OFF THE SIDE OF A BOAT SOUNDED REASONABLE IN THEORY. After all, a rope hung over the side would be simple for access and safety. Unfortunately, application of the theory was an entirely different matter.

First, Jenna lost her bar of soap. It slipped out of her hand while she was sudsing her hair and went straight for the river bottom, which she could not touch with her toes. But the water was heavenly, like a pool during a long, dry heat wave. She wished she could let the rope go, but the current was strong and her arms hurt too much from working the hand pump to test her swimming skills.

Feeling fully refreshed, or as refreshed as one could in water the color of a chocolate shake, Jenna wrapped her feet around the rope and pushed upward. To her surprise, beneath the water's surface the thick jute was slick, no doubt covered with the same greenish slime that coagulated along the nooks and crannies of the banks.

A fish jumped a few yards away and her breath seized. Reminded that she was not alone in the water, Jenna tried pulling herself hand over hand. She could get her shoulders up to the ship's side, but there was no strength left to get her bottom half over it. Her bare legs scraped the cracked paint on the planking, searching for a knee or even a toe hold, but all she got was sharp pain in the ball of her foot.

With a startled yelp, she slipped back into the water, panic growing by the heartbeat.

"Adam!"

Oh heavenly Father, help!

"Adam!" she hissed through her teeth.

I won't distress!

She didn't want to awaken her father, or anyone else for that matter.

And I won't despair!

As for Adam DeSanto, it didn't make much difference. He'd make fun of her regardless. Although, she thought, pulling on the rope again with renewed determination, she hated to give him more fuel for his warped humor.

There was a sliding sound from overhead and the light thump of elbows, or, perhaps, knees. Adam's head appeared over the edge of the canopy, silhouetted dark against the moonlit sky.

"Jenna?"

He slid farther over and peered into the darkness of the deck beneath him.

Jenna swallowed the last of her pride.

"Down here...in the water."

"Ah!" He looked down at her over folded arms, head cocked sideways. "Are we skinny dipping?"

"In your dreams."

"In that case..." He yawned and rolled over. "I'll just go back to sleep."

"I *can't* get back in the boat!"

Something brushed against Jenna's foot. It was most likely more of the flotsam, but she couldn't keep the panic from her shrill whisper.

"And there's something in here nibbling on my toes!" *Dear God, please, no piranha!*

With a smooth acrobatic curl, the irascible doctor dropped down from the canopy and onto the stern deck light as a cat. He moved like he was born to the jungle, quick and quiet.

"Grab my arms, Jenna."

With no quirky smile or taunt but simply raw grunting strength, Adam hauled her out of the water. Exhausted from fear as much as effort, she didn't resist when he pulled her to him and held her, trembling in his arms. He was warm, and his embrace felt like nothing could harm or threaten her. She savored it, knowing full well the risk she took was all her own. But recklessness was becoming a growing facet of her personality. For all she knew, it had always been there, leashed by the role of her former life.

Her nose twitched, tickled by the hair on his chest. Without warning, she sneezed. The captivating closeness evaporated. Adam released her. The cool rush of air that filled the void between them struck Jenna at the same time her left foot protested from her full weight upon it.

She gasped and dropped onto the bench, remembering the splinter. Her foot cradled across her leg, she felt for the offending object. It had broken off when she stood up. She shook off a tummy swirl of nausea.

"Let me see."

Seemingly from out of nowhere, Adam produced a small penlight and shined it on her foot. Wrapped around her toe was a piece of river grass. He pulled it away and tossed it over the side.

"I did see a fish earlier," Jenna managed in self-defense.

Adam touched the stub of the wood and swore. "My next project is to scrape and paint this boat!"

"Can you get it out?"

"Have you got tweezers? My bag is stashed forward and all I have is this." He produced a pocketknife.

Jenna nodded. "In the bag."

Ah, the leetle flowered bag on wheels! Adam didn't need to say it. His expression did. He picked it up and handed it to her. Inside an exterior zippered compartment, Jenna took out a leather-encased manicure set.

Adam examined it curiously. "Have you any lotion or an astringent with alcohol?"

"Will triple antibiotic ointment do?"

"For tonight."

Jenna contemplated the rugged profile of the doctor's face as he went to work with the tweezers. He was so gentle, she hardly felt it when he opened the wound a little more to extract a piece that remained behind. His application of the ointment afterward affected her far more than it had a right to.

Adam DeSanto might have the temperament of a jaguar, or *onça*, as Juana chided from time to time, but beneath it was the incredible tenderness that made his former nurse swell with pride. Jenna saw it when he was with patients, especially the children.

And now. With her.

"You continue to amaze me, Jenna Marsten." He shoved himself up from the squatting position in front of her bench.

"I'll take that as an apology."

"For what?"

"For trying to scare me away with that kiss."

Jenna regretted the words the moment they were out, not just because she'd admitted that Adam's kiss had left its impression, but because they brought the *onça* back. Gone was the sweetness, the tenderness. In its place was a predatory, ebony gleam.

Adam tilted his head, like the cat contemplating the mouse.

"You mean, you want me to apologize for kissing you?"

Jenna rubbed her foot and slipped it into her canvas deck shoe. She could tell from the incredulity in his voice that anything of the sort was out of the question now.

"Forget it. It was a dumb joke."

"Well, I am *not* sorry!" He glanced up at the canopy and ran his fingers through his thick hair.

"Fine. It was nothing."

"In fact..." He swung his gaze back to her, jaw jutting in a neck-stretching jerk. "I am so *un*sorry, that I will do it again!"

Frozen like a cornered mouse, knowing there was no escape, Jenna caught her breath. The caress of Adam's skilled fingers along her chin moved her head back to receive his kiss. If the possessive, yet tender claim on her mouth could be called that. Its completeness spread through her veins with a jalapeño effect, warm, elusive at first, then demanding recognition of all her senses.

And she thought feelings like these existed only in romantic movies! She'd never known the like with her ex-fiancé, Scott. They begged her to abandon reason and will. The only course was to go into his embrace. Jenna moved closer until she could feel the counterpoint of thundering hearts.

Suddenly, Adam tore away, staring at her as if she'd grown two heads. He raised his finger at her and then dropped it as if he had second thoughts.

"And for the love of Pete sake, put some dry clothes on!"

Reaching up, he grabbed the lip of the canopy and curled up and over it.

If she weren't in such a twist herself, Jenna would have corrected Adam's misuse of the English expression. But considering the fire of his kiss still ravaged her senses, proper speech was the *least* of her problems.

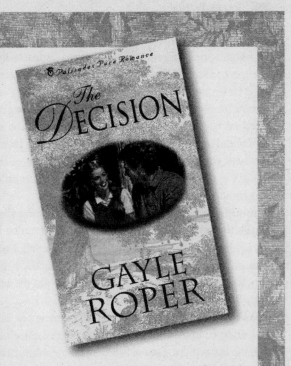

Palisades Pure Romance

The DECISION

GAYLE ROPER

When a car bomb kills Nurse Rose Martin's cancer patient, Rose faces a difficult question: who could have done this? She escapes into the arms of Jake Zook, a man struggling with his past and his Amish heritage, yet decisions come hard in matters of love and forgiveness. Can the living find God's forgiveness for themselves and justice for the dead?

Available in October! At a bookstore near you.
ISBN 1-57673-406-4

THE FORCE OF THE BLAST KNOCKED ME TO THE GROUND.

I fell into Sophie Hostetter's beautiful red impatiens lining the front walk, breaking off the brittle stems with my legs, torso, even my head.

Being thrown to the ground by forces too strong to counter was beyond my experience. When the displaced air pushed ahead by the expanding gases of the explosion hit me in the back and sent me sprawling, when the heat of the resulting fire scorched me through my sweater and turtleneck, I couldn't comprehend it.

Instinctively I raised my hands over my head and pulled my knees to my chest, belatedly protecting myself. I tried to think, to break through the gray fog of shock. After all, I was a nurse and an EMT. I was used to catastrophe, but I was usually the one who bound up the wounded, not the one who lay flattened, deafened, and blank-minded.

Slowly I uncurled and pushed myself to my knees. The great roaring continued to fill the air as I forced myself to look at the fire, a pulsing sea of flames, writhing, consuming what had been Ammon Hostetter's car.

And Ammon Hostetter, nice guy and ineffectual CEO of his family's highly successful toy business.

And Sophie Hostetter, his mother and my patient. Sweet Sophie who had suffered so long and so devastatingly with cancer.

Oh, God! My mind could form no other words. My eyes shut to block out the devastation of the fire. The Town Car was totally engulfed.

I steeled myself and staggered to my feet. I moved toward the fire, but the intensity of the flames made a close approach impossible.

I circled the car at an awkward run, hand held before

my face to protect my eyes from the staggering heat, trying to see if there was some way I could offer help.

Smoke ascended, twisting and wrapping in on itself like some mythical monster. The flames were undulating arms raised skyward, awful in their red, orange, and white glory. The air was acrid with the raw odor of hot metal and burning tires.

My heart fought the realization that there was no life-saving care I could give here. Finally, sobbing, I stumbled toward the house to call 911.

I'd almost reached the front door of the Hostetters' great home when a second explosion rocked the late November afternoon and knocked me down, causing me to strike my forehead against the shallow cement front steps.

Pain lanced across my skull, along my neck, and flashed down my spine. Groaning, I rolled on my side and reached up a shaking hand. I found broken skin and blood. Swelling had already developed, but I felt no pain. Shock, I diagnosed.

I turned back to the blaze, pulsing with renewed life, and saw with horror that pools of fiery gasoline were spreading from beneath the car, rivers of flame racing across the drive toward my car. I raced to move it before it, too, was lost.

"911," I whispered as I rested my aching head on the steering wheel for a minute to ward off vertigo. I grabbed the car phone and punched in the emergency number.

I looked at the scene and beyond to the house and froze at what I saw.

Standing at the front door of the mansion, mouth agape, shock in his eyes, was Peter Hostetter watching the conflagration.

"*Oh, God!*" I prayed inarticulately once again. Tears of

sympathy wet my face and a vise gripped my stomach, tightening until I felt I might implode from the pressure. His mother and his older brother!

I skirted the site of the accident and raced up the front steps

"Peter!" I laid a hand gently on his arm as I shouted to be heard above the roar of the fire. "Let's wait inside until help comes."

He looked at me without recognition, confusion struggling with vagueness in his eyes.

"Peter! It's me, Rose! Come inside while we wait for help!"

His eyes slid from me to the car. "Ammon." His voice was barely audible through the ringing in my head. "Mother."

I swallowed against my tears. "I know." I pushed him, trying to move him away from the terrible inferno. He held his place against me for a short minute, then sagged suddenly against the jamb. When I felt his body give, I pushed as hard as I could. We went flying into the vast entry hall, knocking against the pair of antique chairs.

"Sit here," I ordered when my head stopped spinning. I pushed him down, and he folded passively under the pressure, collapsing on a petit-point seat, disoriented and sweaty, gray.

In the distance we could already hear sirens. Help was near. Peter looked at me and shuddered. "I was almost in that car."

I nodded. "I know."

A uniformed cop entered the front hall and stood with his arms away from his body in that policeman stance accommodating all the gear hanging from his belt.

"Are you two all right?" he asked.

Peter and I nodded.

"What happened?"

"The car exploded," Peter said. "And I was almost in it!"

The officer looked at me. I could see him assessing my grubby clothes and abraded forehead.

"Are you sure you're all right?"

I nodded and glanced down at myself. "I had just tucked a lap robe around Mrs. Hostetter and was walking back to the house when the first explosion came. It knocked me into the flower bed. The second one knocked me into the front steps."

The cop nodded. "I want the two of you to remain here and talk to the detective assigned to the case. Why don't you wait here, Ms.–"

"Rose Martin. I've been Mrs. Hostetter's home health nurse."

"Right." He pointed to the chair I'd just vacated. I sat down again gratefully.

"You, sir," he said to Peter, "can wait in the living room."

Peter hesitated. "But my mother and my brother."

The policeman looked questioningly at him.

"The people in the car," I said to the officer. "Sophie and Ammon Hostetter."

The cop looked at Peter. "And you are?"

"Peter Hostetter."

"Well, Mr. Hostetter, if you'd wait in the living room for the detective, I'd appreciate it. And if there is any news from outside, I'll see that you get it. And I'm sorry for your loss."

Peter blinked. "Thank you." He turned and walked to the living room.

It was almost two hours before the police were finished with me. The detective on the case turned out to be a guy named Lem Huber. I went to school with his younger brother Al at Twin Valley High School.

"Well, well, Rose Martin," he said when he came in.

I felt my tension level diminish dramatically when I saw him.

"So tell me everything you know."

He let me talk without interruption. Then he questioned me politely about what I had said, asking the same questions from several different points of view. I answered as thoroughly as I could, but it all came down to one thing as far as I was concerned: through some terrible accident Sophie and Ammon Hostetter had died.

When Lem finally told me I could leave, I sighed with relief. I grabbed my medical equipment, my purse, and keys and rushed out the front door. Fire equipment and emergency vehicles still filled the drive and lawn. The fire was long extinguished, but all the attendant chaos of a crisis was present, including men and women in a variety of uniforms talking and laughing, now that the immediate need was met.

I was so consumed with relief that I could finally leave that I was unprepared for what I saw. Memories long buried leaped at me, overwhelming me, choking me, a kaleidoscope of emotions tearing reason and control from me. My stomach heaved and I grabbed one of the porch pillars to keep from falling.

"Rose?" Lem Huber spoke behind me and his hand came out to help support me.

I swallowed once, twice, and tried to contain the incipient panic swelling inside, the great beast who waited in the shadows to devour me whenever my guard was down.

I pushed myself away from the pillar. "I'll be all right," I said with what I hoped sounded like assurance, though I suspected I was so white he wouldn't believe anything I said even if my voice had been steady, which regrettably it wasn't. "Too many memories."

Lem nodded as he continued to hold my elbow. "This was pretty bad."

I made a little noise he took for assent, and I allowed him to think that it was the horror of today's events that had overcome me. It was safer that way.

I took my sagging energy level and walked across the yard and out to my car. I got into my blue Civic and started for home.

I hadn't gone very far when my mind, never very quiet at the best of times, exploded. Images flashed through my brain with the relentless pulse of the light strip on a police cruiser. Fire, crushed impatiens, sirens, static, yellow police tape.

And rushing white water, swollen and angry, creaming over rocks.

And the inevitable, "Rose, what have you done!"

It didn't take much intelligence to realize just how close to the edge I was.

I'm fine. Really. I'm fine. I repeated it aloud to myself like a litany. Maybe if I said it often enough, it would become true.

But coming out of the house and seeing those lights and hearing that static had brought such a rush of agony that I was unlikely to feel fine for quite some time. I hadn't had this strong a flashback in years.

You're being stupid, I told myself. *You're a nurse and an EMT. You deal with emergencies much too frequently to be spooked like this.*

But that's when I'm the healer, the helper. I fix the problems. I don't cause them.

But you didn't cause the problem today.

No, I didn't, but I didn't prevent it either.

Like you could have. What are you, prescient? I shrugged away that bit of logic and went back to the real crux of my distress.

But I was the cause then.

The little voice that had been answering me back was uncomfortably quiet.

Suddenly I knew I wasn't going to make it home. I felt the bile rise in my throat and swallowed desperately against the impulse to vomit. I felt the tears begin, blurring my vision until I could barely see the road. I felt the shaking start deep in my stomach, and I knew it would radiate outward until my whole body shook.

Oh, God! I have to get off the road before I fail again, before I'm the cause again.

And I saw the answer to my prayer loom out of the darkness, a white farmhouse with green trim, clean and orderly and known. I pulled into the Zooks' drive, shoved the car in park, and fell to pieces.

I don't know how long I sat in the Zooks' drive. It was one of those terrifying times when thinking is too horrendous and your mind copes by going blank. I sat gripping the wheel, unable to do anything but sob for a long time. At least it felt like a long time. In reality it may have been only a few minutes.

I felt the pain. Oh, how I felt the pain.

I saw Sophie's smiling face, full of excitement over her foray into the real world.

I saw Ammon's kind face as he helped his mother with the seat belt.

Then the image jumped, and I saw my mother's ravaged face, my father's terrified face, Rhoda's dead face. The ache in my chest expanded until I could barely breathe.

Oh, God, I cried for what was surely the millionth time, *Help me! I don't want Rhoda to be dead! I don't want Sophie to be dead! Or Ammon! Please! Oh, God! Please!*

A sharp rap on the driver's side window made me jump, and a small scream erupted like a little verbal geyser. I spun and saw a shape made blurry by the condensation formed on the window by my weeping and harsh, heavy breathing.

I was too emotionally drained to feel fear though I wondered resentfully just who was insensitive enough to bother me while I felt like this.

"Roll down the window," a man requested, his voice made hollow by the glass between us.

I was so depleted with my personal agony that I couldn't respond. All I could do was stare. Tears still streamed down my face and the relentless pounding in my head continued unabated, but I didn't seem to be shaking anymore, a fact that gave me a strange, foolish pride.

"Open the window!" the voice said, this time an order, courteous but implacable.

He spoke with such quiet authority that I struggled to obey with hands so uncoordinated that I could barely push the little button on the door panel. After long moments I managed to lower the window a couple of inches.

"What?" I asked in a thready whisper. I began to yearn desperately for a tissue, for several tissues, for a box of tissues as tears dripped off my chin onto my chest. I grabbed the edge of my cardigan and wiped ineffectually across my face.

The man leaned over and peered at me. "What are you doing here?"

Now there was a foolish question, I thought.

"Crying," I said and sniffed. I lowered my head to my hands where they again rested on the steering wheel. It was too great an effort to hold myself upright. "Crying."

Suddenly a flashlight was shining on me, or rather on the top of my head and what little of my face wasn't blocked by my arms.

"Rose?" The man's voice was hesitant, disbelieving.

I nodded without lifting my head.

"Is that you, Rose?"

Now I recognized the voice of Jake Zook. I was parked in his driveway, or rather that of his father, John. I leaned back wearily against the headrest and looked toward the partially opened window, blinking in the glare.

Jake rolled closer to the window in his wheelchair. "Rose!" His voice was appalled.

Well, now I knew what I looked like.

I smiled, or at least I tried to. I always smiled at Jake, prickly, handsome, marvelous Jake. "Hi, Jake," I managed. "I'm—" I swallowed against the constriction in my throat. "I'm just borrowing your driveway for a few minutes. I won't be long." I tried to sound like it was an everyday occurrence that I drove into driveways, parked with my motor running and my lights on, and sobbed my heart out.

He muttered something harsh under his breath. "Lower this window," he ordered.

I didn't move.

"Rose," he growled. "Lower the window all the way."

I nodded but still didn't move.

Jake made a disgruntled noise and grabbed the door handle. He pulled. Nothing happened. "Unlock the door, Rose. Now."

What a good idea, I thought, but what came out in a weak, quavering voice was, "Stop yelling at me."

"Rose." His voice was full of exasperation and warning.

"Right." I looked at the door. It seemed miles away, but I wanted to make Jake happy. I always wanted to make Jake happy. I studied the buttons, trying to decide which one was the door lock. With great resolve, I reached and pushed. The window slid all the way down.

I sighed and smiled weakly. "Sorry," was all I could manage as two big tears slid down my cheeks.

Jake looked at me and shook his head. I couldn't tell if it was in pity or exasperation. He reached inside the car, pushed the right button to release the lock, and pulled open my door. He maneuvered around it and wheeled his chair right to the edge of my seat. He sat there studying me for a long minute.

"Hi," I whispered, rolling my head toward him and trying to smile. Without warning my voice broke off in a great sob. I felt myself begin to shake again.

"I'm s-sorry. I'm s-sorry!" And I shook harder. "You're so brave and I'm—"

"Rosie!" The distress in his voice washed over me like a soothing balm, but I couldn't stop the tremors or the tears.

He reached across me to where my hands lay limply in my lap. He grasped them, held them between his palms, and rubbed until they felt warm for the first time in hours. Then he grabbed my wrists and pulled.

"What?" I mumbled as I automatically pulled back.

"Come here," he said as he continued to tug.

I hadn't the strength to continue fighting him. I let him draw me out of the car and onto his lap.

"Jake! I can't sit on you! I'll hurt you!" I tried to pull away.

"A little thing like you?" he said. "Never." He put a hand on my waist and held me in place.

"But your legs!"

"They can't feel you, Rose. Don't worry."

So I sat stiffly on his knees with my tear-ravaged face, my wild woman hair, and a bad case of the hiccups I'd gotten from all the crying. I put my hands to my face to block Jake's view of me. I wasn't surprised to feel tears slide between my fingers. At the rate I was weeping, I'd be suffering from dehydration momentarily.

Jake pulled my hands from my face and held them again in his strong ones.

"Tell me what's wrong."

"Oh, Jake. It was awf—I s-saw—" I took a deep breath. "Sophie and Ammon. And the lights! The static!"

He put a hand under my chin and turned me to face him. He looked at me like what I had just said made sense.

"If it's got you this upset, it must have been rough." He reached out to push my hair off my face. For the first time he noticed the abrasion on my forehead.

"Rosie!" He ran a finger softly over my skin, being careful not to touch the injury itself. "What happened? Did you fall? Or have an accident?"

"No," I said, answering the last question. It was too difficult and too confusing to remember everything he asked. I was too tired. "I didn't have an accident."

"Then what?" His voice was so gentle. If I weren't already crying, I'd have burst into tears at his concern.

My feelings for this man were so complicated, yet so fierce. I'd known him for two years, ever since the night he was nearly killed outside my mother's home in Honey Brook. The accident had left him a paraplegic. I had sat with him in the street in the pouring rain that night while we waited for the medevac helicopter to arrive to transport him to the trauma unit at Brandywine Hospital in Coatesville. I'd felt his failing vital signs and watched the emergency techs shake their heads. I'd thought he died. I'd even planted a little cross by the site as a memorial.

It was a year before I learned he was alive. I took down my little cross, but almost another year passed before I actually met the man. When his mother took a terrible fall on the cellar stairs during the summer, I'd been on the emergency crew that took Mary to the hospital. Then I'd been the home health nurse assigned to her care when she returned to the farm.

Often on my visits to Mary, I'd talked with Jake, lingering after I should have left for my next case. I enjoyed our conversations and apparently so did he. He made it a point to be around when I had a visit scheduled. We talked about everything from his parents' strict faith to why I liked being a nurse to how his life had changed in the past two years.

After my official visits to Mary ended, I stopped by unannounced two more times, ostensibly to check on her but really to talk with Jake. He'd been home one time and we talked for an hour. He was absent the next time, and I was appalled at the disappointment I felt at missing him. I knew I couldn't stop again unless he specifically invited me. Otherwise, I was setting myself up for heartbreak.

Jake called me after that second visit saying Mary had told him I'd dropped by. His voice on the phone made my mouth go dry and my palms sweat. Since then he called at infrequent intervals, always surprising me, always causing the same physical reaction. We talked every time for an hour or two. But he never mentioned meeting or my coming to the farm or his coming to my place. Just friends talking.

Only it always felt like more. Or maybe, more accurately, *almost* more.

Now as I sat in his lap, I was thinking only about the comfort he was to me. If I couldn't cope with the memories that plagued me, he would handle them for me. He would take my pain and transfer it to his strong shoulders, barely bending under the load that was driving me into the ground. Against all reason I knew Jake could fix my troubles. I didn't understand how he could do something that monumental. I just knew that he could.

If he wanted to.

The problem was that he'd never shown in the slightest fashion that he wanted to do anything as personal as cope on my behalf. He never showed he wanted to be anything more than my casual friend. It was in my dreams that he was interested in being God's man for me, not in real life. In real life he wasn't even interested in being God's man, let alone God's man for me.

"What happened?" he repeated softly, studying the edema on my forehead in the renewed blaze of the flashlight.

"I fell. When the second explosion came, I hit my head on the step."

"The second explosion?"

I nodded. "The first one just knocked me down. It didn't hurt me, really it didn't, but it didn't do the impatiens any good."

"Uh-huh," he said, just like he understood what I was talking about. "And that's why you're crying? It hurts? Did you see the doctor about it?"

The man has to stop with these multiple questions, I thought as I reached up and felt the knot gingerly. I shook my head ever so slightly. As pain shot through my temples, I winced, stilled, and forced myself to say, "No."

"No, what? No, it doesn't hurt? No, you didn't see a doctor? No, you're not crying because you hit your head?"

"No, I mean yes, it hurts, and no, I didn't see a doctor."

"So why are you crying?" he prompted when I fell silent. His voice was a shade less patient. "Because you fell?"

"No." I took a deep breath. I could tell this. I could. But for some reason, I couldn't.

"You're crying because of the second explosion?"

"No."

"Because of the first explosion."

"No."

"Were you on an emergency call?"

"No."

There was a short silence. I could almost feel Jake's tension building.

"Come on, Rose, help me out here."

Just then, Jake's brother walked up to the car. I could tell he was hesitant to disturb us but concern was written all over his face. Elam glanced at me then said to Jake, "You'll bring her in when she's feeling better? Mom'll be very upset if you don't."

Jake nodded and Elam walked toward the house where the soft, gentle light of Coleman lanterns and kerosene lamps glowed in the windows. No electric lights for the Zooks. No curtains to block the light, either. They kept the *Ordnung*.

All except Jake. He'd rebelled, and the rebellion had led to his injury. His mother thought his paralysis was his punishment from God, but she loved him fiercely anyway.

Jake rolled his chair—and me—back until there was room to shut the car door. The overhead light went out and the darkness of the autumn night wrapped around us.

"Oh, Jake." I sighed, my voice ragged.

"It'll be okay," he whispered, lifting a hand to wipe at my tears. His other hand continued to rest on my waist. Hawk sat beside us and stared at me.

"No." I whispered, disconsolate "Never."

"Come on, Rosie, tell me." His voice was gentle again. "What happened?"

"Lights," I said, trying to explain. "Static. They died!" And I grabbed him about the chest and buried my face against his denim shirt. I couldn't stop the tears. He wrapped his arms around me and held me, waiting for the storm to pass.

"It's all right," he whispered over and over again as he gently stroked my hair and patted my back. "You're going to be fine. It'll be all right."

"No." I drew a deep, quivering breath. "Even God can't make it right."

I felt his surprise. "Is this Rose the Evangelist making such a statement?"

Immediately I tried to cover my faithless tracks. "Not that God can't get me through it. It's just that what's done is done."

"Ah."

We were silent for a little while. I rested against him, drawing strength from his strength, until I became so self-conscious that I had to sit up. In fact, I needed to get off his lap completely. I needed to remind myself that his lap wasn't mine.

I straightened and stood. He let me.

"Why don't you sit in the car?" he suggested. "Then we can be eye to eye."

I nodded and opened the car door. I fiddled with the dash until I found the knob that turned out the overhead light. I wanted the cocoon of darkness for a while longer.

I levered my seat as far back as it would go, then sat sideways, facing him, my feet resting on the ledge of the open door. Our knees met between us.

"Okay," Jake said briskly. "Suppose we start with the first explosion."

My smile slowly faded as I watched this man I was afraid I loved. "Sophie was in the explosion."

"She died?" Jake's voice was gentle.

I felt the tears again. "Yes. She and her son Ammon." I cleared my throat, pushing down the welling emotion. "It was her car that exploded. I was there."

Jake, who had been leaning toward me while we talked, fell back in his chair as if someone had pushed him. "Rose! You saw this?"

"Well, I didn't actually see either explosion. I had my back turned. That's why I was knocked down on my face instead of my bottom. But I saw the fire." I started to rub my aching forehead only to wince when I dragged my fingers over the lump. "Oh yes, I saw the fire."

"I don't know what to say!"

I shrugged. "I've seen terrible things before. Scraping up people after accidents or shootings isn't exactly pleasant. But I *knew* Sophie." Again the welling of tears. "And there were all the lights and the static from the radios." My voice faltered and fell silent. I gripped my hands and pressed them to my chest. I started to tremble again.

Jake reached out and took my hands in his. He pulled them down to his knees and began to rub his thumbs absently over the backs of them.

"You mentioned the lights and the static before." He looked at me closely. "Why did the lights and static affect you so much? You're familiar with them from your emergency runs."

"Rhoda," I said in a whisper.

"I thought her name was Sophie."

"It was. But it reminded me too much of Rhoda."

He shook his head in a flash of irritation. "Rose, you're rambling again. Who's Rhoda?"

"My sister."

"Was she with you? Was she hurt?"

"Rhoda's dead. She's been dead for fifteen years. This just brought it all back." I started to sob. "I'm sorry. I feel like such a baby." Normally I rarely cried, but tonight I couldn't stop.

"It's okay," Jake said. "Memories can be very painful things."

I glanced at him through my tears. His memories must be excruciating at times. I wondered which hurt him more, the memories of running or of the agony of rehab? And I cried harder.

Somehow I found myself on Jake's lap again, his voice gentling me, his hand soothing me. I don't know when I realized that I wasn't crying for the past anymore. I wasn't even crying for Sophie and Ammon or for Jake. I was crying for myself and the fact that it had been fifteen years since anyone had rubbed my back and told me everything would be all right.